THE AIMS OF ANTHROPOSOPHY
AND THE PURPOSE OF THE GOETHEANUM

Eleven public lectures given in Basel, 9 April 1923, Dornach 14, 15, 20–22 April 1923,
Prague 27 and 30 April 1923, Vienna 26 and 29 September 1923 and Paris 26 May 1924

TRANSLATED BY MATTHEW BARTON

INTRODUCTION BY MATTHEW BARTON

RUDOLF STEINER

RUDOLF STEINER PRESS

CW 84

The publishers gratefully acknowledge the generous funding by the
Anthroposophical Society in Great Britain of the translation for this publication

Rudolf Steiner Press
Hillside House, The Square
Forest Row, RH18 5ES

www.rudolfsteinerpress.com

Published by Rudolf Steiner Press 2020

Originally published in German under the title *Was wollte das Goetheanum und was soll die Anthroposophie?* (volume 84 in the *Rudolf Steiner Gesamtausgabe* or Collected Works) by Rudolf Steiner Verlag, Dornach. The text is based on shorthand notes that were not reviewed or revised by the speaker. This authorized translation is based on the latest available (second) German edition (1986), edited by Hella Wiesberger and Konrad Donat

Published by permission of the Rudolf Steiner Nachlassverwaltung, Dornach

A catalogue record for this book is available from the British Library

ISBN 978 1 85584 571 8

Cover by Mary Giddens
Typeset by DP Photosetting, Neath, West Glamorgan
Printed and bound by 4Edge Ltd., Essex

CONTENTS

LECTURE 1

BASEL, 9 APRIL 1923

The Purpose of the Goetheanum and the Aims of Anthroposophy

The name of the Goetheanum in gratitude to Goethe. Knowledge of the world of spirit alongside the scientific worldview. People are asking for knowledge of the world of spirit. Ordinary memory does not take us back into worlds of spirit. Activated thinking brings us perception of the etheric world. If we deepen our inner silence, the spiritual world begins to speak. Overcoming egoism enhances powers of cognition. Mathematics as elementary anthroposophy. The whole of the human organism participates in retaining what has been spiritually perceived. Notebooks. The Goetheanum building as sheath or shell for what was cultivated there. The Group with the Representative of Humanity. The future needs anthroposophy.

LECTURE 2

DORNACH, 14 APRIL 1923 (LECTURE 1, SEMI-PUBLIC)

Enhancing Human Powers of Perception to Develop Imagination, Inspiration and Intuition

The outer world is available to us through sense impressions. Thought refers us outwards, feeling refers us inwards. Engagement of the will at the transition from sleep to waking life. Thinking, feeling and will during waking life. Feeling as diluted will. Thinking and etheric body during sleep and waking. Connection of the astral body with feeling and dream. Interaction of the nerves with blood circulation. Activity of thinking as content of Imagination. Relation of the astral body to Inspiration and of the I to Intuition.

LECTURE 3

DORNACH, 15 APRIL 1923 (LECTURE 2, SEMI-PUBLIC)

Human Soul Life and the Development of Imagination, Inspiration and Intuition

Dream images from the perspective of waking reality. Thoughts in waking life. The 'noise of thoughts' drowns out subtler perceptions. Suggestions for meditation and activated thinking. Experience of formative forces in the temporal realm. Thinking as sum of growth forces. The outer sense world alone inhibits cosmos-forming powers of thought. Concentration exercises enable us to perceive the world's etheric. Thoughts as shadow image of the etheric body. The etheric body as part of the cosmic ether. Thinking and holistic thinking in the world. The life of feeling in relation to Inspiration. Moral and physical aspects in the Inspiration content of the world.

LECTURE 4

DORNACH, 20 APRIL 1923 (LECTURE 3, SEMI-PUBLIC)

Experience and Perception of the Activities of Thinking and Speech

Activity of thinking when engaged in geometry. Thinking as inward activity. Activated thinking allows us to experience the temporal body as part of the universe. Interplay of nutrition: physical nutrition for the body, etheric in the place of secretions. Living our way into the world's etheric realm. Speech activity and also learning to be silent, and perception of our astral aspect. Reflection of natural laws from the cosmos back to the earth. The cosmic ether as thought-creating world. How the ether sucks out space. The physical is reflected back from the cosmos as etheric configurations. The experience of a world of spirit.

age of seven. What is the significance of the educator's authority for the child? The transition from natural laws to inwardly configured content, and from science to art.

LECTURE 11

PARIS, 26 MAY 1924

How Do We Gain Knowledge of the Supersensible World?

Thinking, feeling and will in relation to the human body. In the ancient Mysteries, outward processes and rituals gave rise to higher knowledge. The activity of thinking engenders imaginative knowledge. Retrospective view back to birth, time becomes space. The second stage of knowledge, spiritual worlds in consciousness. Intuition as enhancement of knowledge. Recognition of pre-earthly and also post-mortem spheres. The task of the First Goetheanum. Humanity's quest for the spiritual, for new Mysteries.

EDITOR'S PREFACE

After the destruction of the First Goetheanum at New Year 1922/
23, Rudolf Steiner focused his efforts on rebuilding, and on reorga-
nization of the Anthroposophical Society. This necessitated trips to
Germany, Czechoslovakia, Norway, England, Austria and Holland,
during which he gave numerous lectures for members of the
Anthroposophical Society as well as courses for various professions. A
synopsis of these lectures can be found in GA 259 (not translated).
The public lectures also given in 1923, and those given in Paris in
1924, are collected in this present volume. Of these, the Dornach
lectures were semi-public, in so far as they formed part of the regular
weekend lectures for members of the Anthroposophical Society in
Dornach to which participants of a public course for Swiss teachers
were also invited (see GA 306*).

The theme of the first lecture in this volume ('The Purpose of the
Goetheanum and the Aims of Anthroposophy') was presented in
various cities following the fire (between 5 and 12 April in Bern,
Basel, Zurich, Wintherthur and St. Gallen). We have chosen the
Basel lecture for this volume.

---

* *The Child's Changing Consciousness*, Anthroposophic Press 1996.

INTRODUCTION

The first Goetheanum building burned down in an arson attack at New Year 1922/23—the devastating loss of a building that had physically embodied, in its forms, spaces and colours, all the teaching of anthroposophy. Though this loss was a terrible blow to Rudolf Steiner, and must surely have sapped his strength, he rallied and went on to increase the intensity of his activities to an extraordinary degree in the last two years of his life. The lectures in this volume are one testimony, despite all adversities, of his continuing labours and hopes, of his extraordinary determination to root and embody anthroposophy in the world.

Steiner had in part attributed the destruction of the Goetheanum to the failure of his followers and adherents to 'wake up'. In a conversation with Count Polzer-Hoditz the day after the fire,[*] he said that this 'House of the Word', as he had conceived it, 'can only exist if it finds its corresponding, living reflection in the heart, in world conscience—that means, if the human being doesn't just listen but is also willing and able to be responsible to the "Word of the world".' It is striking, therefore, that in several lectures in this volume, given in various European cities only a few months after that terrible loss, he speaks a great deal about sleep and waking, and about possible stages of spiritual awakening. When we awaken in the ordinary way from dream and sleep, we can reflect on the meaning of our dream experience. This being so, says Steiner, why should we not also awaken a second time from this same ordinary, limited waking consciousness, and look back on it from a higher vantage point. This

---

[*] See Emanuel Zeylmans, *Who Was Ita Wegman*, Vol. 1, p. 112, Mercury Press 1990.

enhanced vision—and Steiner goes on to describe precisely how we can work to achieve it—enlarges our human integrity, our wholeness, by enabling us to act in free conformity with our higher nature and in affirmation of it. In this sense, the Goetheanum building itself, which as he says was intended to embody and reflect the human activities within it—in lectures, gatherings, artworks and artistic performances of all kinds—can also exemplify our 'congruence' as human beings: our truthful expression of our being's spiritual reality and the way we manifest this in our thoughts, feelings, words and actions.

'If we only lived in a dream world', says Steiner, 'we would have a dream reality before us . . . we would never think of breaking through this dream reality into a different one.' To me these words immediately beg the question of how awake we actually are, nearly a hundred years after those words were spoken. Though partial spiritual awakenings have indeed broken through into our evolving consciousness in some respects, as witnessed at least by growing concern and awareness of, and sense of responsibility for, the ecological plight of our planet, this is matched at the same time by an ever greater addiction to virtual realities, to somnolence-inducing technologies, to 'connectivity' that may resemble but surely cannot replace true human connection with our greater selves, with each other and with the sustaining natural world. Speaking of the way we are given up to the outer world in modern culture, Steiner goes on to describe how, in a first step, we can silence these outer stimuli and come to real awareness of the life of thinking in us. Through the exercises he offers, he shows how we can reach behind or 'beyond the mirror' of the senses to the other side of thinking where we connect with real forces in the world. The screens that surround us in ever larger number, by contrast, while mimicking an inner life, are surely in fact mirrors that draw us into an addictive world of superficial appearance, that drown out deep silence of reflection with their continual outward 'noise'. Thus we can become caged within physical forces, cut off even from real sense perceptions of the world through whose gateway we can learn to divine or discern hidden qualities and realities.

In progressing into awareness of the life realm, the etheric, on the other hand, we no longer feel ourselves 'shut off from the world' (Steiner's words) as we do in the physical body. Instead we can 'feel the outer world stream into us, and our own being stream out into it'. The inner practices Steiner describes here require an enormous intensification of quiet within, for living reality, he says, or what he calls 'the active Logos', only speaks to us out of such deep stillness. As I read this I was reminded of a fairy-tale I used to love as a child: to free her brothers from the spell that has turned them into swans, and make them human again, as beings fully of the earth, a sister must keep silence for seven years while weaving them each a cloak of thistle-down. Wrongly accused of a terrible crime, she is condemned to death because she cannot speak out to defend herself. Intent only on her task, and her silence, the pyre is lit beneath her at the very moment she has fulfilled her task, and her brothers swoop down to extinguish the flames. The silence and the weaving could be an image of the dedicated work of meditation, which may take long years to come to fruition but is ultimately redemptive, and can bring the otherwise floating and evanescent life-realm of spirit to full, grounded embodiment in us. The tale also reminds me of Steiner's repeated dictum in these lectures: that ultimately we reach our own true core of being, the I, through selflessness, through a love in which our own being is devoted to another. For Steiner, as he makes clear in this volume, love can become a 'power of cognition', of perception of realities other than our own through devotion to them.

The Goetheanum was destroyed by fire, but the pain and cata-strophe of its loss fired Steiner to re-embody its message and mission in words of spirit that are eternally beyond destruction and convey a sense of our task as human beings. The building was irretrievable in its original form, but Steiner, instead of dwelling on the loss, here re-enlivens, re-affirms and re-imagines the spirit of the Goetheanum in words that can summon us to heartfelt and wholly congruent activity, can encourage us to become free, moral and empathic beings who may therefore bring blessing to the world.

Matthew Barton

Lecture 1

THE PURPOSE OF THE GOETHEANUM AND THE AIMS OF ANTHROPOSOPHY

BASEL, 9 APRIL 1923

THE catastrophic fire on New Year's Eve a year ago[1] destroyed the Goetheanum which many, to whom it was dear, remember now with pain and sorrow. The talk I will give today on anthroposophic insights and outlooks refers back to this catastrophe, but is not intended to dwell upon it at length. The lecture today will not differ greatly from others I have given for many years now in this same hall in Basel.[2] In fact, the devastating fire revealed what outlandish ideas people in general hold about everything that the Goetheanum was intended to embody, and all that should have taken place there; they speak of the dire superstitions that were to have been disseminated there, the anti-religious impulses and spiritualist invocations, the nebulous mysticism that we were supposedly going to propound, and so on and so forth. Today, responding to some of these things, at least, I'd like to consider what the aim is of the anthroposophy to which the Goetheanum was dedicated.

The very name 'Goetheanum' was a cause of annoyance to many who failed to reflect on the deeper aspects giving rise to this name, and how they relate to the anthroposophy cultivated there. This anthroposophy itself emerged for me in a living way over more than four decades through my preoccupation with Goethe's worldview and his whole oeuvre.[3] But it must be said that mere consideration of Goethe's worldview and his works will not immediately and logically give rise to what we mean by 'Goethean'. This alone will not reveal what led to us choosing the name Goetheanum for the building in Dornach. I'd put it like this: there is a logic of thinking and then also a logic of life. And if, rather than engaging with Goethe merely through an intellectual logic but instead embracing Goethe's thought with all the vital stimulus contained therein, trying to gain from it what can be gained now that so many further decades of humanity's evolution have passed since Goethe's death, we will find—however we may otherwise regard the truth and value of anthroposophy—that it arose only by virtue of the living impulses of Goetheanism, through a living necessity, through experience of what does actually lie germinally in Goethe, and by cultivating, in all modesty, the plant that grows forth from his work.

Now the original name of the Goetheanum was the Johannes (or John) building, given it by friends of the anthroposophic outlook who, more than ten years ago now, instigated the building project. This name, the Johannes building, has nothing whatever to do with the Evangelist John but was taken—not by me but by others—from one of the protagonists in my Mystery Plays,[4] Johannes Thomasius; and this was because the Goetheanum was, among other things, intended for staging these Mystery Plays. Naturally a misunderstanding arose here, and it was thought that a reference was also intended to the author of the Gospel of St John.

That is why I often said—in this hall too, during the years when the Goetheanum was under construction—that the building took its name from Goethe because I derived my outlook in a living way from him. And then this name was officially taken up too by friends of the anthroposophic movement. I have never regarded this in any other light than as a form of gratitude toward what we can gain from Goethe, an act of dedication towards the towering individual, Goethe. It is not, though, as if what lies in Goethe's works themselves should be cultivated in the best or loveliest way at the Goetheanum in Dornach but rather that the anthroposophic worldview feels the deepest gratitude toward what Goethe brought to birth.

Thus if we see the name of the Goetheanum as originating in an act of grateful dedication, I do not think this can give cause for offence. At the same time it is understandable if someone with no knowledge of the anthroposophic outlook, encountering this building on the hill at Dornach, were to be oddly struck by the double cupola form, by the unfamiliar and seemingly odd forms of both the exterior and interior of the building and so on. And yet this building emerged with inner, artistic coherence from what is intended as the anthroposophic outlook. And therefore I can best describe the purpose of the building if I now try—in a somewhat different form from accounts I have given over many previous years—to answer the question, What is the aim of anthroposophy?

Anthroposophy seeks firstly to be knowledge of the world of spirit—a knowledge of the world of spirit that is fit and able to stand alongside the magnificent edifice of modern science. It seeks to stand beside modern science both in terms of its scientific rigour and by virtue of the fact that those who wish not only to inwardly absorb anthroposophy but also to develop it, must above all first have passed through the school of serious discipline as this is practised today in scientific enquiry.

Hence anthroposophy seeks to be the very opposite of how, as I described it, the world views it. It is astonishing, really, that ideas the very opposite of our real underlying intentions can become fixed in public discourse. The views of the world about anthroposophy, as I described them, are certainly *not* anthroposophy, which seeks, rather, to be serious enquiry into, and knowledge of the world of spirit.

Now as you know, everything purporting to be knowledge of the spiritual world is regarded somewhat disparagingly, or at least dubiously, today. The scientific education which humankind has enjoyed for the past three to four hundred years gradually culminated in the nineteenth century and the beginning of the twentieth in this view: that the rigorous methods of modern science enable us to study the world around us as it is available to our senses, and as human reason can derive from sensory perception with the help of empirical trials and observational methods. Wherever people believe themselves to draw on the strictest scientific foundations, they reject the possibility of perceiving spiritual realities. With a certain pride, or maybe with a certain humility, they hold that there are limits to our knowledge and as far as spiritual matters are concerned, we are compelled to resort to faith and belief alone.

But for a great many people whose education is underpinned by what is nowadays popularized everywhere as science, this gives rise to a serious inner conflict. Articles of faith have been passed down to us from olden times. People are unaware that these actually correspond to insights gained at earlier stages of humanity's development, which then became enshrined in tradition. If they are simply taken as professions of faith, the psyche becomes subject to conflict with everything that it otherwise engages with as it absorbs the rigorous findings of scientific methodology, and its consequences for humanity and practical life.

These scientific conquests are truly not merely the possession of a small, privileged group of human beings. No, this particular way of thinking that derives from science has already worked its way into primary education. And this outlook will go on spreading, right down to underlying strata of human existence; not science itself perhaps, but the kind of inner condition that arises from it. While many are unaware that their inmost longing is to gain ideas about the spirit that are as clear-cut as scientific ideas about the natural world, they do still suffer an inner conflict that comes to expression in all kinds of dissatisfaction with life. People feel a sort of restlessness and insecurity. They do not know how to integrate their thoughts and feeling with the life they live. This condition is ascribed to a variety of causes, but its real cause lies here.

Nowadays people demand real knowledge, in fact, not articles of faith about the world of spirit. Anthroposophy seeks to formulate such knowledge. In doing so, however, it has to resort to a very different concept of knowledge from the one that has become habitual today. In trying to characterize this concept of knowledge,

I'd like firstly to do this with a kind of metaphor, though it is more than a mere comparison; it is something that can lead us directly into anthroposophy's efforts to perceive supersensible, spiritual realities.

Consider first that strange world which all of us know as the other side of human existence—the world of dream. Each one of us can picture these colourful, manifold, rich and vivid images that dawn for us out of the dark depths of sleep. When we're awake and look back upon our dreams, we find that they are in some way connected with our waking condition, with what we are in waking life. Even if—and this is true beyond doubt—our dreams are sometimes prophetic, they are still connected nevertheless with what we have experienced. But this life experience is here subject in a sometimes excessive degree to what I might call a naturally configuring imagination, to a riotous kind of transformation. And in another way such dreams relate to diverse bodily conditions in us—to shortness of breath, to a rapid heartbeat. Disorders of the organism are experienced in dream in symbolic form.

Just to develop a little the idea we need here, imagine that we lived only in this world of dreams and had no other existence. Imagine that we could not step out of this dream-world ever, but that we regarded it as our reality. If in these circumstances our lives continued to be governed by some kind of outer powers, so that we went on living as we do, if the actions of spirit beings enabled us to go on walking about in towns and cities, to go on working and yet still dreaming, we human beings would regard this world of dream as our only reality, in the same way that dreamers regard their richly furnished dream-world as the only reality while they are caught up in their dreams. On awakening, the perspective of waking life, the way we then relate to our surroundings, enables us to form a view about the reality and meaning of the dream we have had. But caught up within a dream we are unable to form a view of the meaning and reality of the dream itself, of the degree to which it relates, say, to physical states of the body. We can only make such a judgement from the perspective of waking life. We have to wake up before we can judge the nature of our dreams.

Now we live primarily also in our will, since on awakening our will engages with the phenomena of the outer sense-world; it lives in the pictures this sense-world conveys to our psyche. We can form no judgement about reality other than through feeling our way into the sense-world and experiencing our connection with it. And from this perspective, which one can describe as a state of complete engagement of the soul with the sense-world via the body, we initially view this world of the senses as sole reality, as opposed to the phantasms of dream that seem not to belong to it. Yet everyone will ask themselves, sooner or later, especially when they survey all the pictures offered to them by the outer sense-world, how the soul and spirit they inwardly experience relates to the transformations and flux of this outer sense-world.

The great questions of existence emerge as we compare what we perceive in the outer world of the senses with what we feel arising from the depths of our human nature, within our thinking and whole sensibility, and our will. The reality of soul experience is one such question, and leads on to the greater question of the soul's immortality; then there is the question of human freedom, and numerous others. You see, we soon feel how different our experience is depending on whether we look outward into the world and receive sense impressions, or when we look inward and dwell within soul experiences. This inevitably elicits the question as to whether it may be possible to awaken in a higher sense so as to gain insight into sense reality from a higher perspective, in the same way that we gain a view about the dream-world from the perspective of the sense-world upon awakening naturally each morning.

If it is clear that the nature of dream images can be evaluated by comparison with reality when we awaken, then we can seek similarly to gain a point of view that can teach us something about the relationship of sensory experience itself to a higher level of reality. Thus the great question of spirit knowledge can be formulated as follows: Can we awaken, as it were, a second time, to a higher degree, out of our daily, waking consciousness; and will this second awakening give us insight and knowledge about the sense-world, in the same way that this sense-world provides insight into our dream life?

We can already sense how dreamlife works, and precise observation will give certain confirmation of it. When we dream, we feel our whole life of soul to be possessed by inchoate powers. As we wake up, we feel that we now have our physical life in our own hands again, to some degree. We feel that the physical body then subjects the riotous images of dreamlife to a greater discipline. We feel too that these dream images are riotous because we can experience, as we wake up or fall asleep, a moment when we no longer have the physical body fully in hand. Is it possible, in the same way as the powers of our organism forcibly pull us back into waking life in the sense-world, that conscious soul activity can induce a higher or second awakening in us?

This question can only be answered by, as I would put it, testing, trying out whether the soul finds powers for this higher awakening within itself; and only by answering it can a different concept of knowledge be created than the one we are used to today. The latter leads ultimately only to the 'ignorabimus' formulation,[5] the assertion that we cannot know a world of spirit.

To enquire into these questions we will first need to draw—as anthroposophy does—upon the faculties of soul that we already possess, asking whether these soul faculties can be developed into something higher and stronger, in the same way that waking life is stronger than dreamlife. We might say that this waking soul life we possess in adult life gradually itself developed from a dreamier life of soul that we possessed in infancy and early childhood. If we had remained at the phase of consciousness that we had in our first three years of life, we would still see the world as a kind of dream. But as we grew, we awoke from this dreamier existence.

This can give us the courage to seek, to start with, for certain powers of soul that can be further developed than they so far have been since infancy. And if we seriously tackle this question we will first of all turn to a faculty we possess which even the more significant philosophers of today[6] admit, on purely philosophical foundations, points to a spiritual or mental activity that is more or less independent of the body. This is the faculty of memory.

Let us recall, once again, what lives within our ordinary memory. This power is of course not initially one that can penetrate supersensible worlds of spirit. We are aware that this power of memory is only in full working order initially insofar as the psyche comes to expression within the body. And yet something remarkable can be discovered here. Our memories also include pictures of experiences that may have occurred decades ago. Depending on our particular constitution, manifold images, very similar to those of dream, but just more ordered and disciplined, arise in us of the experiences we have had of the sense-world and of ordinary life. And if our memory is reliable, a living knowledge rises in us today from depths of soul of things that existed many years ago but no longer stand before us in sense reality. I'm putting this in an easily accessible way, for we have to start from some sort of sure perspective. And so we can say this: in memory we possess thoughts and images that inwardly reflect what once existed, things that occurred in life but no longer presently exist.

And in this way a question can arise that is vague initially, and naturally only acquires importance if it can be answered; but we will see that it can in fact be answered: Is it possible, through inner soul-spiritual work, to acquire an additional power of soul, in a sense a transformation of the power of memory, by means of which we not only picture what no longer exists, but by means of which we think or picture something that does not, for now, exist at all in the sensory reality of earthly life, nor, either, by virtue of logical deduction. This question can be resolved only through serious inner work, which involves taking in hand and inwardly developing the faculty upon which memory relies, that of thinking and picturing itself.

How do thoughts unfold, and how does the picturing, thinking activity operate in ordinary life? Well, outer things make an impression upon us. Initially we have our sense perceptions. Then we form our thoughts from these sense perceptions, and carry these in our memory. And we know of course that it requires a certain effort to recall something that we were involved in years ago, a context we were part of, something that occurred. But we also know that in order to possess the world faithfully within our thoughts and not to introduce fantastical elements into these images of the outer world, we must surrender ourselves passively to the outer world. This passive surrender, supported additionally by all possible empirical and experimental methods, is indeed the right approach for natural science. But it is possible to begin to do something else with our life of thinking and picturing. We can try to take up pictures, thoughts, with inner activity, whatever their content might be; the content need only be one easily surveyed, and not suggestive in nature. Ill-defined thought contents, those we draw up from the depths of the soul, can easily have a suggestive effect. So we can try now to inwardly and actively assimilate a simple thought content of this kind, surrendering our whole psyche to this content time and time again.

In my books, *Knowledge of the Higher Worlds* and *Occult Science* I described this technique in more detail. Here I will only give the principle. If we repeatedly surrender ourselves to this chosen thought, quite irrespective of the outward significance of this thought that we inwardly assimilate, upon which we inwardly dwell, that we inwardly connect with others and in which we immerse our whole soul, then we will gradually begin to notice a remarkable enlivening of our thinking and picturing that comes about by such inner work. This living quality that develops is one that must be experienced to be evaluated. If we experience it, we will also begin to think in the following way. As a muscle strengthens when we exercise it, so the power of thinking within the soul is strengthened when, instead of surrendering ourselves passively to external impressions we undertake this inner work of picturing, repeatedly and in very vivid fashion bringing about a certain state within our soul. By this means we will at last succeed in filling thinking, which otherwise appears shadowy and vague even in memory pictures, with a soul-spiritual quality that possesses a sense of vitality similar to that we experience in relation to

our breathing and blood circulation. If I can put it like this, life
force streams into our now activated thinking.

Yes, true anthroposophy as spirit knowledge is something that
depends upon intimate inner methodologies of soul; not upon
invoking spirits in some way but on the soul itself reversing its
faculties of cognition and changing them. And if, in this way, we
increasingly empower our thinking then eventually—and it may
take years—we come to a very distinctive inner experience, one that
can be described as follows: If we only recall outward objects or
actions, we delve only to a certain depth in the soul, a level from
which we draw our memories and recollections. But if, as I have
described, we work upon our thinking in a living way, then eventually we arrive at the point of achieving a very precise form of
knowledge with this thinking; we delve deeper than the power of
memory is able to.

This is an important experience: to regard memories as lying at a
certain level to which we delve in the ordinary mind, drawing from it
our memory pictures, but then sensing that there is another, deeper
level in soul life. To this we can now descend, and we can then draw
from it thoughts through the power of an invigorated thinking that
are not the same as those to which we first surrendered ourselves. No,
they are of a quite different quality. Whereas memory can provide us
with pictures of things that are no longer there, by drawing on this
deeper level we now find that we can arrive at thoughts and pictures
we never otherwise possess in life.

Through this door of perception we have now penetrated the
world of spirit. And the first experience that arises is to gain a really
tableau-like retrospect of the whole of our earthly life hitherto. We
can say that in a single momentary vision—to put it somewhat
radically but this is pretty much so—we have time transformed into
space; we have our life on earth up to now spread out before our
mind in mighty images. And these images are different in quality
from recollections we might gain by sitting down and drawing them
forth by the power of our ordinary memory: pictures that we could
form of the continuity of our life back to nearly the time of our birth.

The panoramic tableau that we acquire in this way is very different in kind from those ordinary memories. The pictures passively formed in ordinary recall are distinguished by the way in which the outer world has impinged upon us. For instance, we remember meeting someone, and the impression he made on us; how someone showed us friendship, say. Or we recall the impression made on us by a natural phenomenon, the pleasure or pain caused either by this natural occurrence or by a human encounter and suchlike.

What we possess in the tableau I am speaking of, acquired through strengthened, invigorated thinking, is a vision of ourselves, of how, say, we approached another person with our particular qualities of temperament, our character, with what lived in us as longing and love. Whereas ordinary memory presents us with what approaches us from without, this memory tableau shows us more what we ourselves contributed to this experience, what emerged from within us. And whereas an ordinary memory will show us how, say, a natural phenomenon gave us pleasure or sorrow, how in other words the external world acted upon us, in the memory tableau we find more what moved us to go to a particular region of the earth where this experience was granted us. Thus we experience in this memory tableau more of what we ourselves contributed to the impressions we received. In brief, it is a total overview, removed from the outer world, of our life and all its activity. Really we now see ourselves as another, a second person. In this memory tableau we do not so much have the sense of our physical, spatial body, but we feel ourselves to be immersed in everything we experienced, and at the same time we feel that everything we experienced is in a sense a streaming etheric world. At the same time we learn to perceive in this streaming etheric world, which contains our own life in mighty images, as in an onrushing river, how this flowing etheric world of our own existence is connected with the etheric world in general. When, as a physical human being, we stand before the external world with our physical senses, we feel ourselves to be enclosed within our skin, and regard all other things as external to us. We feel a clear

contrast between subject and object, to put it more philosophi-
cally. But this is no longer so when we now embark upon invigorated thinking and enter into the volatile, fluctuating world of
what I will call the 'second' human being, the human being of
time as opposed to that of the physical, corporeal realm of space.

We can really speak of a time body, for we can feel here how, as if
suddenly, this whole life on earth we have spent hitherto is moving in
a broader world of which it is part. It starts to make sense to say that
the dense, solid physical world is complemented by a finer world in
which we have spent our flowing, streaming life—an etheric world.
Only now do we come to discern what an etheric world is, and what
we ourselves are as a second person, as second human being, within
this etheric world. And in doing so we have reached the first level of
supersensible spirit. In direct perception, more or less, because we feel
ourselves now to be a being of spirit-soul within a world of spirit-
soul, we know that the whole world is pervaded and interwoven with
the soul-spirit nature that we contain within ourselves. But as yet we
know no more than this. And above all we are as yet unaware of any
other soul-spiritual world than the one connecting us as earthly
(etheric) human beings with the surrounding etheric world.

But we can make further progress. Having once acquired this
capacity to experience oneself within the etheric realm, to experience
the etheric world through oneself, we can then ascend by developing
another kind of soul faculty. This involves engendering in the soul
what I would call the opposite process to the one first described. First
we attempted to render thinking very active, very alive within us so
that, instead of passive thinking, we possess an inwardly active
stream of surging, weaving energy. And now we must try to suppress
again in turn these thoughts freely hovering in the soul, doing so
with the same inner intentionality and power of will.

Everything I am describing must be undertaken in soul exercises
with as much exactitude as a mathematician tackling equations. We
undertake this in full deliberation so that it is not distorted by any
kind of false mysticism, dreaming or even suggestion and suchlike.
We must undertake these exercises in the soul with the same sober

coolness—for the warmth and enthusiasm that arise are engendered by what we then see, not by the method we employ—as we would use to solve problems in geometry. But despite this, one thing becomes apparent. Once we succeed in having these invigorated thought pictures, especially of our life so far, which can fill us entirely when we dwell upon them, it is hard to detach ourselves from them again. We have to develop the inner strength to suppress these thoughts once more, having first elicited them through our own activity. In other words, we have to gain the ability to extinguish all thinking and picturing, having first kindled it in intense activity. Erasing our ordinary thoughts is already hard enough, but is relatively easy compared to extinguishing thoughts and pictures of this kind, which we have first entertained in the mind through enhanced, intensified activity.

For this reason, this extinguishing signifies something quite different. And if we succeed—again through long practice (though we can undertake such exercises at the same time as others, so that both capacities are developed simultaneously)—in achieving this, in engendering in the mind strongly active thinking processes, and then extinguishing these again, then something comes over the soul that—since words are needed to describe these things—I would call the soul falling inwardly silent.

Such inner silence in the mind is something we simply do not know in ordinary life. The spiritual enquirer who wishes to pursue the anthroposophic path of investigation needs first of all an enhanced life of thinking and picturing, which gives us the kind of self-knowledge I have characterized. The next thing is to create a completely empty mind, so that everything otherwise existing in the soul as thinking, feeling and will, falls silent, but only after we have first enhanced and intensified this soul activity to the highest degree. Then this silence of the soul will be something very special. I can describe this stage, which can be called the second stage in spirit knowledge, roughly in the following way.

Imagine you are in a large city, surrounded by a cacophony of noise that deafens you. Now imagine leaving this city: as we get further away the tumult quietens somewhat. Though we still hear its gradually fading noise and alarms, the quietness increases. And the further we go, the quieter it becomes. Eventually we reach the silence of the forest, and perhaps find ourselves surrounded by tranquillity. We have made this journey from tumultuous noise to outward silence. But now I can go further still. This is not something that occurs in outer reality, but the idea gains full reality if we come to what I have called the 'soul falling silent'.

I'm going to use a very mundane comparison: you can have a certain capital and keep spending it. Then you have less and less, and finally nothing left at all. Then you have 'zero' capital. But this may not be the end of it: you can go on to incur debts, and then you have less than nothing. We're familiar with this idea from mathematics. The same can be true of stillness, silence. Passing from the noise and tumult of the world, we can enter complete silence, as it were, 'zero'. But then we can go further still, gaining greater quiet than quietness: we can descend below this zero point to become quieter and quieter, a negative quiet, negative tranquillity that is deeper than tranquillity. And this is what does happen if we extinguish this intensified soul life, falling to a deeper silence than mere 'zero silence', if I can put it like that. We create in the soul a tranquillity that goes to the other pole, a silence that is more than the silence we possess when the ordinary mind is tranquil.

And once we enter into this silence, when the soul feels that it has, if you like, distanced itself from the world, not only because the world grows still around the soul, but by virtue of the soul feeling that, though the world cannot become more tranquil than 'zero', the soul itself can delve deeper into silence than the silence of the world can be. And when this negative stillness arrives, from the other side of existence the world of spirit starts to speak to us, really it starts to speak. Otherwise as human beings, with the words we form outwardly upon the air, we keep interrupting the tranquillity of the world. But by engendering in ourselves this tranquillity that is deeper than mere silence, deeper than zero quiet, the world of spirit begins to utter itself in a language, a speech we must first become accustomed to, which does not in any way resemble the language of words. This language shapes itself for us so that we gradually become accustomed to it, hearkening to qualities we know well from the world of the senses—to colours, tones and in short everything we are familiar with from sense perception. We have to resort to these sense experiences if we are to describe the distinctive impressions we can receive in this way from the world of spirit.

I want to draw your attention to a few aspects here. Let us assume that in this inner silence of the soul we have experienced the following: an impression that from depths of spirit there rises a power that, as it were, approaches us assertively, and acts upon us with a stirring or arousing force. Initially this is a spiritual experience: we know that the spirit is manifesting. By comparing what we experience in this way with an experience in the sense-world, we can recognize that the comparable sense experience is, roughly, one we have when meeting the colour yellow. Just as we coin a word or phrase to express something in the sense-world, so now we can take the yellow colour as an embodiment of this spiritual experience; or in another instance we take a tone to express this spiritual experience. In the same way that we use language to speak of the sensory world, so we employ sense qualities, sense impressions, to speak of what we receive in a spiritual manner in the silence of the soul from the world of spirit.

This is how we characterize spiritual realities, and how I described them in my books, *Theosophy* and *Occult Science*. But such accounts have to be rightly understood. It has to be recognized that a new kind of language emerges in relation to the deep silence of the soul. By contrast to the external, articulated speech that we possess as human beings, that we use to speak to others, something now resounds toward us and into us from the world of spirit which we have to clothe in tangible words in some way; but then, in turn, such words must be understood, perceived, with the necessary subtlety of vision; these perceptions must be translated into human language, must be conveyed in words that are, of course, coined within and for the realm of the senses.

In entering this experience of the soul fallen silent, we can then come to recognize that what we first possess, this world of intensified thinking, is basically only a picture, a picture of what we only now perceive and for which we now have a language; a picture that served as the starting point for penetrating the soul's deep silence. Now the world of spirit speaks to us through this silence of the soul. And now we become able, too, to extinguish this whole life tableau we first formed, which conjured our life on earth before us etherically, so that the inner silence of the soul can also come to bear upon this life of ours as we lead it here on earth. The illusion of the I that can live only by virtue of the physical body also now ceases.

If we adhere too strongly to the ego due to theoretical or practical egoism, we will not succeed in establishing this silence of the soul in the face of our own life-tableau. If we battle with this theoretical and practical egoism, we will come to see that initially we possess this ego because we can make use of our body in physical life, and that this body enables us to say 'I' to ourselves. If we then take leave of this corporeal sense of ego and enter into what I described as the etheric world, where we flow and merge with the world, where the world is etherically one with our own etheric, then we no longer hold fast to this ego; and then we can experience the reality of which this life-tableau, to which we raise ourselves, is an image, a reflection. We experience our pre-earthly existence. We experience this pre-earthly existence in which we inhabited a world of spirit before we descended into a physical human body through conception and birth. Anthroposophy does not speak of immortality, of the human soul's eternal existence, out of merely philosophical speculation, but it speaks of how, by particular development of our soul faculties, we can forge a path to vision of our being of soul before it descends to the earth.

Now, indeed, direct vision is vouchsafed to the hushed, silent mind of the eternal soul existing in the world of spirit. Just as, in memory, we can look back upon what we have experienced on earth so that past occurrences in our life awaken in the mind, so now, after we have learned the language of the spirit world within the silent soul, as I described this, there awaken in us occurrences that do not pertain to earthly life at all, through which we prepared ourselves for this life on earth before we descended to birth.

And now we can look upon what we were before we descended to life on earth. While contemplating the life-tableau still, it is clear that we ourselves are pervaded and interwoven with spirit; but although this is a subtle, etheric spirit, it is nevertheless in some respects still of this world's nature, natural spirit if you like, that we experience ourselves to be. But now, as we gaze into pre-earthly existence and see ourselves connecting with what father and mother endow us with at birth, we also see the unity between the moral world order and the physical world order. In this pre-earthly existence lie all the powers that subsequently elaborate themselves as echoes or after-images during physical life on earth. We see how, in physical life on earth too, spiritual powers hold sway upon the human body. We can admire the structure of the human brain as it is gradually configured. We can turn our attention to the undifferentiated nature of this brain when we were first born, how it was shaped by our seventh year, round about the time of the change of teeth. We can turn our gaze to inner, plastic, configuring forces. Thus we do not have to make do only with vague generalities concerning 'forces of heredity'.

What we develop in the first few years of life alone by way of plastic configuration of the brain and the whole organism, is the echo, the after-image of universal, far-reaching occurrences experienced in the world of spirit, where we were surrounded by spirit beings in the same way as we are surrounded by the kingdoms of nature and other human beings on earth. And we now come to discern how the world of spirit works into the physical, earthly world, and how in everything inwardly and actively organizing us we find the after-effects of this pre-earthly existence at work. Here we learn to know the soul and spirit as they work within the physical.

And in the further course of spiritual development, a third element must be added to what I have already described. I have already shown that we must overcome the illusion of the ego, must overcome ordinary, everyday theoretical or practical egoism and come to see that this ego of earthly life is bound up with the physical body, where it initially manifests in a sense of the physical body. But here already something arises in physical life on earth which, if I name it, may cause some to feel a little philosophical discomfort since it is not usually counted at all among the faculties of cognition. Yet it must be named; and those who have invigorated their thinking in the way I described, and then succeed in hushing or silencing the soul, will recognize the need for this. The third quality that must join the others is a higher enhancement, a more intense development of something that exists in ordinary life as love, as love of people, love of nature, love for all our works and deeds. All of this, already existing in ordinary life, can be kindled by discarding theoretical and practical egoism in the way described. Love must be enhanced, and as it intensifies, as the power of love—the surrender of oneself to other things and people—is joined by invigorated thinking and the soul's deeper silence, we arrive at a third level: we come to perceive and comprehend the true form of the human I, now not only acquainting ourselves with pre-earthly existence but also coming to discern that an enhanced power of love further energizes the other enhanced and intensified powers of cognition that we have developed. We arrive at the point of this specific experience: everything we have so far achieved has nothing more to do, now, with the physical body; instead we now experience ourselves outside the physical body, we experience the world in a way it cannot be experienced through the physical body. Instead of natural phenomena we experience spirit beings. We no longer experience ourselves as a natural being between birth and death but now as a spirit being in pre-earthly existence.

If we have achieved this, and add to our capacities an enhanced, strengthened power of love, the ability to surrender ourselves to what we perceive, to offer ourselves up to it with our whole, body-free being, then perception arises of what we possess in the immediate present, independent of the physical and also etheric human body. We gain direct vision of what dwells within us and passes through the portal of death into post-earthly existence when we return to a world of spirit. By acquainting ourselves with what we are in a body-free condition, we also learn to see what continues to exist in a body-free state once we lay aside the physical body at death.

You see, everything turns upon gaining perception of the eternal nature of the human soul. But only in this way do we come to discern the true I that passes through both birth and death, and that rests or dwells—we cannot say 'lives'—within the body. But at the same time we come to see how this I moves and is active in the world of spirit in pre-earthly existence. We come to see this in a way that resembles how we become acquainted with the human being here in sensory, physical existence through sense perception. Just as we walk about here amongst natural things, amongst natural occurrences, amongst other people, so we come to see how the soul in pre-earthly existence moves around, if you like, in the world of spirit. And we also come to see how its motion there, its conduct there, is dependent on a previous life on earth. As I said, we learn to perceive the unity of moral and natural worlds, and how, in pre-earthly existence, we are not only pervaded by spirit but also by moral impulses. When we have the etheric life-tableau before us we can discern only that the whole world is pervaded by spirit. Now, on the other hand, we also come to recognize that our being of soul and spirit was impelled and imbued with moral impulses which then surface in the memory, and altogether in our moral predisposition during physical life. We learn to see the unity of the moral and physical world.

But we also learn to recognize that in this moral-physical world which the soul has passed through in the spirit—where the physical world appears only in images that shine into the spirit from physical existence—that the soul, that the true I of the human being in the spiritual world, lives in accordance with its previous existence. Indeed, once we overcome the illusion of the ordinary earthly ego, when we come to spiritual vision, then we can perceive the I as it passed already through the world of spirit between death and rebirth, how it conducted itself within this world informed by moral impulses in accordance with its previous life on earth; and how it then carries with it all this into the new life on earth as an inner destiny, which comes to expression in a person's inclinations, in the particular nuance or longing through which a person is drawn or driven to one thing or another in earthly life.

This does not impair our freedom, though. Within certain constraints, freedom still exists, just as, if we build a house, we are then free to move into it or not. But we *will* move into it, for we built it for ourselves for a particular reason. Similarly we remain free, even if we know that we possess certain drives in our physical body, to turn in one or another direction in life, or to decide to live in a particular place. We may regard it as the destiny we have woven for ourselves from previous earthly lives out of the world that contains not only laws of spirit but also moral laws through which we passed and which imbued what we have been in a previous life on earth with particular spiritual impulses, thus creating our new destiny for this life on earth. But in the same way, if we consider what originates from our last earthly life, as described, we will notice that the soul's eternal nature has determined our destiny during this life. We carry this eternal nature out into the world after we cross the threshold of death, uniting with our soul what possesses the nature of soul, or morality, so as to bring it into further harmony with the requirements of the moral world; and then, in turn, bearing what you might call the resulting outcome of what we were in our past life, and what the world of spirit makes of us between death and rebirth, we enter again upon a new life on earth.

Thus it really is a matter of first developing a certain capacity of perception and cognition by means of which we can look upward into the world of spirit. Consider this: not every person is naturally gifted as a mathematician. In fact most people find it very difficult to entertain geometrical thoughts that can be drawn only from the imagination. Geometry as such does not exist directly in nature, though it can enable us to understand nature. But we first have to engender geometry within us, and through geometry we create forms that lead us into dead structures. With the same inner rigour we create inward vision by developing intensified thinking, the silence of the soul, the love that becomes a power of perception. But the difference here is that we then grasp life, living things, sentience and self-awareness. In the same way that we comprehend lifeless things through mathematics, so, by proceeding rigorously and precisely in a mathematical way, we can develop a form of vision that comprehends life, sentience, self-awareness.

And so we can say that if we pursue and cultivate anthroposophy with dedication, we do so as if we were obliged to account to the strictest mathematician for what we develop through our powers of perception and cognition. The development of mathematical thoughts is, if I can put it like this, elementary anthroposophy. And once we have learned to develop this self-creative mode of mathematics in relationship to dead things, then we also gain an impetus to develop the modes of cognition that will lead to perception of what I have here described. We become acquainted with a different world content: first the dead world, perceived through mathematics—for mathematics is elementary anthroposophy—and then the living, sentient, self-aware world as it can reveal itself to us if we investigate it with anthroposophic insight.

Thus it is important not to confuse what is ordinarily thought of as 'clairvoyance' or suchlike with the pursuit in anthroposophy of perception of the world of spirit. If we refer to knowledge of the spiritual world as this appears in anthroposophy as clairvoyance—and we can of course use this term—then we must qualify it by speaking of 'exact' clairvoyance, just as this term is used in mathematics: exact clairvoyance as opposed to the confused, mystic clairvoyance that people usually think of when this term is employed.

Now my account may have given you the sense that this is a difficult undertaking. Yes indeed, it is difficult, not easy! That is why a great many people who want to form a view about what goes on in Dornach do not try to acquaint themselves with things that are difficult for them to fathom, instead viewing them as trivial, confused clairvoyance and suchlike. And then everything I spoke of at the beginning of my lecture arises. Yet the anthroposophy worthy of its name, which I am speaking of, is an exact mode of cognition, albeit one that everyone can understand with their healthy human reason—just as you can understand a painting without necessarily becoming a painter. To pursue anthroposophic enquiries, you have to be an anthroposophic investigator just as you have to be a painter to paint a picture. But everything I have described today can be understood with sound human reason and common sense—as long as we ourselves do not place obstacles and preconceptions in the way of it.

To paint a picture you need to be a painter. But to judge a painting you need only invoke sound common sense and human perception. To contribute to anthroposophy you have to be a spiritual investigator. But to understand anthroposophy you need only bring to bear upon the accounts presented of it—though some of these will naturally be better than others—your sound, independent human sensibility, unsullied by 'scientific' and similar prejudices. Anthroposophy is only in its infancy as yet, and matters that I may not have described very well today will grow clearer, will be better described as it develops. And then a time will come that eventually comes for everything new in the world. It took a long time, after all, for the Copernican worldview to gain acceptance. No less than this new outlook, it overturned all the ideas people previously possessed. Today this worldview is regarded as self-evident and is taught in schools. The Copernican worldview was once upon a time thought to be ridiculous fantasy and nonsense. And anthroposophy is now seen in this way too, but will eventually become self-evident. And anthroposophy can wait to be accepted as self-evident.

This anthroposophy is to be cultivated initially in the Goetheanum at Dornach. I will just conclude by saying that over ten years ago friends of our movement formed the plan of building a centre for our anthroposophy, and asked me to implement it. This became the Goetheanum. If anthroposophy were only a theoretical worldview or merely a reform movement, how would people have responded to the idea of building a home for anthroposophy? They would have gone to a building company, which would then have built something in whatever traditional classical or more modern style might be required. But anthroposophy is not a merely theoretical matter. It is not simply a body of abstract knowledge but it involves and encompasses the whole human being. The anthroposophic investigator very quickly discovers this.

You see, one needs one's head to form thoughts about external nature, and even more so to engage in philosophical speculations. The things we perceive in the way I described for the world of spirit in relation to the hushed soul, manifest in a more fleeting way. For this we need presence of mind to catch it as it flies. But we also need our whole human nature. The head alone is not enough. The whole human organism has to place itself at the service of the spirit so as to summon into the memory what we perceive without the body. In order to illustrate this, let me offer my personal experience, a personal note related to it.

For instance, it is not my custom ever to prepare a lecture in the way this is usually done. Rather, I customarily experience the thoughts and ideas necessary for a lecture in a spiritual fashion, in the same way that one must spiritually experience any results of spiritual research. But mere thinking, into which, after all, we must convey and relocate what we experience through intensified thinking and in the human soul, mere head thinking, is not adequate for this. One must be more intimately bound up with the whole human being if one is to express what one experiences in the realm of spirit. There are various points of reference to really also introduce this into the ordinary mind so that one can speak of it. It is my custom to record with a pen everything that dawns on me from the world of spirit, to formulate it, write it down by hand, either in words or in sketches. This means I have wagon-loads of notebooks.[7] I never look again at what I record in this way. These writings and sketches are there, but only in order to connect what I investigate in spirit with my whole human nature, so that, as it were, I do not simply comprehend it with my head in order to convey it in words, but with my whole being.

Anthroposophy takes hold of the whole human being. And in

consequence it becomes an expression of the Goethean worldview in another respect too. It is so initially by taking inspiration from the way in which Goethe observed the metamorphoses of plant and animal life. In these observations of Goethe, thought becomes very alive as he attempts to intensify it in the way I described. But Goethe was also the one who forged a bridge between cognition and art. In his artistic conviction, Goethe coined this lovely phrase: Art is the manifestation of secret laws of nature which would never be revealed without it.[8] In other words, Goethe knew that in real knowledge we encompass the sway of spiritual activity that is then embedded or implanted in matter—whether we are a sculptor, musician or painter. Goethe knew that the imagination is a kind of intentional projection of what we can experience with the spirit in its pure form.

Knowledge such as anthroposophy, which is rooted in the life of spirit, flows by itself also into artistic creativity. It flows into artistic creation if we perceive the human being, in the way I described, as influenced by pre-earthly powers that play into our earthly and corporeal existence. Then we have the sense that mere concepts, mere reason, cannot encompass human nature. At a certain point, instead, we have to let our abstract concepts pass over into artistic vision so that we can feel how nature has created the human being as an artwork.

Naturally this is open to ridicule in some quarters, for people find nothing worse than hearing that something should be grasped artistically for a full understanding. But however much it is claimed that logic, not art, should be paramount when studying the world, we will not come closer to understanding the artistry of nature in this way. Here we have to pass over into artistic perception to perceive the real secrets of nature. This is what Goethe meant when he said: Art is a manifestation of secret laws of nature which will never be revealed otherwise. He held the same view when he at last reached Italy after long desiring to go there, and believed he had found his artistic ideal. He said this: When I look at these artworks, it strikes me that the Greeks, when they fashioned their works of art, obeyed the same laws as creative nature: laws which I am intent on tracing.[9]

Goethe is someone who always seeks to enhance a merely cognitive apprehension into a work of art. And because anthroposophy is of like mind it was not possible simply to go to an architect and request some building or other as a centre for anthroposophy, executed in some neo-classical style. No, a quite different outlook on life and art underlay this endeavour.

The underlying impulse for this is something I have often compared, somewhat trivially, to the relationship between a nutshell and a nut. The nut that we eat has been formed according to particular laws of growth and development, as has the nutshell likewise. You cannot imagine a nutshell being adapted externally to the nut, made to fit it, as it were. The shell develops according to the same laws of development as the nut does. In the same way, the building's external, visible forms,[10] and the paintings of the cupolas, the sculpted motifs as well, were developed according to the same laws as the words proclaimed within it in speech and song—a fitting shell for them, if you like. Like the nutshell to the nut, this building had to relate to what was cultivated within it. And in the view of many, not only my own, this is also indeed what was achieved. With eurythmy presentations, performances of this special art and language of movement—where scenes are enacted by people or groups of people in motion: not dance movements or mime but really speech made visible in gesture—we developed an expressive art of movement[11] on the stage of the Goetheanum. And the forms in which the human soul expressed itself in the art of eurythmy were in lovely harmonious accord with the lines and forms in the building's architraves, the capitals and columns, the whole form of the building including its painted surfaces. There was a single unity between what was cultivated inside the building and its exterior, enclosing form. When a speaker spoke from the rostrum, when things that had been apprehended in spirit were formed into words, and resounded into the auditorium, what was spoken from the podium was the nut, the kernel living at the centre. The building's artistic form had to correspond and match this kernel. The architecture, in all its details, had to proceed from the same impulse, the same sources, as anthroposophy itself. You see, anthroposophy is not an abstract, theoretical body of knowledge but involves encompassing life itself, life in its entirety. It therefore inevitably comes alive. It fulfils what Goethe likewise said: Those who have science and art also possess religion. But for those who have neither, religion is essential.[12]

A nine-metre-high wooden sculpture[13] was intended to embody and encompass everything that lived in the forms of the Goetheanum, and all that could ever have been said or artistically presented there. This sculptural 'group' depicts Christ, the Representative of Humanity, whom Ahriman and Lucifer seek to tempt. Now it is not that anthroposophy has anything sect-like about it. Anthroposophy has no interest at all in opposing any religious conviction, let alone in establishing a new religion. But it is able to show how true spirit knowledge tends toward the highpoint of religious evolution, toward the Representative of Humanity, Christ, toward the divine Christ incarnated in the body of Jesus of Nazareth, and how this picture of the midpoint of all earth evolution, this picture of the mystery of Golgotha, is needed in spirit cognition. Anthroposophy certainly does nurture a religious mood, but it does not seek to establish a new religion.

What anthroposophy sought to achieve in the Goetheanum was intended to proceed from the same impulses from which also the spoken word, and song, emerge. And it can be even said that when one stepped up onto the podium—and I say this in all modesty—the forms of the pillars, the whole architectural form of the interior, the sculpted and painted interior, were an admonition to summon words that would really engage with the true nature of the human being. It was like a continual prompting to the speaker to place words into this space that would be worthy of it.

Thus the building was to be an outward sheathing for anthroposophy, proceeding entirely from the spirit of anthroposophy but present to sensory perception. There was nothing symbolic or allegorical about it. The whole building's architecture, sculptural forms

and painting were created to give expression to things that had been
encompassed and comprehended in living spirit vision: not in
rationally conceived symbols, but to convey living ideas, fluid inward
thoughts about the world of spirit. All this came to expression
through the immediacy of artistic sensibility, through direct vision.
There wasn't a single symbol in the whole building. And if people say
the edifice had a symbolic quality, they are talking in the same way as
those who speak about anthroposophy without familiarizing themselves with it.

And thus the building was to the outward eye what anthroposophy is intended to be for the human soul. Anthroposophy is after
all meant to be the mode of apprehension that recognizes the longing
flaring and flickering in people today to find the realm of supersensible spirit; that recognizes how modern humanity, through the
scientific education now becoming so widespread, can no longer
make do with traditional tenets of belief but inevitably now seeks to
know things, to find knowledge that also ascends to the supersensible
world. At the same time anthroposphy recognizes how an inner
restlessness and dissatisfaction emerge from the absence of such
thoughts and knowledge.

Anthroposophy seeks to serve the present moment, the modern
era, so as to properly serve also what human beings need from this
era to develop on into the forthcoming future. What anthroposophy
seeks to be invisibly for human souls, as nurturing sheath, as inner
homestead, the Goetheanum was to be for the outward eye. If the
Goetheanum had been only a symbolic building, the pain at its loss
would not have been nearly so great, for one could still have
repeatedly re-awoken it in one's memory. But the Goetheanum was
no such matter of mere recall. It was something which, like every
work of art, seeks to offer itself to immediate sensory vision, that
seeks to proclaim the spirit to the world of senses. When the Goetheanum was burned down, therefore, everything the Goetheanum
sought to be was lost. And yet it may nevertheless have shown that
anthroposophy cannot be something narrowly theoretical, not mere
knowledge, but can and should be living content in all directions,

and that this is why it had to build its home in a unique and distinct manner.

The Goetheanum sought to present to the outward eye the spirit that anthroposophy presents to the soul. And anthroposophy should offer to the human soul what this soul really demands out of the inmost need of the modern age: a perception, a knowledge, an artistic apprehension of the world of spirit. Souls demand this, long for it, because they increasingly feel that they can only come to a full sense of their human dignity by experiencing the full scope of their human destiny.

The Goetheanum was something that could burn down. A catastrophic fate robbed us of it. The pain of those who loved it is greater than words can describe. Something that was configured from the same sources from which anthroposophy also flows, and through which it seeks to serve humanity, had to be formed of physical material. And in the same way that the human body itself, as you will have seen from my account today, is the sensory image and the sensory effect of an eternal spirit, but then lapses at death to enable the spirit to evolve in other forms, so—and I will close these observations now by comparing the misfortune at Dornach with other processes at work in the cosmos—it was possible for flames to devour forms that had to be material in order to be available to the outward eye. But what anthroposophy should be is built of the spirit, and only flames of the spirit can engulf it. Just as the human spirit-soul is victorious over corporeality when this is destroyed at death, so anthroposophy still feels itself to be alive despite losing its home in Dornach, the Goetheanum.

We can say that physical flames were able to destroy what had to be built for the outward eye of outward physical material. But the anthroposophy that must exist for humanity's further evolution, is built of spirit, and the flames of spiritual life will not consume it since these flames are not consuming but strengthening ones; they are flames that give more intrinsic life. And the life that is to manifest through anthroposophy as a life of perception and knowledge of the higher world, must be tempered in the flames of the greatest human enthusiasm of soul and spirit. Then anthroposophy will go on growing and changing.

If we live in the spirit in this way, the pain of earthly things passing away will not affect us any less. But we will realize, nevertheless, that we can lift ourselves above all this if we know—and spirit perception gives us this knowledge—that spirit will always vanquish matter, and continually transform itself into matter once again.

LECTURE 2

ENHANCING HUMAN POWERS OF PERCEPTION TO DEVELOP IMAGINATION, INSPIRATION AND INTUITION

DORNACH, 14 APRIL 1923

DURING this course[14] for teachers and those interested in education, the special anthroposophic courses I will give alongside it are intended to be accessible also to people who have only recently encountered anthroposophy, or who are right at the beginning of studying it. Much of what I will say here therefore will be a kind of repetition for those more versed in anthroposophy. And yet I think that such repetition can also be very useful in various respects.

The subject I will speak on today is intended as a kind of further elaboration of what I presented in the public lecture I gave last week in various places in Switzerland.[15] It will follow on from that lecture, and develop it in certain ways.

If we survey the whole compass of human life, we find that it can be divided into two strictly separate parts: a life we lead when awake, thus our ordinary waking consciousness; and the other aspect of life, usually shorter, when we are asleep. This part of our life is one plunged in unconsciousness, in which consciousness only flares up momentarily in the colourful variety of our dream world. Thus if we speak from the perspective of human consciousness, we have to say that during waking life our mind is filled with a content supplied by our senses. What we learn about the world through our senses is, we can say, present as images in our mind. We experience this. Whether in ordinary life or in science, we connect what our senses tell us with our ideas, our thoughts. That is, we combine our sense perceptions, seeking to discover lawfulness within this sensory world we apprehend.

The faculty of thinking is what we use to do all this. We connect the ideas and thoughts we can acquire by means of our thinking capacity with our sense impressions. And then there is something else we also elaborate during waking life. One impression may be pleasant to us, another unpleasant. Sympathy is elicited in us by certain impressions, antipathy by others. This sympathy and antipathy is present in the most varied ways and nuances. We refer to this inner experience of things, the pleasure, pain, elation or sorrow they give us, as our feelings about them, and we distinguish clearly, no doubt, between our feelings and thoughts, with the latter offering us something more in the nature of outward representation of the world. Our thoughts do not live only within us, but represent something outward. Through our thoughts we acquire something of the outer world. The very word 'picture', as a verb, means that we gain an impression from outside ourselves. What we picture inwardly comes from without, initially. Thus picturing and thinking point us outward, whereas feeling points us inward. We have the definite sense that what we feel is experienced in a more inward way, and that it is not as directly connected with outer things as the mental picture or thought.

But there is something else we experience too. An angry dog will cause some people to run away. Some people even run off if they catch sight of a mouse. And other outward impressions and realities similarly instigate actions. In this case we speak of our will being activated. Whereas feelings can unfold in us without external motion, through our will, to put it very roughly for now, our whole organism comes into activity or motion relative to the outer world.

Thus we speak of the conscious mind as it functions during the day. And we distinguish between the waking state and the unconscious, which is also part of our life, in which we are immersed during the hours of sleep. And out of this unconsciousness also rises the colourful variety of our dream life.

But now let us consider for a moment matters of importance for ordinary human consciousness. The ordinary mind can see how the world of dreams rises out of unconscious sleep and glimmers into consciousness. And then, in waking experience, we become aware similarly of thinking, feeling and will.

How can we give an easily accessible account of this difference between our unconscious state, from which dreams emerge, and our fully waking condition?

Well, it will not take long to realize that in waking life we feel ourselves to be involved, engaged with, what we call our physical organism.

Then consider the dream world that unfolds before you in pictures: in this condition you are not involved in your physical organism. On awakening, we feel especially that the will penetrates our physical organism again. Our senses too need to be controlled and managed by the will in waking life. And thus we can say that the sleeping state, from which dreams emerge, passes over into the waking state by virtue of the fact that we engage the will, if you like, in our physical organism.

Let us therefore look at this physical organism for a moment. Even just in saying this I am appealing really to your capacity for sense observation. I'm appealing to what you know as a result of this capacity for sense observation. Initially, indeed, you can have no knowledge of this physical organism beyond what the senses furnish you with and what you can think about it. No school of anatomy or physiology knows anything about this physical organism other than what the senses teach us to know, and what can be comprehended through thinking as it combines and interrelates sense perceptions.

But this will draw our attention to the fact that we must first have recourse to the senses—and we become aware of this as we employ the mind—if we wish to know anything about the world in general and the physical human organism in particular: the senses and thinking.

So let us now examine the senses for a moment and consider, in an easily accessible way, what our senses show us in relation to two characteristically different states, those of waking and sleeping.

People generally reflect too little on these matters since, if they are not actually blind, they receive the lion's share of conscious experience from their eyes, which are precisely the organs that close when we are asleep, so that outer impressions are kept at bay. But think now of the other senses. Can you believe that your ear, if you do not plug it, provides you with experiences during sleep that are different from those you have in waking life in the physical body? If you properly consider the physical body, and do not stop up your ears at night, it is impossible to think that something different occurs in your physical ears when you sleep from what occurs when you're awake. There are no grounds for this to be true. But the fact you're unaware of it is a quite different matter.

Or let us enquire into the sense of warmth. We perceive heat and cold. Do you think that the temperature you perceive when awake, the heat, stops short of your skin while you are asleep? It will naturally exert the same action upon your skin at night as it does during the day. Thus with the exception of the sense of sight, you are exposed to the very same impressions while asleep as when you are awake.

If that were not the case you would have to assume that while asleep you were covered by some kind of warmth-shield that keeps the heat away. You would have to assume that some good spirit plugs your ears so that external impressions are no longer able to enter them. Considering this, you will realize that the eye is so sensitive that the human organism has arranged matters so that, by an act of will, we close the curtains of our eyelids at night while we're asleep.

However, it is true to say that the external world does help a little to keep sense impressions at bay while we're sleeping. Recently there was a newspaper article saying that it would be more pleasant for people in Basel who live near music venues, and want to sleep at night, if concerts would end at half-past ten in the evening instead of eleven. This is a clear indication that people would prefer to have their ears spared, but this can only be done in an external way. To sum up, the outer world continues to act upon all our senses while we're asleep, apart from the eyes.

And then we must go on to ask what happens with our thinking, our thoughts? We might start from various angles in tackling this question; but in our era modern science has gained widespread acceptance, and so modern people are aware that every sense transmits impressions on into the body via nerves, and that these impressions therefore continue inward and connect sensory perception with thinking.

You see, if it is the case, even in the relative stillness of the night, that your ear remains open to auditory impressions in your surroundings, in the same way as when you are awake, then why should these impressions cease to continue via the nerves into our thinking?

In other words, your physical organs, with the exception of the eyes, do not fend off sense impressions at night, nor do they keep thoughts at bay. And you can see—though this inevitably remains a little hypothetical for outward observation, even if social customs do allow for certain senses to be undisturbed at night—that this does not apply to other senses, such as the sense of temperature, heat and cold, nor to the sense of touch. If you press your thumb on the table you feel the pressure, don't you? So why would you not perceive pressure also when you lie on your back in bed? Naturally you must perceive this pressure, mediated by the sense of touch, throughout the night. Likewise, if you place something on your hand, you feel it; so why would you not feel the blanket too while you are asleep? And as well as this, why would the senses not continue to convey sense impressions to your mind and thoughts?

Thus if we observe things with an open mind we have to say that even when the physical body lies in bed during sleep it still goes on receiving sense impressions in the usual way. We still have the same experiences that we are conscious of in the day as thoughts. And just as we know nothing of sense impressions despite them existing at night, our thoughts still exist although we know nothing of them.

People are not usually aware of the fact that they keep thinking all the time they are asleep, but do not know it. Just as little as we are aware of the pressure of the blanket on us, so we know nothing of the thoughts that go on unfolding in sleep. We keep thinking all our lives, not only when we are awake. Though these thoughts are not conscious during sleep, they still live in us. And therefore we are pervaded with a world of thoughts also from the moment we fall asleep to the moment of awakening.

Now let's consider a person just waking up in the morning. We wake up. Let's say we awaken from our dreams. By studying certain dreams, we can very easily discover how quickly a dream runs its course, so that as we awaken it has come to its end. Everyone is different of course, but let's imagine that something like this happens in a dream: that you get into a fierce argument with someone and this degenerates into a shouting match. As you know, we are sometimes far less polite in our dreams than we are in daily life. So this degenerates into a shouting match. Let's say the other person in your dream punches you, and at that moment you wake up to find . . . that a raindrop has fallen on your cheek. In fact, this was what woke you: the raindrop. The whole dream, that seemed to have lasted a long time, was actually caused by the raindrop at the moment you awoke.

We can observe very similar things in countless dreams. They actually take next to no time, instigated by some cause, and may have a dramatic content. So let's say you wake up with a dream. You will find, if you really examine it closely, that a dream provides something that you could not have otherwise thought, based on your experiences; you would have entertained other thoughts than these when awake. As we know, dream clothes in a sometimes fantastical guise the experiences it brings to our sleeping mind.

Take the example I gave you just now. If a raindrop falls on your cheek in the daytime, you have a quite different picture of this than the dramatic one of getting into a fight and an argument with someone. The heated exchange of words may take a rather long time, seemingly, culminating in the slap or the punch, which is when you wake up. During the day this experience would have been a very simple one, a sense impression and a thought that follows from it. But in the dream, as you awaken, you have a very dramatic experience, far more elaborate. And yet what you are dreaming will almost invariably be composed of sense experiences that you have already had, or might have, or also inner experiences in the body and suchlike, all of which can give rise to dreams.

The more dreams you study, the more you will come to see the actual nature of dreaming. When you're awake, you see colours, bright and dark; you hear sounds, you perceive temperature, hot and cold. You interrelate these sensations through your faculty of reason. And in doing so you have a clear sense that you are working from within outwards. Within you is your will, through which you engage with all this, working from within outwards. Let us leave aside for now what exactly it is that is working from within you. What is clear is that you feel you take hold of your sense impressions and in some way order them by means of your thinking. You combine and interrelate them, and so on, doing all this from within you. And when you dream, you will see if you reflect upon it, that you have images in you similar to those of sense impressions. You need only think of a vivid dream you have had and you will recall images, colours, someone moving and so forth. Images are there as they are for us in our sense perceptions. The difference is that in sensory experience these images, as it were, overlay the solid objects around us, whereas in dreams they hover and float freely. And the dream also reveals thoughts, even invoking the cause and effect of which science is so proud. We do not only dream in images but in connections and contexts. All this is present.

So if you carefully study dreams you will acknowledge that the experiences of dream are the very reverse of your waking life. The reverse. While I'm awake I know that I am receiving sense impressions and that my thoughts are ordering them. When I dream, sense impressions initially overwhelm me, and in these sense impressions lives a kind of context and interconnection that is otherwise given by daytime thoughts. Just as we assign sense impressions to a larger context, the same is true in dreaming. And if you think properly about these things you will find that, in dream, things are actually reversed. You encounter sense impressions for which you cannot easily grasp the thinking correlate. That is why the sense impressions of dream are so inconsistent and illogical. You cannot get a hold of the thinking that will order them. In waking life, depending on whether you are more prosaic or more imaginative, by and large you hold sway over your sense impressions. You know that you possess thinking and by using it you can master the impressions you receive, which are at somewhat more of a distance from you. In brief, if you reflect carefully on this, you can sense that you live from within outward during waking life, the sense impressions are outside you (yellow arrows); and within you is thinking (purple arrows).

The reverse is true when you dream (red arrows): then you first encounter sense images but cannot get hold of the thinking underlying them. You can't find the way to it properly. This is why thinking in dreamlife is so haphazard and various.

By properly observing, you can distinguish the nature of dream

and sense reality. In ordinary, waking sense reality, you live from within outward, in intimate proximity with your thinking. Thinking is closer to you. And you employ it to interrelate and coordinate your senses impressions.

When dreaming—and we can discover this by observation—we must be outside ourselves, for we cannot properly approach thinking. This is why such a curious logic is at work in dreams, because thinking is on the other side. Thus when awake we are *here*, and when we sleep we are out *there* (see drawing). But we have just come back in, for we pass over then into our ordinary waking state, where we are intimately connected with thinking. Try to feel this: when dream unfolds it is running toward ordinary day consciousness. You are rushing back in to your ordered thinking, travelling through the surface of your body. You pass through your eyes, but from without. You have not reached the optic nerve. You have the eyes, through which you pass. And the optic nerve acts from the other direction, from a kind of beyond, is still conjuring images as you come back in. Then you become intimate with the [optic] nerve again, which makes an ordered world from these images. And the same is true with all the other senses.

Thus simply by noting facts, you can see how waking up actually involves slipping back into the body. So what is the nature of sleep? You need only properly consider these realities and then you will acknowledge that a sleeper must in some way be outside of the body.

And now let us reflect again upon ordinary, waking consciousness. Those in my audience familiar with anthroposophy will find me repeating what I have said elsewhere. If we examine thinking, we will discover that this is where we are really awake, we are intimate with our thinking and are fully awake. So the thinking we possess within us is something we intimately accompany when awake. That's where we really are awake.

But now let us consider feeling. If you carefully observe your own experience, you will not be able to locate feeling as a presence in you as keen as thinking. You will find that feeling is already less logical than thinking. In feeling, after all, we permit ourselves to be far less logical than in thinking. We allow ourselves far greater scope and indulgence to react with sympathy or antipathy to things than we would permit in the pursuit of mathematics. If it were a matter of feeling, a housewife would far prefer two pounds and another two pounds to make five pounds. Not just housewives: everyone would prefer this. But thinking would not allow it. Thinking depends on exactitude and precision.

Briefly, while the content of dream may be different from that of feeling, the vagueness and indeterminacy of feeling is equal to that of dream. When we feel things we are in the same condition as when we are dreaming. While feelings do not unfold in images as dreams do, their quality and character are certainly a kind of waking dream.

As we know, if we want to embed or immerse our logical thoughts in the realm of art, we have to resort to feeling. Art does not exist without it. We have to invoke feeling, lend thought an element that resembles dream. By this means we create inwardly something similar to what the dream world presents to us, as it were, from without. Inwardly we do not create logical thoughts but imaginative pictures. And in all ages people have felt that dreams seem to approach us from without, in unknown and strange or striking guises, and yet that they resemble the inward pictures we can conjure in the imagination.

And if we now turn to the will, it is perfectly apparent that our waking mind knows nothing of it. We first have a thought, the idea that we wish to go somewhere or other. Even if we must specifically speak of the will when we wake up in the morning, because we feel that we are taking control of the body again, nevertheless we know nothing about this will. We have some thought: to go somewhere or other. But we do not know how this thought shoots down into our organism and moves our legs, so that this will is enacted. You can observe yourself moving of course, but the mind remains unaware of what occurs between having the thought and the manifestation of will—as unaware as if one were asleep. In fact you are asleep as you unfold your will and as it acts within your organism.

So we can say that feeling is dreaming while we are awake, and will is sleeping while we are awake. As far as will is concerned, we never awaken at all in the ordinary waking mind. During the day, too, in waking consciousness, this activity of will occurs in a sleeping condition. Thus while we only actually sleep a third of our lives— some more, some less of course— we recoup this imbalance by sleeping in waking life too, that is, in our will. If you work this out, we therefore sleep a good deal more than a third of our lives.

And feelings: they are the dreams that rise up out of the will and stimulate thoughts. Just as dreams emerge from sleep, feeling emerges from will. You can actually observe this. Imagine you have a flower in front of you. You could pick it and carry it away and then you *possess* it physically. In doing so, you have used an impulse of will. If you can't carry it away with you, instead you can make do with its fragrance, its pleasant scent, the sympathy it elicits from you. You experience the flower only within you, in your feeling life. But then we might perhaps ask: What is a pleasant feeling? A pleasant feeling is the inner, diluted experience corresponding to the stronger experience that we actually seek, which is an act of will. We wish to possess something that engages our sympathy; but if we cannot have it, it remains merely pleasant, sympathetic to us. Thus feeling is a weaker will. It is just that dreaming occurs in a different way in us when we are awake than when we're asleep. Dreaming while we're asleep is sleep held back. Feeling while we're awake is will not fully enacted.

If there were no inhibiting factors in us, we would want everything

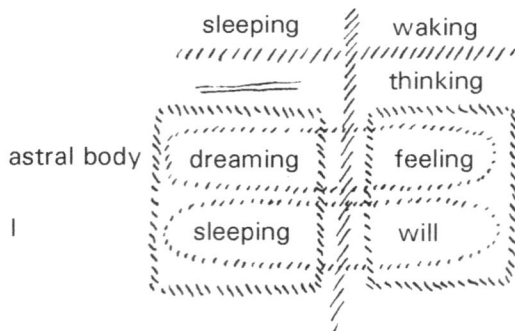

that we find sympathetic, and push away from ourselves everything, including expressions of will, that we do not like. But when we feel, we keep our will constrained. When we feel we merely dream of wanting instead of really wanting.

Now if we indicate the division between sleep and waking life with a simple vertical line, you can see that we have thinking while we're awake, with nothing corresponding to it while we're asleep. During sleep we have dreaming, which corresponds to feeling when we're awake. Then we have will in waking life, and this corresponds to deep sleep, real sleep—dreamless sleep.

Thus we see that feeling and dreaming really live in the same element, as do will and sleep. Dreaming is what we do at night which corresponds to the feeling life we have during the day. They are the same conditions. At some point, what feels in us during the day must dream, and what wills in us during the day must enter upon dreamless sleep. Thus the alternation between feeling and will during the day, or dreaming and manifesting this sleeping condition of the will, depends on being inside or outside the body. You can gain a view of our core being as able either to be inside or outside the body. When it is outside the body it is either in dreamless sleep or it allows dreams to rise up. When it inhabits the body, it wills, or feels. But when it enters the body it encounters thinking. Thinking is not something that can be outwardly seen. Throughout life it exists within us, but is invisible. Now, because it is invisible alongside what is physically visible, we refer to what thinks as 'etheric body' (though as we will see we can call it this for another reason as well). Throughout life, this etheric body remains within the human body when we are both asleep and awake.

The element that feels does not remain inside the body, but strolls out of it when we sleep, and allows dreams to arise. We call this the 'astral body'.

And the element that wills, and dwells in dreamless sleep, we call the 'I'. And so, simply through careful observation, we discover these three invisible aspects of the human being: etheric body, astral body and I. There is of course no doubt about the reality of the physical body.

We see the physical body with our physical senses. The other aspects that constitute us are imperceptible to the physical senses. Can they in some way be rendered visible, perceptible, tangible? Yes, this can be done by undertaking the following.

As I said, when we are awake, we live from within outwards. Now imagine the eye or some other sense organ, from which nerves radiate. Nerves end in the eye. Now let's consider the waking state, when we are living closely bound up with our thinking, that is, with the nerves in our physical body. We are bound up with these nerves. Yet we do not live only in thinking but also in our sense impressions. We can say that a nerve radiates into the sensory impression or picture. We can also express this physiologically: the nerve connects with blood circulation, and by this means it enters into the sensory image. And then we perceive the outer world.

But consider what happens when, instead of perceiving the outer world we develop only the life of the nerve itself, and only go as far as the end of the nerve. We stop short of the blood circulation but go only as far as the nerve's endings. Then we have a memory picture, that is, a thought that remains memory. It is shadowy, therefore, pale, because it does not reach the blood.

In ordinary life we have sense perceptions which pass into the nerves, whose ends lie in the body. We also experience memory, which goes no further than the nerve ends. Here thinking is invoked, becomes a memory picture—whereas if it pushes on further and connects with the blood, it becomes sense perception. If it only pushes through as far as the nerve ends, and does not push further, it becomes memory. But initially we cannot remember anything other than what we already bear within us. Now imagine that, through certain practices, we become able not only to push to the end of the nerve that we bear within us, but also that we absorb from the other direction, from without. So imagine that you not only push to your nerve endings what you have first allowed to enter your head but also what you absorb from the world without sense perception, or what

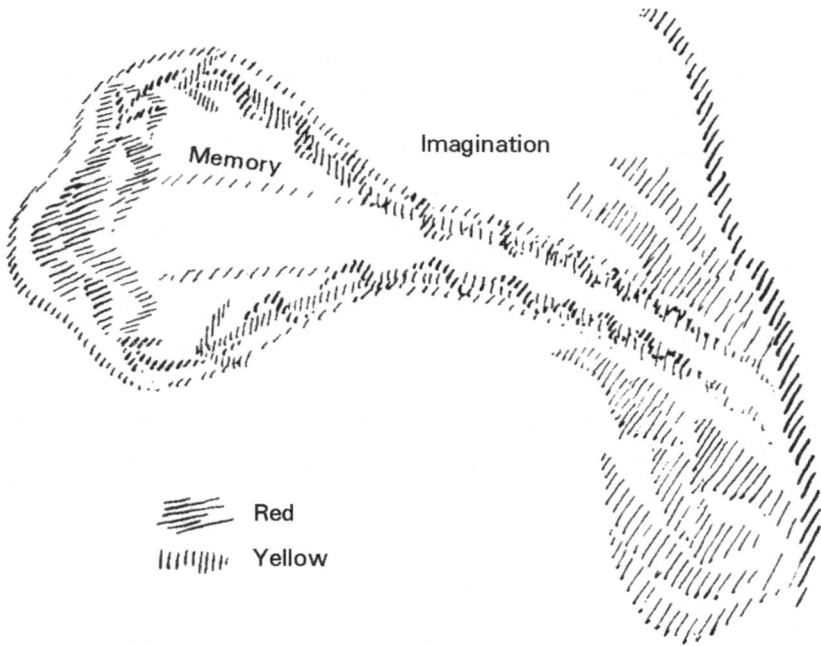

Memory   Imagination

≣ Red

||||||||| Yellow

you absorb without sense perception via your spinal cord. Then this experience pushes into the nerve from the other direction (see drawing).

Then you gain the pictures we call the content of Imagination, which will enable you to perceive this etheric body, which contains within it the activity of thinking.

And, as we will see tomorrow, we can also take up into our feeling something that does not first come from outside us and is reflected in us but that we take into the body as if in reverse. Then comes Inspiration. This does not enter the nerves but the breathing process, and by this means we comprehend the astral body. And finally, when we develop Intuition, no longer experiencing only what we ourselves have learned in life but feeling ourselves as the other person's living reality, when we entirely enter into the other person, then Intuition arises. And by this means we comprehend the I, and the will. And so we can say this:

We comprehend the etheric body through Imagination
We comprehend the astral body through Inspiration
We comprehend the I through Intuition

In ordinary life we do not have the I, but the I sleeps. We know only as much about our I, which is asleep, as we know of darkness when we are in the dark. The objects are there but we do not see them. In the same way we are asleep to the I.

By means of the most rigorous thinking we can in a sense discover the things that are described fully in my book, *Theosophy:* the physical body, the etheric body, astral body and I. And then we can also show how these aspects of human nature can become apparent and perceptible to us through Imagination, Inspiration and Intuition.

LECTURE 3

HUMAN SOUL LIFE AND THE DEVELOPMENT OF IMAGINATION, INSPIRATION AND INTUITION

DORNACH, 15 APRIL 1923

YESTERDAY I tried to examine some aspects of the nature of the human being and human life from the perspective we can gain if we consider the whole compass of human life. Besides the life we lead while we are awake during the day, about a third of our life is spent in sleep. And if we consider only the ordinary human mind, then, as we look back on our life, we have a memory really only of our days, the experiences we had while awake. We tend to overlook or discount the periods during which we were asleep. Of course it must be said that waking life is paramount in relation to outward life and culture. But we can also ask whether the thoughts that unfold in the mind in daily waking life are the only ones that have importance for human interiority too.

Even superficial observation can teach us that this is not so. The reflections I will present today and in the next few days will in fact show that, while the occurrences experienced by the human soul during sleep remain hidden, these occurrences are far more important for our inner human nature than the events that occur during the day.

Today, to continue what we described yesterday, let us initially return to a comparison between sleep life and waking life. Sleep occurs partly in fully dreamless sleep. Anything that occurs during this dreamless sleep is entirely unconscious for us, even if it has an effect on our earthly life. Out of this unconsciousness, this complete darkness of the mind, dreams then emerge, and from dreams we either awaken to ordinary consciousness, where we possess earthly reality via sensory perceptions and by connecting and combining rational thoughts, or we plunge away from this reality again into dreamless sleep.

Let us once again pinpoint the difference, for ordinary outward observation, between dream and the sense perceptions that live in images and logical concepts.

For many people, the contents of a dream often contain a more vivid reality than the one we know in waking life. Yet this is a reality of images that we do not direct by our will but are compelled to follow in the soul. And the difference between following these dream images and following ordinary images of reality in waking life can be precisely described. We will refrain here from specifically philosophical speculations. We could offer them here, but they take us beyond the scope of what we wish to consider. Let us simply consider generally accessible insights. Dream images are ones in which we can dwell. We dwell within these images themselves. We live with them. In waking life, we naturally have colour images, tone perceptions and so on in the same way as in dreams. But we necessarily relate these images, whether they are visual images, tones, sensations of temperature, touch and so on, to what one might call 'harsh reality'. In our daily lives we are always confronted by the need to bring our will to bear on whatever sense images we perceive.

This is not so in the case of what we might call 'dream reality'. The perspective from which we judge the meaning of a dream relative to our reality can be found only within waking life. As long as we dream we regard the dream as reality; and if we were to dream our whole lives through, dream reality would be our only reality. There is no need for us to think that in that case our outward lives would be completely different from what they are now. We could easily imagine that people would still meet one another, though not now by volition but simply pushed toward each other automatically by natural forces, or if you like by higher beings. We could also imagine people being forced to do their work by the compulsion of, again, higher beings or natural forces. In brief, everything we find before us in waking life could still continue, without us knowing anything about it. If we only lived in a dream world, we would have a dream reality before us. We would never think of breaking through this dream reality into a different one. But by the natural dictates of our organism we wake up again, and then, within sense reality, gain a perspective by which we can judge the relative reality of the dream.

Thus only by accomplishing this sudden transition from dreaming to waking do we gain a perspective for judging the reality of a dream by comparison with it.

But now let us ask this: is everything that we experience while awake truly a waking condition? Yesterday I showed in some detail why this is not so. Specifically, I described how it is only really our thoughts that wake us up, and these only in so far as they depict or reflect outward reality. Thus we are only really awake in our thoughts. In our feelings we have no other reality before us than we do in dream, as far as our condition of soul is concerned. It is just that dreams appear to us in images whereas feelings emerge with a characteristic lack of definition from the depths of the soul.

Ordinary psychologists often judge everything according to certain preconceptions. If, instead, we observe the content of feelings with an open mind we can see how, as they shoot upward toward the life of thought, if I can put it like that, they display a swimming vagueness, a fluctuating interplay, like dream images. In our feelings we are also dreaming while awake. But because what we might call the substance in which dream images appear is different from the substance of feelings, we do not see that really all feeling possesses only the reality of dream. While we think in full wakefulness, our thoughts are also continually interwoven with the undefined subjective contents of feeling.

Just picture vividly how, when you wake up, dream images can continue to play in to waking consciousness. Recall how in dream images everything is in flux, larger than life, or perhaps smaller, and you will see that something seemingly comes toward us in pictures that otherwise approaches us from within in feeling life, once again in blurred or erratic fashion, subjectively either enlarging or diminishing things.

And as far as the will is concerned, in waking life we are in the deepest sleep. We know nothing of the will except our intentions, which are thoughts, mental pictures. If I decide that I'm going for a walk, I first picture this. It is my intention. But the ordinary mind shows me as little of what happens as this intention passes into my organism as it does of what occurs while I'm asleep. The success of my intention can only be measured in terms of the movements I actually perform, the changes to the scene in front of me while taking a walk—which are also a matter of thoughts and mental pictures. What happens in the organism between picturing the intention and picturing the outcome is the same for the ordinary mind as everything that occurs without my knowledge during sleep.

Thus we can say that in our will we are in deep, dreamless sleep even when awake, and that we are awake, in a sense, when we live in thoughts. But if we look inward with penetrating honesty we will notice that these thoughts are also only awake as far as outward nature is concerned, not in respect of their own life. As far as the intrinsic life of thoughts is concerned, we cannot remain properly alert. There is no thinking, picturing activity whatever, going on in most people if they cannot picture or think something outward. But this is really only because people nowadays, in our modern culture especially, are given up to the outer world. We can compare this passive surrender to an existence in a thunderous, roaring world.

Imagine that someone is playing a piano here, or another instrument, but that outside some kind of machinery is making a racket. You would hear the machinery far more than the piano, especially if you were some way away from it. The same is true more or less of the thinking activity that lives within you. But we must apply this comparison in the right way. The concepts nowadays disseminated by science, which we all absorb, that are taught us as, say, external doctrines of evolution, are basically a kind of thought racket, a lot of noise. And this thought racket to which we surrender ourselves nowadays, especially if we are scientists, hampers and hinders our subtler perception of the inner activity of thinking.

In my book, *The Philosophy of Freedom*, I described this pure kind of thinking, that does not think anything outward but unfolds entirely within us. Yet I am aware that in describing it I presented something whose existence many contemporaries dispute. They are like someone who hears a machine outside making a racket which drowns out the piano so that they do not believe there is any piano music at all.

This being so, we can see something of great importance: that we are awake when we reflect and think about an outward phenomenon in the world, but that we dream, at most, when it comes to the inner activity in which we are engaged in thinking. Likewise we dream in our feelings and are asleep in our will. Thus the soul activity, what lives within us, is not really awake when we are awake to the sense world. We go on sleeping, even while awake during the day, as far as our activity of thinking is concerned, and our feeling, and will. We only awaken to external nature. And this awakening is something we also cultivate through instruments, through empirical methods of research, and by this means achieve modern science, which is important and significant. Science must develop by reflecting outward phenomena and processes in our thoughts. There are differing degrees of wakefulness in our thinking, feeling and will. And if you can observe without preconception how dream differs from the outer, physical-sensory world of perception, you will not regard the soul faculties of thinking, feeling and will as resembling external sense impressions but, at most, as resembling what they most pertain to, dream. As far as our contents of soul are concerned, we are dreaming and sleeping continually. We awaken only to nature's outward content. We do not awaken at all to our inner soul content in the ordinary mind, but there we sleep on soundly. As we saw, dream images are flimsy, have no hard, outer, underlying reality beyond them that is subject to the will. The same is true of our soul's content, which lives in images, pictures. And if we have the ability to compare qualities with one another, not only quantities, we will find that, if we assign to dreams a pictorial character that does not initially point to any underlying reality, then we must also assign a pictorial character to our own soul content.

But this gives rise to a question of much importance. When I dwell in dreams, and afterwards wake up again to physical reality, then, by virtue of engaging with my body through my will, I feel myself to be connected with the physical reality of the world. From this perspective of a sense of reality in the physical realm, I will speak of dream as having only a relative and different mode of reality.

The question is this: Can I in the same way awaken to soul life as I wake up to the natural, physical world? Just as I connect dream images to the structure of my waking reality by engaging my will in my body, can I similarly, by a higher awakening, connect thinking, feeling and will to a corresponding reality? That is the question. Can I waken for soul life as I waken for the natural world? The natural context I experience during life on earth in the form of outward, physical sense reality appears to me in dream in the form of images. But the whole of my soul life also only appears to me in pictorial form, as in dream. Can I waken to it fully?

Yes, I can. I can wake in this way through exercises such as those I have presented in my book, *Knowledge of the Higher Worlds* and *Occult Science*. I first sharpen and internalize my thinking, no longer only developing a thought content through outer stimulus, but instead giving myself from within a clear—not a vague, suggestive—thought content. I dwell upon this thought content, concentrating on it as a content actively given from within me, within my soul. In this way I gradually come to real awareness of thinking.

You see, we are not conscious of thinking at all if we only allow our thoughts to be stimulated in us from without. Only if we stimulate thought from within, time and time again through meditation, concentration upon a thought content, do we become aware of, and within, our thinking activity. Then it becomes apparent to us that we live, really, in this thinking and that we do not know this when we seek only outer stimulus for it. In this way thinking comes to life whereas otherwise it remains abstract and dead. Thinking becomes something that no longer consists only of thought shadows, as it were, that come from outside us, but rather something that stirs inwardly in us like our soul's very blood. We are filled with what seems a second, higher human existence.

Thoughts become living powers, formative forces, as I also called them in my book, *Theosophy*. And we become aware that we bear thinking within us really as a second body, the etheric body, the body of formative forces. You see, it becomes apparent that what otherwise only exists in shadowy form in thoughts, are in fact forces that cause our growth. We withdraw into the growth of our human organism and come to see that the processes that would otherwise only occur chemically according to the properties of the substances we ingest, are assimilated by this same inner spirit corporeality, etheric corporeality that forms our thoughts. And we discover that we become a unified inward human being by virtue of these inwardly living, inwardly stirring thoughts. In this way we come to recognize the existence of a second human being within us.

But we discover something else as well. This second human being we come to know is not like some kind of static cloud that vaguely fills the spatial physical body. This second human being is actually in continual motion, and it is not possible to fix it and hold it fast at any particular moment. I can put it like this: At any particular point or moment in life we could draw (see drawing) our experience of the human physical body, which is identical with our thinking—except that in ordinary thinking we possess only thought shadows, not the living thoughts themselves. The second body that pervades us as etheric body or body of formative forces can only be held fast for a brief moment. The moment before it was entirely different, and in the next moment it will be different once more—and so on, both back into the past and forward into the future.

But this means that, for inner, beholding experience, this body of formative forces—apparent to the ordinary mind only in the form of shadowy, abstract thoughts—is found to be nothing spatial at all; it is, rather, something, that unfolds through time. This leads us back in a living-tableau to a certain moment of our earliest childhood. I will draw this schematically here.

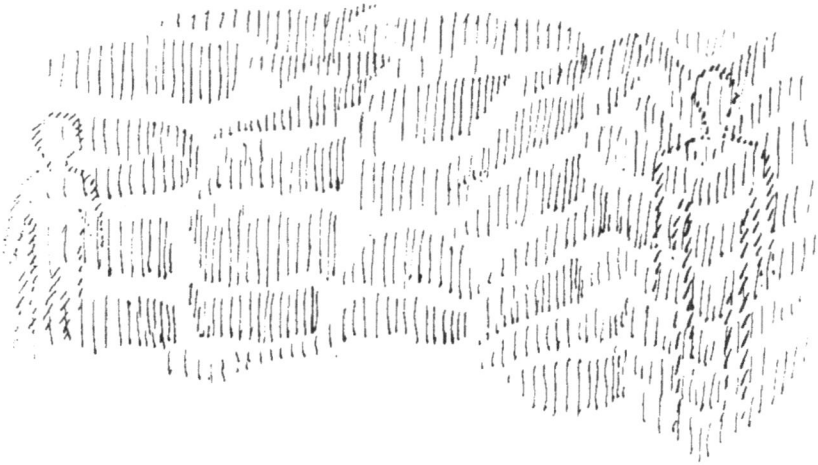

Let us say that we are by now an older person at a particular moment. Yet this body of formative forces is not restricted to one period but leads us back to childhood. We do not survey our life through ordinary recall but like a tableau in which everything is simultaneously present. What I am drawing here as spatial con-figuration is in fact temporal. This leads us back to our childhood, to the point in our childhood which we can normally remember back to, our earliest memory.

There too we find our etheric body, this body of formative forces. But if, through carefully practised exercises, we acquire the ability to look back to this point, then we arrive at the time when we learned to think as a small child. Then it seems as if our thinking, our ordinary thinking initially, comes up against a barrier. The ordinary mind, ordinary memory, meets a barrier here. Through Imagination, however, we reach further back beyond this. We gaze upon the soul content of the child who we were before we were able to think, while, as a young child, we still dreamed into the world. You see, thinking only emerged in us at a particular moment, after we had begun to speak.

Now by this means we gaze into a period of our early life and see the nature of the soul before we possessed shadowy, abstract thoughts. Back then we still had a living thinking. And this living thinking worked very strongly to configure and sculpt the human brain, the whole human organism. Later on, when much of this thinking is absorbed into abstraction, into what is dead, only residues of it remain for working upon the human physical organization. While we are a dreaming child and cannot yet think, thinking itself is active in us. In later life the hubbub of the world prevents us gazing upon such thinking, and so we cannot look back either to the thinking that was still active in early childhood. But now [through these practices] we can look back. And then this thinking appears to us as the sum of forces that actually formed and configured us, growth forces, forces of nutrition and so on. We now see that the human organism is built up out of the etheric nature of the world, for this is where these forces originate. Increasingly we become able to approach the etheric body. We see that this etheric body is most active, working into us from without, in our earliest years, before we have learned to think and while we still experience life as a dream. In this way we have worked our way through to imaginative perception.

Something of this early thinking can remain in us. Given the hubbub of our modern scientific culture, we do not notice it if we do not undertake exercises such as I have given in the books I referred to. But if we do, we find that something of this thinking we once possessed in infancy, before we can remember, remains to us. This thinking that builds up our organism and to which we therefore owe our outer, physical organism, this active, living thinking is what I spoke of in my books as imaginative thinking. Something of this imaginative thinking remains to us, and with practice we can also enquire into it in our later life and in this way come upon the etheric body.

I spoke of this yesterday but not everyone was present, so I'd like to mention it again. Imagine the human eye, and then the optic

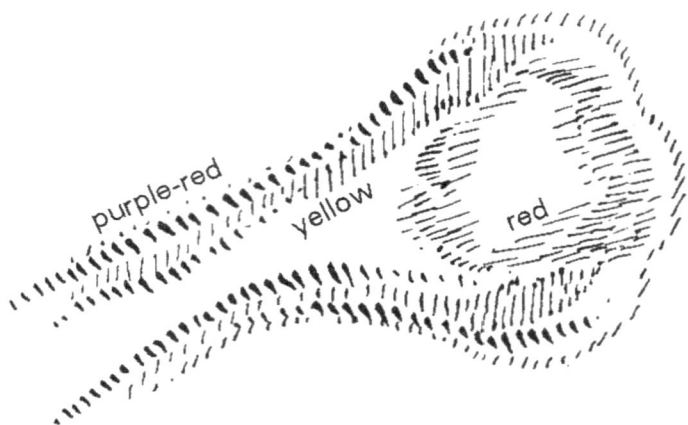

nerve that passes from it inwards and spreads out in the eye. If you trace the body of formative forces (purple-red)—that largely follows outer physical neural activity—to the point where you arrive at processes (red) where the outer world is reflected through the eye, then you have a perception of the outer world. And what is then established or fixed in the body of formative forces by the optic nerve—I am giving only an approximate account here, it would take too long to describe this whole process accurately—can always in turn be stimulated to activity again. Thus with the activity of the body of formative forces, the neural system, we come to the point where the nerves end (yellow). It is not that we intrude into the neural processes that reflect the outer world; we only give an impetus to what lives in them as the body of formative forces, pushing this body of formative forces through to where the nerve stumps taper off, and then we have a memory impression. The memory image largely consists of reaching only as far as the nerve ends with our inner activity. By contrast, in the case of sense impressions, we push through to [and beyond] the nerve endings, and advance to sensory processes largely engendered by the blood.

Here you see the living activity of the body of formative forces. But everything that you imprint in memory in this way has to have entered the nervous system, and thus it originates from no further back than that early period when we learned to think, in infancy.

What predated this is as follows—and if we have schooled our thinking through exercises I referred to, and then look back, we can discern this as we look back through the second human being in us who unfolds in the temporal realm: we become aware that by the same paths by which impressions entering us from without are turned around, reversed, by memory, something enters from behind that is also an activity of the body of formative forces. Continually we have both these activities really. But in the ordinary mind we only know about the first, about memory. But these two activities are present: what originates from outer sense impressions that are pushed back, pushed forward again to as far as the nerve ends so that memory images arise; and then also something that, as it were, pours in a human-creating way into the whole nervous system, from the direction in us where we do not perceive with the same sensory strength as we do in the front of the body.

From behind—of course I am not speaking precisely—creative powers enter us: in the earliest infancy, before we can think, they pour in very powerfully, and later do so in a weaker fashion. And this is the thinking that does not originate in the sense world but from the whole cosmos, that is taken from the cosmic ether and that we appropriate when we descend from pre-earthly existence to earthly life. We retain it as a higher gift up to the moment when we learn to think. The moment we learn to think you can say that, in the ongoing stream of our life, we close the door to this living thinking activity, this development of human formative forces in the body of formative forces, in the etheric body. To learn to think in relation to the outer world of the senses means to close the door to universal, cosmos-forming powers of thought.

In childhood, therefore, we closed the door on cosmos-configuring powers of thought. They remain within us, for we need these formative forces continually in the first part of our life, as growth forces while we go on growing, then later as powers to assimilate the food we take in and so on. But we do not notice them. We only notice what the body of formative forces reflects of the impressions we receive, which then, in memories, push through to our nerve endings.

But through exercises in concentration and meditation, we can come to perceive what now comes from the realm of the cosmic ether and enters us to develop and configure us ourselves. In our self-observation we become aware of processes that also unfold in time, that we have not absorbed through outer impressions but which possess only the stream in one direction. If we then pursue these to the point where the nerves end, where we otherwise have memories from outer impressions, we not only gain a picture of our etheric body but of how we are embedded as human beings in the whole cosmic ether. We perceive ourselves as a second human being. We come to discern how etheric forces enter and depart from us, and how the whole play of universal cosmic forces that lives outside us and enters us is of the same nature as the thoughts in us that are like a shadow image of the etheric body. We discern that our thoughts are the shadows of the etheric body, and that the etheric body is really something living, a part of the whole cosmic ether. Here we have reached the first level of supersensible perception.

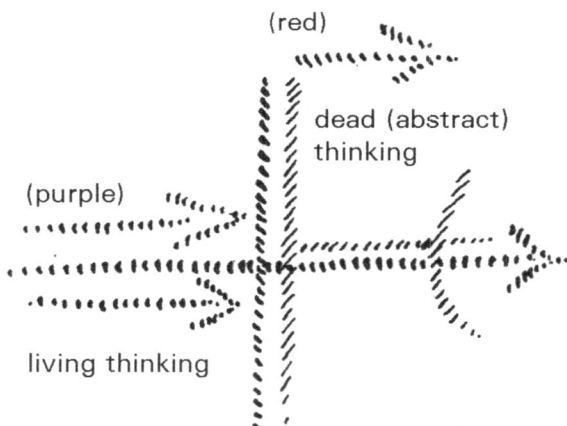

(red)

dead (abstract) thinking

(purple)

living thinking

We could say that what manifests in thinking is really a kind of mirror image (see drawing). Here is the surface of the mirror. It faces forward, toward the senses (red arrow). What is absorbed by the senses is reflected, comes to consciousness when it arrives at the nerve ends. But there is also an inner activity that does not work like this but passes through the mirror (purple arrows). If we follow these, then we have a body of formative forces that is part of the formative forces of the whole universe. In this way, though, we have in a sense reached the other side of thinking.

What is the nature of the exercises to reach imaginative thinking? It is like this: whereas normally we only see as far as the mirror surface within us, looking upon what is reflected outwards, which is in fact nothing other than outward nature, we now acquire the ability to look behind the mirror. What we find there is not the same as outward nature. We find there human-creating powers. That is the other side of thinking. Here we have dead thinking, also called abstract thinking. There we have living thinking. And in living thinking, thoughts are forces.

This is the secret of thinking: that what we possess in ordinary thinking is only the shadow of true thinking. But true thinking pervades the world, exists as the world's structure of forces, not only within us as human beings.

It is not very bright to think that thinking is only inside us. That is roughly like saying, after drawing water from a brook and drinking it, that my tongue produced the water I drank. We draw water from the earth's whole fount of water, and do not think for a moment that out tongue produces it. We only do this in the case of thinking. We say that our brain produces thinking, whereas we merely draw from the totality of thinking spread out everywhere in the world, and then have it within us as a sum of thoughts.

Human beings succumb to another illusion when thinking of their thinking, one that I can compare with the following. Imagine that we have here a path roughly like the one that goes down to Arlesheim and Dornach, which is soft underfoot! Imagine that I'm walking along it, and you see my footprints (see drawing, red). Now imagine that a Martian arrives on earth, never having seen anything like these footprints before. Imagine that he knows nothing of the existence of human beings, and perhaps he's arrived too early in the morning to see anyone yet. So he looks at these footprints and thinks: Aha, here is the earth and here are these tracks in it. The earth there is substance—he already knows this from Mars—and in this earth substance are all kinds of forces, vibrating forces or whatever, ions or electrons. These forces, he thinks, are at work down there, and they have created these tracks, these markings on the earth.

The Martian is of course wrong. He is unaware that I passed that way and made the prints, and the earth did not produce them from below; that the earth all the way down to Arlesheim is innocent of making these prints. There are no forces down below that have shaped them—they were made from without, from above, by me.

But this is the same illusion people have in relation to the brain. There are structures, shapes there too, and they think that these structures are created from within, and that this manifests in thoughts. In the brain we do indeed find the full imprint of thinking. It is a fine thing to trace how a person's thinking is reflected in the forms of the brain, down to the tiniest convolutions. But just as little as footprints in the earth emerge from below, so the convolutions of the brain do not arise from anything other than impressions which living thinking, coming from the universal ether, weaving and alive in the universal ether, engraves into it.

What I'm describing here becomes vivid apprehension when we develop this imaginative thinking. And just as we can grasp thinking from, as it were, the other side, so now we can also grasp from behind, if you like, another element that arises somewhat earlier in ordinary human life: the element of speech.

Let's picture for a moment what happens in speech. The airstream from your lungs passes through the larynx and the other speech organs. The shapes of the larynx, of the tongue, the hard palate and so on, give rise to the sounds of speech that emerge from your mouth.

But now instead of tracing this path of the airstream through the organs of speech and out into the world, you can trace the whole process in reverse (see next drawing, red). Again, this cannot be done with the ordinary mind but must be accomplished by means of exercises that enable us to follow earthly speech to the point where it forms outwardly: we trace the inner nature of speech to the point where it outwardly forms. This is not found in the physical body, nor in the etheric body, but in a higher aspect of the human organism than the etheric body or body of formative forces: in what I called in my books the astral body.

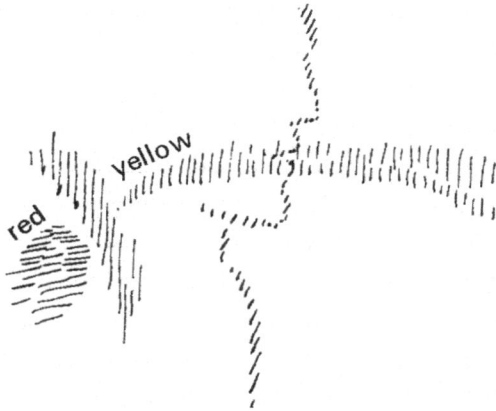

What is spoken outwardly is speech for earthly life. But what comes toward us as it were from behind, reaches as far as the organs of speech but does not resound outwardly as speech; what speaks into us and thus does not arise as earthly, audible speech proceeding from the larynx and issuing forth outwardly, but ceases at the larynx, becomes mute there, as opposed to the earthly language that starts there and issues forth into the world; is a spiritual speech. It is something we can call spiritual speech, which is spoken to us from the world of spirit.

What informs and imprints us in this way is Inspiration, meant now in an entirely rational way. We have to bring about this Inspiration by withdrawing our consciousness—again through exercises I have described in my books—from our full engagement in outward words. What approaches the larynx and organs of speech in this way from the wider world and speaks to us—whereas we normally think of speech as us speaking out into the world through our speech organs—will have been especially pronounced in childhood: this element of Inspiration up to the point when we learned to speak. As we learned to speak outwardly, these forces ceased being active in the same way. But they exist in us still, and we can find them if we raise ourselves to the gift, the boon of Inspiration.

Then we become aware of a third element within us, a third human being, who does not belong to space nor time, but nevertheless acts within us in a strongly configuring way. This is the astral body, whose processes are Inspirations, where we experience what actually underlies our life of feeling. Our feeling life is a dreaming of what flows into us as Inspiration. And this feeling life is intimately related to the process of breathing and speaking.

This is why, in more ancient times, when people sought to reach the world of spirit in a different way, they used specific exercises to work upon the inner process of breathing. And the old yoga exercises were calculated to turn attention to what lies behind speech. By replacing natural breathing with a specially cultivated form of breathing, they became aware of this, as we inevitably become aware of something else if we modify what is habitual.

Imagine for a moment that you perceive the water in a river, as you swim in it, differently depending on whether you swim at the same speed as the flowing water, or slower or faster than the river current. If you swim at the same speed as the water is flowing, you do not perceive the counter-pressure that you will notice if you swim more slowly than the current. By configuring breathing differently from natural breathing, the Indian yogi perceives the spiritual element present in the stream of breath: the spiritual element that endows us with our astral body, and by means of which, in turn, we reach up into a higher world than the world of the etheric.

We regard these exercises, that I described in *Knowledge of the Higher Worlds*, as right and fitting ones, for humanity advances and progresses. You see, we can point everywhere to tangible processes that underlie things which the world at large finds so fantastical about anthroposophy: that we do not consist only of a physical body but also of an etheric and astral body, and I. Next time we will speak more of this. But these things are not just shaken out of a sleeve. They arose through careful and detailed enquiries, taking scientific method and developing it further to embrace the full scope of human nature. The difference, though, is that such enquiry depends on continually heightening and enhancing human capacities of perception.

What therefore is the nature of Imagination, whereby we penetrate the etheric world and etheric life itself? It involves tracing further than the senses processes that have first pushed backward through the senses, and can then in turn be pushed forward again as far as the nerve endings; it involves us becoming aware, as we otherwise only are of memories, of what originates in the universe, the cosmos, and is of the same nature as sense perceptions but now belongs to the supersensible world.

If we come to perceive world-creating powers in the same way as we perceive memories, then we have the being of Imagination, we experience the etheric being of the world. If we learn to perceive behind speech what now does not proceed outwards from the larynx but speaks into us, rather, from the other side, from the universe, the cosmos, and falls silent when it reaches the larynx, then, through Inspiration, we become aware of a further world to which we belong with our third human organism, the astral body.

At the same time, however, something else becomes apparent. Here in the physical sense world we have on the one hand physical processes and on the other, moral impulses that rise up from within us. They stand alongside each other in such a way that even theologians nowadays urge us to apprehend the sense world in only sensory terms and to see the world of morality through a quite different mode of cognition. But the moment we advance as far as Inspiration, where we not only dwell in the world in which one speaks outwards, forwards from the larynx, but in a world that speaks through our entire being and falls silent on reaching the larynx—because we close the door there when we learn outward speech, replacing the language of the heavens with outward language—then, at the moment we live our way into this other world that ceases at the larynx, we experience the Inspiration content of the world, the mysteries of the world; and then we no longer experience only a nature that moral impulses cannot penetrate. Behind natural existence we then experience a world where natural impulses, natural laws and moral laws are interwoven, are one. We have lifted the veil and have found a world in which morality and physical reality resound in accord. And we will see that this is also the world in which we lived in our pre-earthly existence before we descended to earth, and into which we enter again after we have crossed the threshold of death.

Lecture 4

EXPERIENCE AND PERCEPTION OF THE ACTIVITIES OF THINKING AND SPEECH

DORNACH, 20 APRIL 1923

In my last few lectures I have described human nature in a way which, it seems to me, may also be comprehensible to the visitors who have kindly come to join us for the teachers' course, and whom we are pleased to see here. At the outset I remarked that much of what I had to say would be a kind of repetition for those already well-versed in anthroposophy. Today I will continue these reflections firstly with a brief recap of salient points, and will then move on to matters that take yesterday's lecture further.

When engaging in outward vision, as I remarked, in everything we understand as sense perception, which our reason can then combine and interrelate, perhaps also with the aid of experiments and empirical research, only the human being's physical body is initially involved. But underlying this physical body is what we can call the etheric body or body of formative forces, a subtler entity within the human being, if you like—a second human being within the first. How do we develop real perception of this second human being? I have to keep emphasizing that it really is not all that difficult to develop true perception of this second person in us, who stands before us with as much validity as what the senses perceive and the faculty of reason combines and connects. In modern times people do not live as strongly as they once did, in earlier phases of our evolution, in the thought element itself. Within this thought element, they tend rather to surrender themselves passively, awaiting sensory impressions from the sense world. And for this reason we have to first strengthen this thought element by practising particular exercises. Of course people still have thoughts, but they can scarcely come to any real insight into the actual nature of thinking, the activity of thinking, since they are now entirely accustomed, on awakening each morning, to allow an influx of external sensory perceptions to enter their thoughts, and really only accord these external sense impressions any value or worth. While this means that their thoughts have a content, that of external sense perception, they do not manage to feel their own thinking activity as such. This can be achieved, though, through the exercises I have discussed, for instance, in my book, *Knowledge of the Higher Worlds*.

Such exercises require us to transpose, if you like, our whole being into thinking activity, giving ourselves up with the utmost inner impetus to thinking. In this thinking, what the senses tell us must become a matter of indifference, so that we then live in full consciousness only in this thinking activity.

If we have studied mathematics, and especially geometry, this can help us a great deal with this inner thinking practice. This thinking activity, which we need to practise in geometry, is something—I would say it jolts us strongly into our own being—that we need only experience in its autonomy, its vivid pictorial quality, its inner life and activity; and then, already when we draw a triangle, we will experience the activity of thinking. Look, you can draw a triangle on the board (draws). But is this a triangle? What you see on the board here is not a triangle in fact but a large number of chalk flakes sticking to the board. If you had a strong enough microscope, you could even count them. It is nonsense to think that what you see on the board is a triangle. The triangle is something you can only have within you, in the thought invoked in you by these flakes of chalk sticking to the board. And if you ignore the chalk flakes on the board, you can still have a mental picture of the triangle within you in thought, without any board or chalk, simply sitting there, or standing, not even moving a finger at all. And then you can trace in thought how you start drawing a line—but only inwardly, in thought—then add a second and a third to it. You can live in this inner activity without doing anything outwardly. You can go on to do more and more of these exercises, in particular more complex ones. For instance, you can draw this form in red chalk, and then this one in green chalk, and then you will have a tangible picture of what you can now do inwardly.

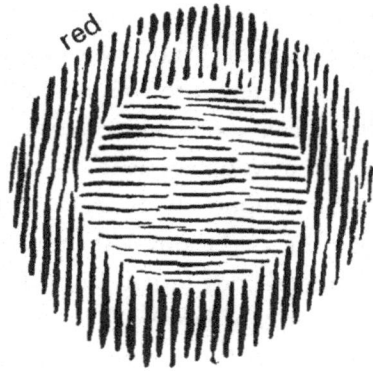

Just as you drew the triangle in thoughts before, so now you can do this: the red grows out here into the green, stops here, and the green pushes itself through and under the red so that *this* figure arises from *that* one—but all inwardly pictured only. So now you have the red in the middle, and the green all around it. And then picture how the red in the middle grows and the green contracts, so that you get the smaller green circle and the red all around it, the red wheel surrounding it. And then you can reverse it again: the red pushes inward, the green expands. You can alternate between these two forms, in rhythmic sequence: inside a sphere, outside a wheel, changing from red to green; from green to red; from red to green; from green to red. You can picture all this without needing to do anything outwardly at all. And then it will gradually become apparent to you that thinking means doing something inwardly in the same way as doing something outwardly means using your hands or arms. When you use your arm, you feel this. Now you must learn to feel what it means to use your thinking powers. When you use your arms and feel them, you experience your physical body. When you begin to use your thoughts in this way, you feel your second human being within, your etheric body, your body of formative forces. As soon as you have gone far enough with this so that you need only give yourself a jolt to pass from that sense of moving your arms or legs to feeling the inner forces of thinking, then you will at that moment experience the etheric human within you, your being of formative forces. And you will experience it as being woven entirely of thoughts. And simultaneously your whole life on earth will become present to you. As if in a single panorama, you will be able to look back upon your whole earthly life, right back to earliest infancy.

What you experience as the second person in you is not a spatial but a temporal body. And, as I already said in these lectures, when one draws the physical human being, one can then also draw this temporal body into it. But this is only to hold fast to one phase of the lightning, as it were. This body of formative forces does not live in space, or only momentarily in space. The next moment it has altered. It continually fluctuates, continually changes, and this flux is what we experience as the life-tableau.

But at the same time we also feel ourselves to be a part of the whole universe, no longer thinking we are enclosed in our separate skin. It now seems self-evident that we ourselves fluctuate within the whole universe, we are only a wave in the etheric universe.

And we gain other apprehensions of this second being in us too: the perception that it continually endeavours to dissolve physical matter into its nothingness. During these days I said to a number of you in a different context that physical matter, physical substance, exerts pressure, while what lives in the etheric realm sucks up what fills space, sucks it all up. And in our life on earth we live continually in this interplay. We eat, and by doing so introduce physical matter into us. This physical matter streams a little way into our body, and there initiates all kinds of processes and occurrences that are oriented to this physical matter. When you eat sauerkraut, as it passes initially a little way into our organism it behaves to begin with as it must according to its chemical and physical properties. When you drink milk, the milk behaves as milk must, according to its nature. But this nature is soon dispelled from both sauerkraut and milk. The etheric body begins its activity on them, and seeks to extinguish their milk-nature and sauerkraut-nature. Thus we have within us a continual battle between the nature of sauerkraut or milk on the one hand and the extinguishing of these properties. This battle exists and unfolds. We can recognize this battle in what we excrete, and in what migrates toward the head as formative forces, as our supersensible human organism. Precisely as much as we excrete through the various organs of excretion is transformed, in the other direction, into negative matter as sucking principle, as negative substance that lives in our nervous system, and especially the brain. We cannot understand the human being if we consider only the physical body, since then we only learn, as it were, from the periphery and a little way into the body, of a small part of the processes that actually work within the human organism. We can learn in this way of the processes that occur along the digestive tract, and of the excretions such as sweat and suchlike. All such processes of excretion, which involve substance lapsing into coarse materiality, are balanced equally by the other pole of what is drawn toward the nervous system as etheric substance. Wherever we excrete external material substance, etheric substance passes into us. This etheric nature spins, spirals and weaves within our etheric body or body of formative forces, which pervades us in the way that I have described.

And, as I have already suggested, we learn to know this second person in us by recognizing how the power and faculty of memory can change. In ordinary life we perceive external impressions. These pass inward into us and are taken up by our thoughts, our mental pictures, and then come to a halt. We can invoke them again. But when we do so, our inner energy reaches only as far as the nerve endings. Thus if we consider the eye and the forming of an outer visual image, we push further, through the nerve endings of the optic nerve that spreads out in the eye, into the eye's blood circulation. This gives rise to a perception. If we only remember something, we only come to the end of the nerve in the eye, to where it runs out if you like. We do not push our etheric body or body of formative forces further through the nerve endings into the blood.

But when we strengthen and invigorate our power of thinking, it is as if we no longer experience this push-back that we have in ordinary memory, in which we have first received a perception, and transformed it into thoughts that come to rest, and are pushed back again. Instead, as it were, coming from behind, we still apprehend the etheric nature of the world. Then we push this etheric content of the world in our organism as far as the point to which we otherwise reach with memories which are, however, only reminiscences of life. And then we acquire consciousness of the etheric workings of the world, and live within the world's etheric activity. Those who experience themselves within the world's etheric activity have an experience of themselves that I will sketch roughly as follows: here is the world's multitudinous etheric activity (yellow). You must imagine it to be configured and formed. Everything lives and weaves here. And then we can experience ourselves within etheric activity. What I am going to draw now will look curious, but it is how things are—the red I'm drawing here must be understood as follows: you hardly notice feet and legs. You experience the etheric activity in such a way that you grow forth from this etheric world at one point. You experience these etheric workings reaching to your nerve endings. This passes through the back and reaches as far as the nerve ends of the front of the body, and in this way you become the last outpost or offshoot of the etheric world. This is how you feel in relation to the presence of the etheric world. You perceive the etheric world very much as seeing yourself pushed out into the last outpost of etheric activity: its last portion still intrudes into you, and then this etheric activity ceases in you. Briefly, in this fashion we can live our way into the world's etheric activity.

And it really is true: it would not be all that hard to achieve if people nowadays were only inclined, as I described, to live their way into the activity of thinking.

yellow

red

The easiest way of doing so oneself is to really dwell fully upon the content of my book, *The Philosophy of Freedom*. There, for example, I point to this thinking experience in relation to the ethical and the moral world. If you study *The Philosophy of Freedom* in the right way, you can develop first-hand experience of the etheric world, the world of formative forces.

The next experience is one you can have by not only engaging this thinking activity but also the activity of speech; by raising yourself to an apprehension of speech activity. You can start even with the very ordinary mode of speech we use in daily life. But again you must get as far with this as you did with thinking activity. In the latter case you have to bring the senses to silence, preventing their impressions on you, so that you live only in active thinking. In the case of speech activity we must come to the point of having a great deal to express—so that we are not poor in words but rich in words, so that we actually have a great deal to say—but can also intentionally not utter it all for a certain period while practising this. I know that some people will find this an extremely arduous exercise; and yet it is essential if we are to become acquainted with the third human being within us. This involves understanding what it means to make all inner preparations to utter a phrase, but to learn to be silent nevertheless; to be actively silent, if you like. To learn to be passively silent when one is in an empty room and no one else is there, will not help at all. No, we have to learn to fall *actively* silent.

You might say this will make you a very boring person if you walk around amongst others saying nothing instead of speaking with them. I won't deny that this might well be rather uncomfortable in a social respect; and yet it could be highly beneficial for your spiritual progress. It could produce very positive results for someone who is not ordinarily silent, who would usually speak, to refrain from speaking in company. We may know a great deal, and what we know may have led us in the past to talk a great deal, to chatter away, but now we do not speak. As I say, we might do this. But actually we do not have to do it outwardly, and though it might be beneficial, it would not get us all that much further in respect of higher intentions. It is much more a question of practising this inwardly: of making all preparations for speaking but then holding back from speech.

You will better understand what I mean if I say to you, for instance, that we do not truly think in ordinary life. We do think in mathematics, if we picture a triangle in the way I described before; and especially if we undertake curious exercises that words cannot convey. But if we only think in terms of things that surround us in ordinary life, we are not truly thinking, for in this 'thinking' the speech organs are continually resonating, albeit so quietly that we do not hear it. Human thinking nowadays, when people have such little inclination to engage in thinking without any outward, sensory correlate, is not real thinking at all. It is only an inner weaving of word shadows. Just study yourself and you will find this inner weaving in word shadows at work in you. Now if we are, on the other hand, able to bring our larynx to full peace and tranquillity within us, and yet still to exercise our inner activity of soul which otherwise underlies the movements of our larynx—and thus if this exercise of leaving words behind remains a completely inward practice, so that we do the same with speech as we previously did with thinking activity, which is a transformation of our capacity of memory, in which we only pushed forward as far as the nerve endings, then we now carry the speech activity only as far as the larynx, specifically to the point where it would seek to speak. If we do this then, slowly, what I recently described in a public lecture as 'the deep silence of the human soul' develops. To hold back even from inner speech enables the soul to fall into a deep silence.

This is how you should imagine the soul's deep silence. Imagine you're in a city—maybe not Basel but London, say, or a still noisier city. You are right in the middle of the hubbub and uproar. But now you leave the city and the noise grows less and less as you leave it further behind you. At last, let us say, you enter the lonely quiet of a wood. You find inner tranquillity there, and you may say that everything is quiet both in you and outside you. There is a point, if you like, where the noise has reached zero, and there is quiet. Let us call it the zero point of quiet. But now you can go further. By refraining from speech despite exerting all the inner activity that can give rise to words, by not involving the physical body, we can come to a deeper silence beyond the zero point occurring when the outer world falls silent in the soul. I described specific exercises for this in my book, *Knowledge of the Higher Worlds*. By practising them we find that we can go beyond the 'zero' point of quiet. In my public lectures[16] I used a trivial example of what I meant. Imagine that you have a certain amount of capital and spend it so that you have less and less. In the end you have nothing at all. But you can go on spending by incurring debts—then you will have less than nothing. Mathematicians have introduced what are called 'negative numbers': -6, -4, $-2\ 0\ 2\ 4\ 6\ 8$ etc. Thus you can picture how from the point of zero quiet we can go on into negative quiet, into a quiet quieter than quietness. That is something you can produce within your soul.

But then, if the outer world not only falls silent in this way but we go beyond this silence, when the response of the soul plunges deeper beyond zero quiet into the negative of outward noise and sound, from the soul's deep silence the spirit starts to speak, and then we perceive the third being within us, whom we call the astral human being. The terms themselves are unimportant; it's just a form of terminology, and we might find other words for it. We begin to perceive this third, astral human being in us when we arrive at the soul's deep silence, and out of the deep silence of the soul something else resounds, the spiritual element, which is a sounding opposite to that of physical tone. And in all respects this astral body leads us further than the etheric body. In order to clarify this, I would like to cite an example taken from the cosmos.

Modern physicists or astronomers, or any modern scientist, study natural laws. They observe and experiment and by this means deduce laws. These laws form a body of scientific knowledge and tell us what is at work in physical things. Scientists should not really go any further than this. But they are so pleased with these natural laws that they can easily start to get a little above themselves, and make an assertion they are not actually in a position to make: that these laws hold true throughout the universe. They say, for instance, that anything they discover in their laboratories could be reproduced on the furthest-flung planet in the universe if conditions could be replicated there: on planets or stars from which light takes so and so many light years to arrive here. People believe they can picture and calculate such things, and that the same natural laws would of course hold good there since they are of absolute validity.

But this is not so. If you have a light source here, it initially shines strongly in the immediate environment. Further away the light will grow weaker in strength, and still weaker the further away we are from it. Once we have left it a long way behind us, the light will be very weak. So light strength diminishes according to our distance from it. This is true of light and, curiously, it applies to natural laws as well.

The natural laws you can observe and formulate here on earth grow ever less applicable the further away you go from the earth. It sounds like a terrible thing to say, and scientists will look at us as idiots if we do so. It is very easy to understand the scientific response to such a statement, we can easily relate to what scientists would think of it. Unfortunately the reverse is not true: scientists cannot relate to what goes on inside a spiritual researcher. The spiritual researcher very well knows how scientists arrive at their findings, but the same cannot be said for scientific understanding of spiritual enquiry. This is why most scientific criticisms of spiritual enquiry seem entirely justified to those who make them. And yet they say nothing more than that the scientist cannot conceive of what the spiritual researcher discovers. Scientists would first have to become spiritual enquirers before any real argument could happen. It is a waste of time to argue with someone who holds fast to their scientific position and is unable to conceive of any meaning in the discoveries of spiritual enquiry.

Now as far as light is concerned, scientists will acknowledge what I say since they themselves have discovered it; but they will not admit the truth of what I say about natural laws. But already as regards light the spiritual researcher has to offer a caveat. In the view of science, light strength diminishes the further away we are from a light source—and eventually a point will come where we can no longer distinguish the light strength from zero. And yet such an assertion is about as wise as saying this: I have here a plastic ball into which I press a thumb. Now as you know, as I do so, the surface of the ball will tend to bulge out on the other side. The ball's elasticity enables us to push the surface back and forth. But imagine someone saying this: when I push my thumb into the ball, it has to go on receding infinitely until the point where it is so weak that one can no longer perceive it. But that is not so. The elastic material of the ball will at some point spring back again. The same is true of light. Light does not spread out so that we can say that it travels on growing ever weaker until it reaches the point of darkness, yet after that travels ever further. That is not true.

It only spreads out to a certain point, a certain sphere, and then it springs back. And as it returns, only the spiritual researcher sees it, not the scientist. You see, once the light has exhausted its elasticity

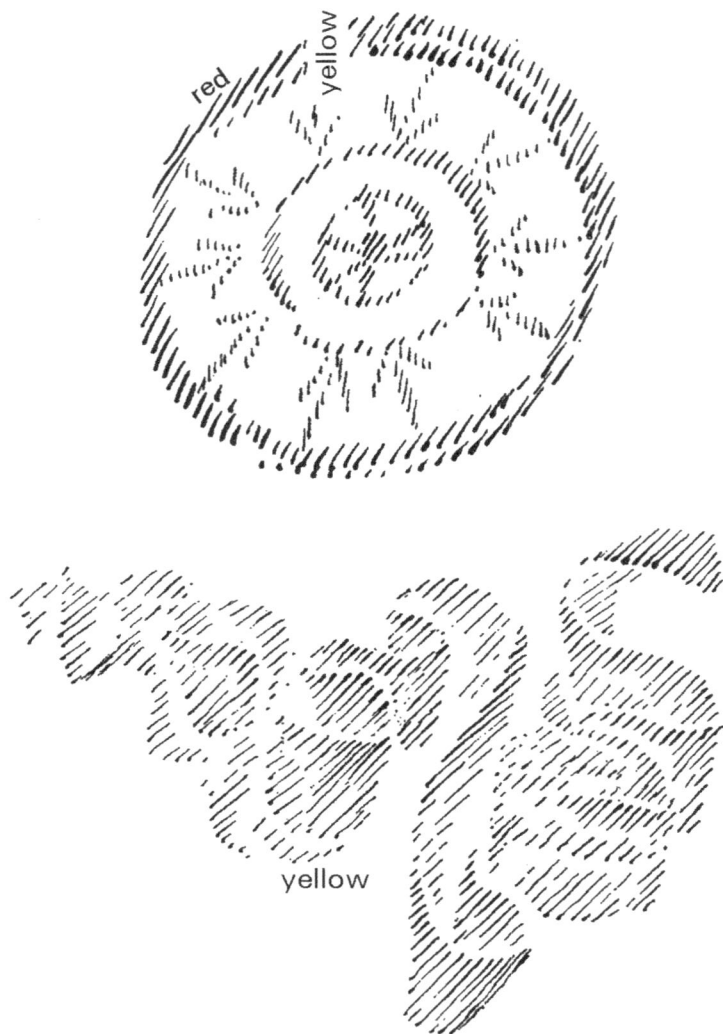

and rebounds, it returns as spirit, as a supersensible element, so the scientist no longer perceives it. No light radiates that does not ray back again as spirit. But what I'm saying here about light also applies to natural laws themselves. Natural laws diminish in validity the further you would move out into space; but this reaches only to a certain sphere and then it all returns. The natural laws return as meaningful thoughts. And this is the cosmic ether.

The cosmic ether does not have a radially emanating or emitting motion in respect of the earth but a motion, rather, that streams in from all sides. And what lives upon the earth everywhere in this influx are meaning-creating thoughts. The cosmic ether is at the same time a world of formative thoughts. But there is a further aspect to this. When I form thoughts here on earth in the way that is done to formulate natural laws, these thoughts make nice straight lines, if I can speak metaphorically. You can say there is a certain constancy of matter, a constancy of energy. In light theories you have a refraction exponent and so on. In thoughts people formulate what lives in the material world. But when these thoughts rebound, spring back, when we experience how thoughts live in the cosmic ether, they are not logical thoughts in the same way, not thoughts with sharp and defined contours. Instead they are picture-thoughts, pictures, imaginations.

In these matters we can experience very curious things concerning modern culture. A few days ago I said to some of those now sitting here that over the last 40 or 50 years theory upon hypothetical theory has been formulated about the cosmic ether. The cosmic ether was regarded by some as a rigid entity, by others as a fluid entity, by still others as cosmic gas, as something that lives in some kind of spiralling motion, and so on. But what actually happens when people formulate such hypotheses? In creating these hypotheses, they simply continue using the kind of thinking they are used to applying to visible phenomena, processes and creatures in the natural world. But what streams back to us as I described, has long ceased to be susceptible to formulation in thoughts such as those used to encompass natural laws. We can only grasp or comprehend what comes back to us in this way by starting to think in pictures, to think imaginatively. So one way of putting it is to say that the content, the formulation of our natural laws, diminishes in validity with increasing distance from the earth, up to a certain sphere. At that point natural laws have entirely ceased to exist. There they all merge and flow into one another, returning as pictures. They come back to us in forms and configurations.

And now, if we have become capable of the kind of supersensible vision I described before, we can regard the world etherically, that is, in picture form; and then you have to acknowledge that as long as we dwell within the etheric, we see nothing of our physical body; and likewise the thinking we normally use becomes vaporous, hazy. Now it is as if the universe were streaming back to us everywhere, sending pictures, imaginations. And so we begin to lead logical thinking over into thinking of a sculptural, painterly kind if we wish to comprehend the ether. And so it becomes quite understandable that the ether cannot be comprehended by all the hypotheses founded on calculation. By the time all calculations and formulations arising in relation to natural physical phenomena reach the sphere from which the ether emanates, they have lost their meaning. No longer does anything radiate outward from there, but there is, rather, an influx towards us, bringing not the thinking that we use here in the ordinary mind but one that, basically, lives only in art, but in art, too, only in an earthly manner.

As paradoxical as this seems, it is simply truth for those who comprehend the world. Imagine that I make a wooden sculpture, and create the form of a human being in wood. I make the form and shape of this sculpture so that it closely resembles the human being. Let us say that I do actually succeed in making the sculpture's outward form correspond to the outward human form. But as sculptor there is one thing I cannot do: I cannot suck out space. As sculptor, all I can do is to master physical matter. But if, at the place where I am making this sculpture, I could also activate the etheric laws of the cosmos, and in other words if this deep silence I spoke of could arise outwardly, then negative quiet not just zero quiet would be there. There would not only be mere space but also something from which space itself emerges; and then my wooden sculpture would not produce a human being but something resembling a plant. The wooden sculpture remains a sculpture because we only reckon with the physical element, thus only make an imprint of form; because we do not also make what the form would actually and intrinsically be, the sucking out of space. That cannot happen, for otherwise my wooden sculpture would be a growing form. And so you have to recognize that ordinary artistic thinking and feeling cannot in fact approach the etheric world since this is something where one would not only project something into space but also encompass space, take hold of it such that the ether would render this space empty, a vacuum. And then we experience the living element in this emptying, sucking out of space. You see, a quite different kind of thinking is needed if we are to raise ourselves into higher worlds.

And then, if one has experienced the other thing I spoke of, the soul falling deeply silent, something else happens too. You will find that etheric configurations approach you from the cosmos. But at the same time you also experience sentient spirit beings within these etheric configurations. Not only etheric configuration but actual spirit beings of the higher hierarchies, as they are called, approach you. Your experience is now that of a spirit among spirits. You experience a real world of spirit that approaches with this influx, this streaming back. And wherever etheric configurations approach us, the world of spirit appears. The physical has gone outwards and returns in etheric configurations. But with these etheric configurations spirit beings can return as well. But if you ask where they have come from, the 'where' actually no longer has any meaning. Their spatial significance is something they have by virtue of coming in from the periphery of the cosmos: they come in from the cosmos from all directions because they are sustained by the cosmic ether. This cosmic ether gives them a spatial 'location', and yet the nature of this spatial quality is their approach to you from without.

These two forms of substantiality that I discover in the world in this way—the formative forces approaching me in etheric configurations and flooding over me, and the living spirit beings—are something we appropriate as we descend from our pre-earthly life into earthly life. We fill ourselves with something that we now hold together within us with a part of the infinite world of formative forces—infinite in a relative sense, that is, extending as far as the universe—which is itself filled with the astral body, with what also enters here and only has a spatial dimension by virtue of the ether.

We bear the physical body that is composed of the earth's physical constituents. We bear within us the etheric body that actually comes to us from the breadths of the cosmos; and we bear within this etheric body the astral body, that is spirit from the spirit of the cosmos. Within us we demarcate and confine something that for the universe appears indeterminate and boundless.

And if we now go on to undertake higher exercises still, where we not only come to the soul's deep silence but also penetrate this profound silence and awaken in our own will—as we otherwise only awaken in thinking—then we experience our fourth human entity, our I. Tomorrow I will speak further of this.

LECTURE 5

THE PHYSICAL WORLD AND MORAL-SPIRITUAL IMPULSES: FOUR STAGES OF INNER EXPERIENCE

DORNACH, 21 APRIL 1923

IN our recent reflections we have been considering the etheric and astral bodies that, besides the physical body, indwell our human being. We showed how the etheric body or body of formative forces can be apprehended if we become aware of the inner life of thinking. The body of formative forces can be perceived when we become aware of this inner vitality of thinking in such a way that we live within it without being influenced by outward sense impressions; when this thinking also is not stimulated by our combining and interrelating of sense impressions but when we endeavour, rather, to experience thinking's intrinsic weaving and surging through our own unsullied activity, without the usual stimulus for thinking from outward sense impressions.

This experience of thinking is at the same time an experience of the etheric world. Yesterday I described how this inner rousing of thinking that we undertake, which really isn't all that hard to achieve, leads us to an experience of the second human being within us; and this experience is also that of possessing a kind of temporal body, which is not so quietly enclosed in space as the physical body but fluctuates continually, is in continual motion. Only momentarily can it be observed in a spatial sense, and then only in the form of contours. But our experience of this temporal body gives rise in turn to the panoramic tableau of our life, which unfolds before our inner eye the whole, unified span of our life on earth so far.

Basically we dwell here within a very soul-spiritual occurrence when, by an inward grasp of thinking, we enter the etheric life of the universe. In this imaginative weaving life of the soul that gives us an experience of the etheric realm, we no longer feel the shadowy quality that the life of the mind normally has for us. We no longer feel the dreamy quality that soul life possesses in ordinary consciousness. Nor do we feel ourselves so shut off from the world as we do within the physical body, where we feel enclosed in our skin. Instead we feel the outer world stream into us and our own being stream out into it. We feel ourselves to be a moving part of the whole etheric universe, to be moving with the world. But nevertheless, what we thus experience can strike us as something frighteningly unreal. By habit we feel ourselves to stand solidly upon the earth in a physical body, but in this experience of the etheric we can feel uncertainty about our own existence. We feel ourselves to be lifted out of the physical world but not yet firmly rooted in the world of spirit.

This rootedness in the world of spirit does however come when the seeker achieves what I spoke of yesterday: the deep silence of the soul. As I described it in *Knowledge of the Higher Worlds*, we must come to a point where we no longer use the power we usually expend, through a modification of breathing, to speak the outward words of language upon the outflow of breath, but we must hold back what otherwise seeks to flow out into words. Nevertheless we must engage this activity that is otherwise expended in speech; we must make the same inner efforts as otherwise used in speaking aloud, and by this means must come to deepened inner silence. And if the soul succeeds not only in coming to, as it were, the 'zero point' of silence, but goes beyond this, goes deeper into what I called negative silence, below the level of mere silence, then we no longer drown out the sound of our spiritual being through the energies that seek to flow into the breath when we speak. Inwardly we keep developing the impetus to speak but we hold speech back before it takes hold of the larynx. By holding speech back in this way and yet still inwardly developing the speaking capacity, we come not merely to inward quiet and stillness but to what I have called the soul's deep silence. This deep silence of the soul relates to speech, to the words that outwardly resound in the physical world, as something that goes beyond the zero point of silence and deepens to a negative depth of stillness. But then, from this deep silence, there resounds what the spiritual world or, to use an ancient term, the Logos, seeks to reveal from the universe. Then we ourselves no longer speak for we have become the instrument through which the Logos speaks. And then we become aware of our own astral body within us, and the astral world of which I spoke yesterday. This astral world is substantially different from the world we experience in ordinary consciousness through our senses and combinative faculty of reason.

In this world of the senses and combinative reason in the ordinary mind, we perceive the solid density of substantial things and material processes that unfold in the spatial dimension. To put it in an easily accessible, though imprecise way, these things impress themselves upon our senses so that we can perceive them. On the one hand, therefore, we have our sensory experience of the world and our logical deductions about material things and processes, and on the other hand we have unreal thoughts, unreal feelings, as we might say, the unreal thoughts and feelings whose relationship to reality has been the subject of philosophical dispute since time immemorial. Those who resort only to the ordinary mind will often regard mere thoughts and feelings that arise in their soul as something that drives them, as it were, to get a quick purchase again on material, substantial things so as to reassure themselves of their real existence.

Thus our existence within thoughts and feelings seems not immediately real; and yet the moral world, the world of moral impulses, issues and flows forth from these thoughts and feelings. So we have before us a dual world: the compact and solid world of matter, which initially strikes us as reality, and then the seemingly less real world of thoughts and feelings, which give rise to our moral impulses. It can seem bothersome and burdensome to recognize that scientific proofs of the constancy of matter and energy lend outward reality a certain kind of eternity, whereas the moral world order rising out of mere thoughts and feelings is simply annihilated again in the great cemetery of material existence that inevitably follows from our hypotheses about natural phenomena. Thus the ordinary mind is faced by a duality between the material world on the one hand and the moral-spiritual world on the other. We stand within this world, or rather within these two worlds that seem to have so little to do with one another. We stand in the midst of this. One aspect of our being is given up to the material world in which our digestive processes act, from which in turn our drives arise, in which our senses receive impressions, and in which our powers of reason relate these sense impressions to each other. We become aware that we belong to this material world; but we also realize that our human dignity only exists if there is real meaning in the moral and spiritual impulses we acquire from thoughts and feelings whose reality appears to be uncertain.

In ordinary consciousness, therefore, we are faced by a need to fill the physical body, by virtue of which we belong to the physical world, with qualities whose reality inevitably appears dubious. We see that moral and spiritual impulses do not prevail in outer nature. The stones follow iron laws of geology—the world of minerals is untouched by moral or spiritual impulses. The world of plants unfolds in its soft quietude, its blossoms called forth by a neutral sunlight and warmth. Here again it is hard for people to see any moral impulses streaming through the awakening warmth of the sun, its awakening light, to sow the tapestry of plants over the earth.

Likewise, beholding the third natural kingdom, that of the animals, with whom our own physical organization has so much in common, it will be said that any moral quality that may be embedded in such forms no longer figures in a moral way. We see predatory animals hunting their prey without any right on our part to judge such seeming cruelty by moral standards. The animal, after all, occupies a place in the scheme of things below the level at which we might assume or require a moral or spiritual impulse to be at work. And then in turn we look upon our own physical, material nature, and we find that we too, in a part of our being, fall below that level as well. Yet, if we are to fulfil our sense of human dignity, we face the need to introduce moral impulses into this lapsed being, into ourselves. Within ordinary consciousness it is not possible to discern any harmonious accord between these disparate levels, an interplay between physical-material impulses and spiritual, moral ones. Spirit and matter fall apart. We can look ahead at the life remaining to us until death and see that we will go on living in this split until we die: that we have this physical, material organization into which we need to introduce moral, spiritual impulses, but that nature shows us an absence of moral and spiritual impulses at work directly within natural laws. We see ourselves as confined within this dualism until we die.

But if, as I have described, we hear our astral body and the world we belong to through it sounding to us out of the deep silence of the soul, then a world arises before the soul that ordinary consciousness cannot reach; a world, though, that we long for in our ordinary awareness when faced by this duality, this gulf between the physical-material world and that of spirit and morality. Then we gain the prospect of a world that is no longer unreal, that appears to us as real as the solid, tangible world of the physical and sensory realm; and a world, also, that everywhere pours moral-spiritual impulses into physical, material ones. Here we gaze into a reality in which it is as if moral impulses at a higher level flowed into chemical processes in this earthly world. We gaze into a world in which there is no such thing as, say, hydrogen and oxygen combining according to indifferent, neutral laws of nature, but where, instead, they follow moral impulses in so doing. Here there are no processes which do not, at the same time, possess a moral, spiritual meaning.

And now we recognize further that the world in which inward interpenetration of a truly creative moral-spiritual potency with an enhanced realm of matter occurs, is also the world we enter on crossing the threshold of death. Out of this world we descended into the physical, earthly world, from pre-earthly into earthly life. Through such recognition we see that only this physical world of earth is one of dualism, where nature and spirit are sundered by a deep gulf. And that we had nevertheless to be set down in this physical earth world in order to experience how spirit makes no headway in approaching matter here; we recognize ourselves to be the only creature within this physical world of earth that can, out of our own freedom, our own intrinsic and inmost impulses, establish this connection and bridge the gulf.

If there were anywhere in this physical world where, by objective laws, a moral-spiritual impulse flowed into a chemical process or into plant growth or into an animal drive, then, since the human being incorporates and encapsulates everything in the cosmos, we could never have attained freedom, could never bring about that connection between spirit and matter that proceeds from our own intrinsic being.

But in human life on earth, we pass through two contrary conditions: that of waking life each day, from waking up to falling asleep, and that of sleep, from falling asleep to reawakening. While awake, we live very much in the world where spirit and matter are strictly sundered, where spirit cannot approach matter, let alone pervade it, where matter is powerless to raise its processes to the spiritual realm. But when we have reached the world I described as sounding up from the soul's deep silence, we can behold the activity to which we give ourselves up during sleep, that of our astral body. And then we know that in these interruptions to earthly life during sleep, we live in the world in which we can initially prepare to connect spirit with matter. During sleep between birth and death we weave within a thin, etheric-astral element: a tissue woven in all our periods of sleep during our lifetime which in turn, each time we wake up again, passes into the duality between spirit and matter. And in all that we weave in this way while asleep lives what we carry over the threshold of death with us, entering the world in which matter is no longer powerless to raise itself, with its processes, to spirituality, where spirit is not unable to approach matter. With everything we have thus woven in sleep we enter the world in which everything that resembles matter raises itself to spiritual processes, in which spirit continually intervenes and engages in matter. And then we see that the duality between spirit and matter is only present in the world which we pass through in successive periods of life between birth and death. Furthermore, we come to know that we enter a quite different world, which appears to us only as if in a fleeting mirror-image while we are asleep, when we prepare ourselves for its other reality.

Once we have passed through the gateway of death, we really do enter this world, and then we weave further at the life we passed through between birth and death. But this weaving is not done in a realm of spirit sundered from matter, free of matter, one free of all connection with the earth and its eventual fate. No, we enter a world where what appeared to us on earth as in a fleeting picture during sleep, a soul-spiritual mirage, now exists in a real world in which there is no duality between spirit and matter, in which spiritual substantiality continually penetrates material substantiality, or one resembling the material; in which there are no mere laws of nature but where the laws of nature are the lowest spiritual laws. Here there are no merely abstract spiritual laws, but lower spiritual processes, spiritual laws, play into material-like processes that are to be found there. Into this world we enter in order to pass through what lies between death and a further birth.

We become acquainted with this world when, out of the soul's deep silence, we hear the spirit, the universal Logos—though in its individual entities—speaking to us: not in a physically audible language but in one that is not only inaudible but less than inaudible, and which for that very reason is spiritually perceptible. As we hear this inner speech, which does not become outer words, and yet inwardly expends the effort that otherwise is only made manifest by means of the breath in outward speech, we come to the point of knowing the world from which we descended, a world of spirit, but one of whose reality there can no longer be the least doubt, no doubt at all that we descended from it to physical existence and will ascend to it again after we pass through the gate of death. In this world, all spirit is at the same time as active and effective as the material realm here on earth. In this world, all matter is raised to a higher level where its density and coarseness no longer resist the influences of moral-spiritual impulses.

If we wish to enter the etheric-imaginative world, we need in a sense to get beyond abstract, dead thinking to a thinking that is inwardly alive. If we wish to reach the world of deep silence, that is, the world where all material-type activity is spiritual, and all spiritual life is creative within matter, we need to go still further: not only reaching beyond ordinary dead thinking to a living form of thinking, but also delving beyond audible speech capacity to the inaudible speech capacity lying behind it. This lives in deep silence, from which not audible words but the active Logos speaks out of stillness, precisely through this intensified stillness.

But if we seek to progress further still, then as well as rising to a living thinking, which is more or less only a process of inner picturing, and coming to what, if you like, weaves and streams through the world—but speaks in this weaving and flowing out of deep silence so that we feel ourselves within it as in an element streaming through the world, in which we ourselves stream with our hearing, with the third human being within us—then, to go further still, we must raise ourselves to another process, to yet another occurrence within us.

In living thinking we live with the etheric. At the second stage we live in the process we ourselves do not set in motion but one illumined by the Logos, which otherwise lives only at a physical level in our speech. At a third stage we must discern something which is a counter-image to a process of destruction in physical life. Here, as well as enhancing and intensifying our thinking, enhancing and intensifying our capacity of speech by deepening it into stillness and silence, we must internalize what occurs when we do something on the earth, when we act. But we must understand that 'doing something' does not any longer now mean mere outward physical action. We act, we do something if we simply work inwardly in thoughts, for will is involved in that too. Everything by means of which we prompt ourselves to activity, whether inward or outward, is action and not mere passivity. But each time such activity is accomplished, even if only within our thinking, a physical process accompanies this action. In the same way that a brain process accompanies physical thinking, and as the breathing process is modified in physical speech, so in a will initiative of this kind that flows into action, an inner process occurs that we can compare with that annihilation of material substance we are aware of in all processes of combustion. If you look at how a flame destroys the substance of a candle—and I'm not going into the precise chemical processes that occur here but just speaking of what we can observe with our usual physical senses—you see how this involves the destruction of something material in nature, irrespective of the fact that there is also a transformation of substance at work into something invisible.

Such processes, that resemble what happens when a flame destroys the candle wax, always accompany any will initiative within us. Usually we're unaware of this, since it occurs below the level of the conscious mind. We know nothing of what happens between the intention we form to do something with our hands, and the actual movement of the hand that ensues. We do not know how the intention, living in our thoughts, enters our muscles and then succeeds in raising our hand. We only become aware that this has happened when our hand moves. Yet between the intention and the action lies a process that resembles combustion. But within the human organism itself we cannot speak in this way if, from a higher spiritual perspective, we observe this process of combustion that is the material process accompanying human will activity. If we observe this combustion process, we cannot ascertain that matter is only transformed; rather processes are destroyed that have first been kindled during ordinary digestion and nutrition. All the physical, combustion-related processes that occur as the basis for will activity, all these processes that resemble combustion, occur between the further course of the digestive process and the formation of blood.

Where the blood forms we can look into these combustion-type processes. And there we can also perceive how the human will sparks and gathers force. We gaze here into a declining material process where, to put it accessibly, matter vanishes. And here we can become aware of something similar to what we perceive when meditating carefully and conscientiously, when we pass from a thinking stimulated from without to one that finds an inner impetus. Then, in these inner impulses of thinking, we have something that we only become aware of through our own activity. In the deep silence of the soul we have something concealed behind our physical breathing process that resounds from the world of spirit and soul into an opposite negative space of stillness, the Logos resounding from silence.

But we also find, if we delve below the processes that act within our organism as combustion, that cosmic will is at work beneath

these processes of destruction. Just as the power of the Logos underlies the breath as it produces an outwardly audible word, so underlying this power of combustion, continually active upon our organism, the creative power of cosmic will continually sparks and effervesces as it works into us.

In the modified breath (red) that unfolds from our larynx to produce an outwardly audible word, we can perceive the spiritual element behind it (light blue, white) which, arising from the soul's deep silence, comes from an opposite direction to that of physical words, and does so in a way we should not allow to issue forth through the larynx. Then we become acquainted with this spiritual element that brings to our awareness the silent, yet for that very reason, clearly articulating voice of the cosmic Logos. In the same way, in all processes that resemble combustion (red, see next drawing) which we can observe within our organism, we can observe the flowing, surging cosmic will (yellow) in which we ourselves participate. This is not Schopenhauer's 'thoughtless will'[17] but a will that is everywhere pervaded by, and effervescing with will.

And now we feel a fourth human being within us. Wherever combustion processes hold sway in the physical organism, we feel creative processes at work. We feel ourselves embedded within the creative world. And within this creative world we now become aware of everything that is also creative in ourselves.

Previously, when we perceived the third human being within us, the astral, we became acquainted with a world in which there is no distinction between matter and spirit. Now we become acquainted with a world in which the spirit not only lives in all processes but in which spirit is the creative principle in all processes; a world in which there are no material-like substances that are not formed by the spirit. Within us we become acquainted with something whose nature is so creative that nothing resembling matter has not been, or is not, created by it within its realm. Before we found a world in which there is no spirit-matter duality. Now we perceive one in which moral-spiritual impulses themselves are the only reality. As we gaze into this world, the corresponding drop of which holds sway within us, as we gaze into the fourth human being in us that participates in this world to which we have now raised ourselves, we come to know in this fourth human being a creative principle in us whose nature is as follows: it is not present anywhere in the world of our natural surroundings, where spirit cannot penetrate matter, nor is it initially present in the world that appears to us within our own astral body. But it does come to the fore wherever a still higher principle, an actual being, enters this astral world. Just as we, as physical human beings, are surrounded by air that is permeable for us, so we become aware of the astral life, a spiritual atmosphere, within which spirit beings wander—in the same way that we wander about in the air, the atmosphere, as physical beings. And now we not only gaze into the Logos of the astral world that speaks in a general way, but we also look upon spirit beings moving and living within this astral world.

And here we come to know our own being as something that cannot now exist at all, but that has passed through this etheric world in pre-earthly existence, and that existed in a previous life on earth. We become aware that moral impulses from our former life, or from several former lives, indwell these destructive processes of combustion; that this fourth human being lives in us and is, at the same time, the creator of our fundamental destiny. Behind the fire in our body, we discover the creative power of the content of our previous life on earth, which has now been able to ascend to the region where, as creative power, it counteracts the destructive power of combustion, because it is not present existence but long-past earth life that has shed everything connected with the duality of spirit and matter, that has passed through the world of spirit and in this world of spirit has assumed the character of creative spirit. Here we discover, within what pulses up in the depths of our otherwise so hidden human will, something that sparks as impetus into us from what once existed in the same way that we now stand within earthly life, yet has in the meantime become different, first being etherized then living in an astral world, and in this astral world rising to a third and higher level. And now it appears to us as something contained in the only shadowy I of our present life as the creative and energetic will from former lives that grounds this I and fills it with reality.

Thus we have risen from the physical nature of our being to our three higher entities: to etheric nature, to astral nature—our intrinsic soul being—and our true I being which is the outcome of former lives on earth, whereas the I that lives in my present earthly life only finds real existence during sleep. I described to you earlier how the astral body weaves and lives in the nature of the astral world while we sleep; but within this astral body, from the moment of falling asleep to the moment of reawakening, we still bear and possess the I as I described. But as yet, insofar as it is the I of our present life, it is not able to work energetically into the physical body, for this is where we share the destiny of the rest of nature, the duality of spirit and matter. Here the human being is confronted by the spirit that is not yet active in matter, and matter that is powerless to approach the spirit.

Behind the curtains of existence, during sleep, there unfolds within us the conflict between spirit and matter that shines into us and consists in a desire to overcome this dualism in the outer physical world. This inner conflict also takes place in waking life in the will. Sleep conceals this from us to begin with, as long as we retain only ordinary consciousness. But in sleep is woven something which, when it is etherized and astralized again after death, ascends to be that creative power which will come to add a new element to us when we have again passed through the period between death and a new birth, adding to what surges in our will from long-past lives on earth.

We can look upon human life with these things in mind. Initially we do not look down into the will, nor behind the veils of sleep. But true spirit vision reveals what is really at work there as creative principle in opposition to processes of combustion from long-past lives on earth.

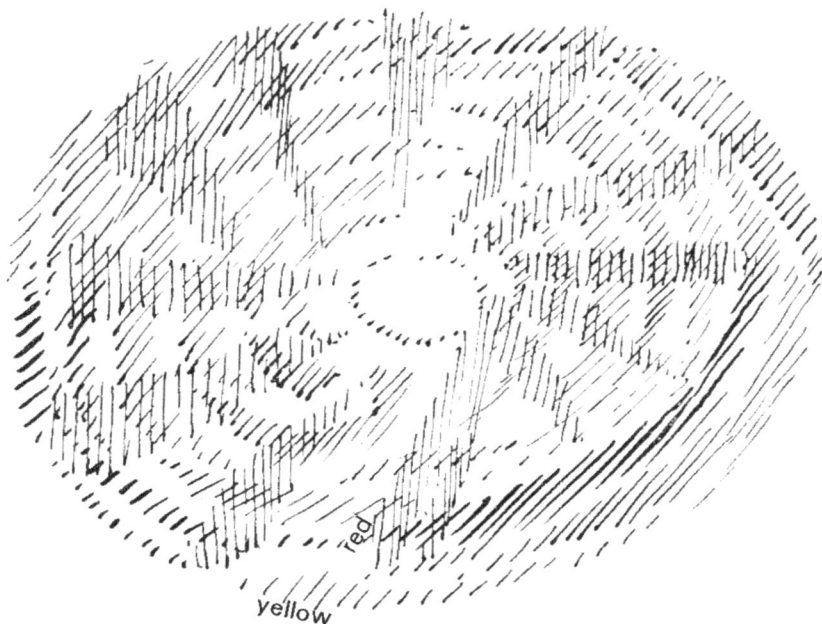

And then we can become aware how former lives pulse as if through our will, preparing our destiny through moral impulses; and how what the human will accomplishes, in a state of sleep even while we're awake, out of drives, emotions, out of conscious intentions, weaves itself during sleep into the being that sleep conceals from us at present. In our next life on earth, this being will unfold as active will, as creative I, pulsing through our blood in the combustion process of our future body: this creative I which will then be enhanced, complemented, by what we have developed in this life on earth between birth and death and have added to what came to us, as described, from former earthly lives.

In this way we can study the four aspects or levels of the human being. And as we come to perceive the reality of these four members, we gain an overview of the whole of human life as well. As I showed yesterday, the nature of life on earth enlarges to encompass life in the cosmic ether which reaches to a certain sphere but reflects back the cosmic astral principle everywhere. We live in our astral body with this cosmic astral realm, which is imperceptible to earthly observation. And if we live our way into this cosmic astral realm as I described it today, then not only does it resound as cosmic Logos, but from the words of the cosmic Logos real beings of the lower and higher hierarchies approach us, as if emerging from real depths of the life of spirit, and amongst these is also our own spirit being from long-past lives on earth.

In this way, as we recognize the human being's nature, our soul-spiritual perception enlarges at the same time to encompass the cosmos, the universe: not only the cosmos as a physical and etheric dimension but also as a soul-spiritual one. Human knowledge thus becomes world knowledge. Just as we could never have only exhalation in physical life without inhalation, the two continually living in us in reciprocal interplay, in a continually alternating rhythm, so, at a higher level, we cannot acquire only knowledge of the human being or knowledge of the universe. As inhalation calls for exhalation, so knowledge of the human being calls for world knowledge, and as exhalation calls for inhalation, world knowledge calls for knowledge of the human being. World knowledge and knowledge of the human being are the systole and diastole of the physical-soul-spirit life of the cosmos in all its grandeur. At a higher level, they cannot stand side by side and distinct but only pass continually in and out of each other in continual interplay, pervading and penetrating each other in an eternally fluctuating rhythm, as the immortal life of the cosmos itself to which the immortal human being also belongs.

LECTURE 6

PERCEIVING THE ETHERIC WORLD

DORNACH, 22 APRIL 1923

IN recent days I have been trying to place the human being into the context of the whole universe, showing firstly how we are constituted of physical body, etheric body or body of formative forces, astral body and the I itself that passes on from one life on earth to another; but then also how these members or aspects of our being each in their own way are connected with the universe. Thus the human physical body is connected with everything in the world that is physical, sensory and earthly in nature. This human physical body belongs to the physical sense world. When on the other hand we enquire into the etheric body or body of formative forces, we have to be aware that it actually belongs to a quite different world—to the one that is itself etheric, and which I described to you as a world that we must feel approaching us out of the far breadths of the cosmos. As opposed to earth forces, that spread outward in all directions from the earth, forces of the physical world within which we live, we must picture the etheric world issuing from the whole compass of the cosmos and approaching us and the physical forces from an opposite direction. This means that the human being's etheric body is subject to quite different laws from those of the physical body. Then again, when we enquire into the human being's astral body, we find it to be connected with worlds that we do not encounter at all in the cosmos encompassed within the physical or etheric realms in which we live between birth and death. We find instead that we belong in our astral body to a world that we enter between death and a new birth.

And with the I itself, finally, we belong to a world that passes like a flowing current through worlds which, like our world for instance, are in turn threefold. Our world is threefold: physical, etheric, astral. The world of the I passes through this world and through other similar threefold worlds. It is, in other words, a far more comprehensive world. It is a world that we must describe in fact as the world of the eternal as compared to the temporal world.

In studying the human being's capacities of perception and cognition, and how these acquaint us with the etheric body or body of formative forces, the astral body and the I, we enter by turn into very different worlds. If we wish to acquaint ourselves with our etheric body we have to enter the sphere of active thinking, an experience of thinking. Here we need to recognize how the world that surrounds us is different in kind from what we experience within the physical sense world. Things and processes we are familiar with from the physical world appear and behave very differently in these higher realms. In the things and processes of the physical world we find only the last effects, if you like, of agencies and activities issuing from higher worlds. In a sense therefore we see a more original and archetypal aspect of these things than we find within the physical world. Dwelling in the physical world, we initially possess the world well known to the ordinary mind, the world in which we are surrounded by the three kingdoms of nature and our own human nature. But when we raise ourselves to the powers of perception— which I have called imaginative perception in my books—that reveal to us our own etheric body or body of formative forces, then we enter the etheric world. And when we have strengthened ourselves to the point of inner illumination, so that we dwell within what I called the second human being within us, in the body of formative forces, then we also enter the world revealed to us at least in pictures initially as the world of the Angeloi, Archangeloi and Archai.

In breaking through into the sphere where we can perceive the etheric body or body of formative forces, revelations are granted us within its flowing world of images of beings belonging to the third hierarchy: of Angeloi, Archangeloi and Archai. Here, therefore, we are surrounded by beings who do not surround us in the physical sense world. The way in which these beings surround us manifests in qualities which, we can say, our senses also give us here in the sense world.

But here in the sense world, colours, for instance, are qualities that adhere to the surfaces of things, or appear in a purely physical configuration such as the rainbow. Tones too appear to us here in their connection with things of the physical sense world. Heat and cold, likewise, issue from sources of a physical, sensory nature. But if we observe this world in which the third hierarchy appears to us, we no longer have colours that adhere to things, tones that resound from things and so on, but instead the flowing colours, the reverberating tones, the resonance of heat and cold, pour not through space any more but within time. A quality of colour does not attach to the surface of things but instead it surges and fluctuates. At the same time, the powers enabling us to transpose ourselves into these worlds teach us that just as colour in the material world conceals a material property, so within a flowing cloud of colour, a streaming colour organism, as we perceive it in this world, a quality of spirit and soul holds sway that belongs to the third hierarchy. At the moment therefore when the life-tableau that I described appears before you, revealing vividly as in an instant everything we have experienced since birth, the third hierarchy is alive within these colours, tones and so on that are now liberated from matter and appear to us within this stream of our own experiences in life.

And when, through the power of our capacity of perception, we raise ourselves to a point where we can survey our own astral body, thus perceiving what existed of us before we descended to earthly existence, and what we will again carry with us when we pass through the gate of death, we can discern a further world, one we do not find in the ether of the cosmos but that exists only behind the gateway of birth and death. We here enter a further world, the world of the astral.

All this does not coincide exactly with what I described in my book, *Theosophy*, where things are characterized from a different perspective. But in the same way that we encounter the third hierarchy when we organize ourselves upward to our body of formative forces, in this further world in which our astral body becomes visible for us, we encounter the second hierarchy, that of Exusiai, Kyriotetes, Dynamis. And this second hierarchy no longer manifests, if we perceive it truly, in flowing colours and streaming tones, but as various meanings that are revealed and proclaimed to us from the Logos that imbues the world. This speaks to us.

We have to use customary words to give some hint or sense of how we can relate to these worlds once we have acquired the relevant powers of perception, and then these words no longer have the same meaning as they do in the sensory world; yet from them we can glean something concerning this relationship to higher worlds. Thus we can say that inner, living thinking becomes a kind of organ of touch for the etheric world. With this inner, living thinking we touch into this flowing world of colours and so on. We should not imagine that the colour red that we see with our senses is the same as the red quality we now perceive: this is not a colour attaching to things, that we see with our eyes, but an apprehension and contact with red, yellow and so on: we touch into them, as it were. We touch into tones. And so we can say that in the etheric world, living thinking becomes an encounter, a contact, with what lives in the world of the third hierarchy.

If we then enter the world to which in a sense our own astral body belongs, we can no longer say that we merely touch it, or touch into it. We must regard this world as the manifestation of the beings of the second hierarchy. We must see each particular expression of it as a part, an aspect of the cosmic Logos. Through the deep silence we engender in ourselves, the speech of spirit beings emerges. Thus after touch, contact, at the first level, comes speech, communication.

And when, in the way I suggested yesterday, we wrestle our way through to an experience of the I that passes from one life to the next, and in the intervening periods passes through those other modes of life between death and rebirth, then we enter a world that is the world of spirit itself, the higher world of spirit. In this world we gain a very particular relationship to our true I. The I or ego we experience here within earth existence between birth and death, is after all bound up with our physical corporeality. It is perceptible for us as long as we experience ourselves within physical corporeality, and we are in a certain fashion compelled to become selfless when we rise into the ether world and the astral world. Here we have at most only something like a memory of this earthly ego.

But we then find the true I as it passes from one life on earth to the next, as I said. We discern this true I initially as a being quite separate from us. We say to ourselves: Here I stand in this earthly life between birth and death, and look back through the portion of etheric world that appears to me, back to my earthly birth. But then my gaze looks still further back into worlds, far regions that really only have temporal existence, and where to speak of space would actually make no sense. I gain a broad vision of the world, with all it contains, as it surrounds us between death and a new birth. As I gaze through the ether, through the world of the third hierarchy, as I gaze through the astral realm, in which I lived between death and my latest birth as in a supersensible world of the revelation of the Logos, a world revealing itself through a cosmic speech—as I gaze through all this, I ultimately look upon a being far distant from me, upon the content of my previous life on earth. Initially this appears to me thus: I stand here in earthly life, with my present, ghost-like I, and then I look far back through all I just described to the content of my previous life on earth. But at the same time I see how the I, winding itself free, has passed through the worlds through which I have been gazing, reaching my present earthly life. To begin with I do really see my true I as a distant, foreign being. And I recognize myself again in this being that is, as it were, an alien one to me.

In this sentence every word should really be taken with great intensity, for each word in it is of quite special importance. It is part and parcel of the whole experience that we wrestle our way forward from perception of our own I as something initially alien to us to the point of recognizing that what first appeared foreign to us is what we ourselves actually are. It appears to you as if another being altogether lived in the distant past, but you are this being yourself.

And then we become aware how this self has streamed in from a previous life on earth into this present life, and in this present earthly life is in some respects covered over and concealed. It would only emerge and appear if all that occurs between falling asleep and waking up again were to unfold before the human soul. Within it there weaves and lives on what has streamed from our former earthly life through the astral and etheric world until it reaches us.

You see, a world of earthly contradictions and heavenly concordances lie in this labour of recognition: earthly contradictions of a kind that mean that everything we initially possess here in daily life on earth cannot basically come near our own true I. Within this earthly I live really only the first rudiments of love. But the fact that this power of love shines into earthly life lends life a shimmer and brilliance. But this love must be intensified and enhanced. This love must be enhanced so that we become able to perceive the etheric world and the astral world, and so that we can overcome what lives in us as our ego, as egoism, as the opposite of love, and in life, as the opposite of love, makes it possible for us to experience ourselves as our own ego within earthly life. Love must grow so strong that we learn to overlook this earthly ego, to forget it, no longer to gaze upon it with such regard. Love means merging our own being in the other. This must happen so strongly that we no longer esteem our own ego, our own I as it lives in our earthly body. Then we encounter the contradictory truth that it is precisely through selflessness, through the highest capacity of love, that we reach our own true I which then shines toward us from the far distances of past eras.

We have to lose our earthly ego to gain perception of our true I. And if we cannot develop this devotional surrender, we cannot approach our true I. You can see it like this: the true I does not wish to be sought, its appearance and emergence will not be dictated. It hides itself when it is sought, for it will only be found in love. And love is the devotion of our own being to another being. This is why the true I must be found, as if it were a being who is other, who is not us.

And the moment we gain perception, vision of our own true I, at the same time we apprehend what henceforth lives in a further world, in the actual world of spirit. We encounter the beings of the first hierarchy: Seraphim, Cherubim, Thrones.

And just as we there rediscover our I, of which we possess only a reflection here in earthly life, so we discover the true spirit form of the whole world of our earthly surroundings. We must also lose the earthly world to gain this perception, to find, at one and the same time, the original world it derives from together with our true I.

And so we can say that what reveals itself in the spirit world is rediscovery, touch, speech; rediscovery and recognition, but of something we previously knew only as a reflection, an image.

In this way, as we experience our own full human nature and perceive our own being, we live our way into the totality of the universe. A full account of the different levels of the human being as physical body, etheric body, astral body and I is only really given if we show, at the same time, how these separate aspects are connected with corresponding worlds of the universe.

What I have just described has to be well understood if we are to be clear what underlies this enumeration of the four members of human nature. It becomes fully apparent here that we not only need to have different thoughts if we are to raise ourselves to an understanding of the world of spirit, but must also think in a different way. We must lead our whole way of thinking, which is really only a dead picturing within merely physical sense perception, into a living apprehension.

And here we can experience something very particular arising from modern culture, which shows us the obstacles that need to be overcome if anthroposophy is to imbue and inform the human soul.

When my book, *Occult Science* appeared, a well-known modern philosopher[18] took it to task. He first read the chapter where I describe the division of human nature into physical body, etheric body, astral body and I and so on. Many ordinary people with sound common sense also read *Occult Science* and were able to make something of it because healthy common sense is sufficient to follow what it describes, in the same way that you can understand a painting without needing to be a painter yourself. But a renowned philosopher may well have greater problems in understanding than an ordinary person. Coming upon these distinctions between physical, etheric, astral and I, he was stumped. What on earth did this mean? The physical body was clear enough of course; and perhaps the etheric body, since he could understand there being a finer kind of materiality than the denser substances of the body—yet still materiality nevertheless. However, he thought this distinction between denser and finer materiality was somewhat arbitrary. Then the astral body—well, this famous philosopher had of course heard of the soul, but astral body, what was that? The soul encompasses the faculties of thinking, feeling and will, which, he stated, are functions of the physical body; and so if we have understood the physical body then we have also grasped thinking, feeling and will. And as to the I, well that is just an aggregation of everything else.

And now let us see how this renowned philosopher responded critically to the book. He regarded what he found in *Occult Science* roughly in terms you might apply to an armchair: he said that an armchair can also be divided into its legs, the seat, and the backrest and armrests—three parts therefore. And then he proceeded to divide the human being, too, as one might an armchair. He thought this a rather good way of considering the human being but did not think it was anything particularly new, just another way of disassembling the human being into parts.

Scientists might get on better. They would not make do with mere intellectual classifications. You see, when chemists consider water they analyse it into hydrogen and oxygen. The scientist will not stop at a merely abstract classification of water into two parts, knowing that hydrogen will not necessarily only be bound up with oxygen as in water, but can also be bound with something quite different, such as chlorine in the case of hydrochloric acid. Thus the hydrogen in water is not just a portion, a part of water but, when separate from water it can form different combinations. And the oxygen, too, if separate from water, can be combined, can bind, with other substances, for instance with calcium to form calcium oxide. Thus hydrogen can form hydrochloric acid with chlorine, and oxygen can form calcium oxide with calcium—and so it is no longer possible to classify water in a merely abstract way as one might an armchair.

With the human being we stand at a still higher level. A mere classification into physical body, etheric body, astral body and I, is not adequate here but we have to recognize that the physical body belongs to the earth. And when a person passes through the gate of death and leaves his physical corpse behind, this passes back to the earth while the etheric body rises into the ether. But the astral body separates from both and enters worlds where the second hierarchy dwells. And the I in turn also belongs to a different world, where the first hierarchy dwells. These four levels or aspects are not mere classifications but each of them belongs to quite distinct and different spheres of the cosmos. Thus the classification into four parts points to the complex nature of the human being and stands at a much higher level than is required for analysis of an armchair, or then also water.

This points us to a significant obstacle in modern academic discourse. If he had turned to chemistry, the renowned philosopher could have discovered that, while abstract classifications may work for an armchair, they don't apply to water any longer. But the philosophy of this supposed philosopher could not extend beyond the armchair even as far as water. It could not carry him from a grasp of mundanities, which can be conceived in abstract ideas, to science. And science, in turn, cannot extend itself into philosophy. Thus chemists today do not include philosophical considerations of any kind in their enquiries.

And so philosophy, which from this perspective we might call a doctrine of armchairs, as yet finds no place for scientific thinking. In chemistry, in science, in turn, there is no place for philosophy. And therefore in the academic world, especially, the conditions that would allow people to penetrate to the deeper inner truth of the universe and its connection with the human being simply do not exist.

This man who offered a critique of my book first sent me his essay in manuscript form. But what was I to make of it? It is impossible to enter into any kind of debate with someone like this, for he lacks even the most rudimentary foundations for discussion. I let the essay lie, and later I discovered it again, in published form, with all the errors and nonsense, really, that was contained in this armchair philosophy. These are the kinds of hindrances that anthroposophy encounters. And we have to acknowledge the chasm that lies here between anthroposophy and those who often present their critiques of it. To begin with at least there is not the slightest chance that we can meet with understanding from academic quarters.

This well-known philosopher does admit certain things that are reminiscent of the customary ideas of modern culture. For instance he acknowledges that there was once a place called Atlantis, a continent between Europe and America, where the ancient Atlanteans lived, precursors of humanity. In this essay he wrote you can find the following question, though not expressed quite as I put it here: Today, when we do have proper fields of physiology and psychology, how does someone still manage to classify the human being in this way? Of course, anthroposophy does not classify the human being like an armchair, but this man thinks that we do. He is a con-scientious philosopher in his own way, and he wonders, questions, how we can have arrived at such a classification. He regards it as very primitive compared with the glories of modern philosophy! Now modern philosophers do not have much access to the truth despite thinking that they do. Two days ago I described to those who kindly attended my course for teachers how we can regard what is nowadays called psychoanalysis. I'll repeat here what I said about it: on the one hand this psychoanalysis has emerged from an amateur under-standing of physiology, which cannot get beyond the psyche and rise to the spirit but instead remains below with the body; and on the other hand it proceeds also from a half-baked grasp of psychology. These two elements cannot combine, and this means that people seek grotesque connections between the half-baked attempts in psy-chology and the half-baked attempts in physiology. This dilettantism is huge in both cases, equally so in both. Dilettantism in psychology plays as much part amongst psychiatrists as half-baked physiology. But if both are equally severe and combine together, this multiplies the problem and the ignorance. Then we get dilettantism squared. Thus psychoanalysis as a discipline multiplies half-baked ideas in the other two fields.

The renowned philosopher I have been speaking of was unable to understand how someone can be so primitive in outlook today as to divide the human being into four portions in the same way that you can identify three parts of an armchair. He seemed baffled by this. He therefore formed the hypothesis that I was a resurrected Atlantean. This is rather inventive of him, it seems to me, especially for an armchair philosopher.

But all these things demonstrate that, if we wish to truly cultivate anthroposophy, there are things we must resolve to overcome. One of these things, for instance, involves learning to discern soul and spirit directly, and then speaking of soul and spirit outside and beyond the physical. We should not speak of soul and spirit through any deductive process but by virtue of observing their reality. There are people today who can no longer do other than allow the soul's existence as an inner need, and yet they say that we have to deduce the soul from its actions within the physical.

As I said, these lectures will be to some degree a repetition of what well-versed anthroposophists have heard before. I am repeating many things you already know—for instance, that there are today natural philosophers who cite this instance: the Venus fly-trap has curiously shaped leaves and flowers. When an insect comes near to it, it opens. The Venus fly-trap catches this insect and consumes it. And if we want to deduce soul from such outward behaviour, we might say that this plant must have a soul; but in this case I can cite another example of something that must assuredly have a soul. There is a little instrument, man-made. You put a piece of bacon in it, and it has a trap that falls when a mouse comes near, attracted by the bacon. When the trap falls, this is just like the Venus fly-trap. And so we might just as well assume the mouse-trap has a soul too, in the same way that a certain natural philosopher ascribes soul to this plant. But deductions cannot be made from external characteristics or behaviour in this way.

We have to recognize that in this domain we encounter something that goes far beyond ideas of ordinary evidence or refutation. If, from this truly spiritual perspective we acquaint ourselves with human nature, we learn what it is that comes to expression as physical characteristics in the human being: in earthly life these are a full imprint or reflection of our spiritual being. In the same way that you find the imprint of a signet in sealing wax, so in the human physical body you find everywhere the imprint of the human being's soul-spiritual nature. The nature of human soul and spirit can everywhere be demonstrated in the brain's convolutions. If you wish to dull yourself to the world of spirit you can say that everything is physical. If you want to be a materialist, you can be. But if not, there is no point in hammering on about evidence or refutation of the ordinary kinds, as these commonly figure in the world, but you must seek spirit, must learn to perceive it as something autonomous in nature. Then you will no longer deny that the imprint in a seal was caused by a signet. The materialist is saying, really, that the signet does not actually exist, but that everything that exists emerged from the sealing wax. He can keep saying that everything appears in the sealing wax by itself, even a whole person. Josef Mueller here for instance.

One can be a materialist if one is unable to find, in the powers of one's soul, in the self-apprehension of the soul and spirit, a point of departure for the path into spirit-soul, into the archetypal realm. Coarse proofs achieve nothing, for you can prove materialism to be true as long as your proofs are founded in the physical world only. By contrast, it is an inner, human deed to find our way from the physical into the spiritual realm, rather than to seek abstract proofs. We only come to true anthroposophy through an inner, human deed which actively cultivates and furthers our perception. All disputation about proof is useless, for those who cite only evidence drawn from the physical sense world consider themselves fully justified, and it is impossible to refute the proofs of those who cannot find the beginning of the path into the world of spirit by the original power of their intrinsic humanity.

We have to recognize this. We have to acknowledge that it is a matter of human freedom to raise ourselves from the physical into the spirit; that unfree proofs do not achieve this, but that only deeds of inner, conscious human experience can raise us to worlds of spirit. If we truly feel this inwardly, only then do we possess what is necessary for understanding in the right way how anthroposophy relates to merely physical modes of perception.

But this is essential in our era. We cannot demand of a philosophy whose analysis applies only to chairs that it truly comprehends matters worthy of our human dignity. Humanity today needs something that will lead human beings to the real nature of the human being, not merely to its imprint. This imprint presents to our eyes everything that is contained as archetype in a person's spirit being, but it does not give us an experience of this. We have to experience ourselves as beings of spirit-soul, and then we will also find the world to be a being of soul and spirit. For this reason, every path of knowledge basically involves perceiving ourselves as an image of true human nature, of what is truly human.

If we enhance our capacity of love to such a degree that our own I appears to us, to begin with, as something separate and foreign to us, which we only begin to recognize; and if we raise ourselves to recognize the earthly world in the surrounding cosmos, then we are no longer caught up in an abstract but in a living process of perception and cognition.

And in this living process of perception, the world reveals itself to us through our own being, and our own human being is revealed in our experience of the outer world. Then we truly become beings who rediscover themselves in the whole universe for, as we come to know ourselves we come to know the world, and as we come to know the world, we come to know ourselves. In this interplay between world and human being is revealed what then connects us with the divine spirit, what inwardly warms us through and illumines us with the religious tenor of all true higher knowledge. If, ultimately, the serious endeavour of enquiry culminates in religious experience, then the lustre of religion is lent to our knowledge, and the transparency of perception is raised to the realm where faith becomes knowledge through the power of enquiry. And then, in our enquiring passage through the world, we find the world in the human being, the human being in the world.

Here, world and human being are united in an all-encompassing, cosmic, spiritual and divine nature, in which we discover ourselves and the world, and only thereby ascend to our true and authentic human dignity, which can then pass over into our religious and moral ethos, rendering us full human beings.

> In the ether world through living thinking: touch
> In the astral world through deep silence: speech
> In the spirit world: recognition

LECTURE 7

SOUL'S ETERNITY IN THE LIGHT
OF ANTHROPOSOPHY

PRAGUE, 27 APRIL 1923

To speak from the perspective of anthroposophy means to face great opposition today, very understandably. Anthroposophy seeks to speak about life and reality in a way that appears to many nowadays as very far-fetched. Especially if we speak of a theme such as the one we will consider this evening, that of the immortality of the soul, weighty objections are raised by voices in scientific or academic circles, stating that such things are beyond the scope of our knowledge and should therefore not be discussed. These things, they say, must be left to the domain of faith: to human feeling that is not founded on direct cognition, for they are hidden from us behind insuperable boundaries to our knowledge and enquiry.

But anthroposophy holds that, on the contrary, we can speak of such matters in life, and can do so entirely in accordance with rigorous methods and with a scientific discipline fully aware of its responsibilities. The only difference is that anthroposophy must summon powers of enquiry which, though they are certainly present in ordinary life and in ordinary science, exist there only germinally and need further development. We have to cultivate such development to delve into the spiritual realms of life from the standpoint of true enquiry rather than from a nebulous mysticism. The starting point for this must be what I would call a union of intellectual humility on the one hand, with, on the other, an unshakeable trust in the possibility of perfecting human powers of cognition. In seeking to unite these two soul impulses, anthroposophy can investigate the supersensible realm, as we will call it, with the same degree of assurance as science today enquires, so ably, into physical existence with the aid of the human senses.

What do I mean by 'intellectual humility' in this context? As we know, our soul life began in a child's outlook, which is very comparable to a state of dreaming, or even in some respects to that of sleep. And in the same way that we wake up each morning from ordinary sleep, so we have awoken from our child's state of soul to capacities of cognition and perception as these figure in science and in practical life. If we adopt the stance of intellectual humility we recognize that the powers we possessed in infancy were perfected by education and the influences of life and our surroundings as we grew up, to the point of our present perspective on knowledge and life as adults. If we feel this with full intensity, then it will not be without intellectual humility, as long as we do not stop short there. During life we have achieved a perspective which, if we apply the right methods current today, we assume must enable us to accept or reject all kinds of things and also determine what lies within the scope of our knowledge and what belongs only to the realm of faith or belief. By contrast anthroposophy asserts that we may also be able to extend the soul powers and faculties we have acquired as adults, in the same way that we developed our cognitive powers from the dreamy state of soul of the young child. Naturally all will depend here on whether we do actually succeed in extending these powers further, and it is of such further development that I wish to speak this evening in relation to the immortality of the soul.

Anthroposophy has full and intense trust in the fact that the powers of perception and cognition each person has so far developed can be increasingly perfected. In consequence, it dares to embark on this path of development, couching this in more or less the following terms: today, through the magnificent achievements of the sciences, we have developed a certain concept of knowledge. But is this concept of knowledge really drawn from the full depths of life? It is certainly justified for everything that is sought within particular fields or disciplines. But does it draw on the full depths of life? Does it address questions of human existence that relate, firstly, to our profoundest human longings, secondly to all that composes a sense of our human dignity, and thirdly to all that signifies and encapsulates the real meaning of life, our moral impulses?

When it is a matter of gaining insight into these most intimate needs and questions, especially concerning the life of the soul, we often resort to certain seemingly marginal or peripheral phenomena in life.

Before I address these questions in a more substantiated way, I want to offer an initial comparison by pointing to a dim and unlit realm of life which nevertheless poses many enigmas for us. We all know this realm well—it is that of dreaming, which we experience during sleep. I want to expressly state that I am not referring to dream and sleep here as a pointer to certain knowledge but only as a point of departure for things I wish to discuss today. Let us first imagine, then, this manifold and colourful world of images that dream conjures before us. We can be sure that these dream pictures arise from the same depths of human life from which our daytime thoughts otherwise arise. But during waking life we are aware that, when plunged in this extraordinarily interesting dream world of ours, we are concerned only with a reality that is relative in nature, and that we can only understand by regarding it from the perspective of, and by comparison to, waking life. Let us assume for a moment that we dreamed our whole lives through and never had anything in our awareness except these colourful, manifold dream images. Could life nevertheless still unfold as it does? Let us assume that certain natural or spiritual powers enabled us to undertake our daily work without a waking consciousness, or even—though some in my audience may consider this misguided—to undertake scientific work. Let us assume we could accomplish such activities in a state of somnambulism, while within us we were aware only of the dream world. In such a case the world around us would be entirely at odds with our sleeping, dreaming consciousness.

If we imagine this and consider it fully, we can recognize that this dream world is one we never really know when we ourselves inhabit it. If, as I described, we were asleep and dreaming throughout life as we went about our work, we would feel this dream world to be our reality. The fact that we can regard dream as having only a secondary reality is due to the fact that we keep waking up; that, by this sudden transition from sleeping to waking life we become conscious, to put it very roughly rather than with any scientific accuracy. In this transition we incorporate something intrinsic to ourselves, our will nature in particular, into our physical body. A close examination of this fact will show that everything mediated to us by the senses in waking life depends very much on our engagement in real life in the physical body while we are awake. By incorporating our will into the physical body, we arrive at the outlook that allows us to distinguish the secondary level of reality of dream from the primary reality that the sense world represents for us in our waking consciousness. Awake, we know that, through the will incorporated in the body, we are connected with an outer reality. I am speaking again of course not from any philosophical standpoint but merely describing what we ordinarily experience in life.

But now this question arises: is it possible that we could awaken a second time, out of this ordinary waking life in the daytime to a higher level of reality? Could we experience a second transition, by means of which we incorporate our life forces into a new element, just as we incorporate our will into the body when we awaken from dream to ordinary, everyday consciousness? Of course this is only a question. And answering it will depend entirely on whether we can embark upon a path that is, first of all, safe and assured, and secondly one that every human being can pursue by their own efforts. But if we succeeded in attaining this second awakening, then it would give us a perspective enabling us to discern the reality of our ordinary waking life from a higher standpoint, in the same way that we observe our dreams from a higher standpoint when we wake up each day.

To bring about a second awakening, anthroposophy first addresses powers of the soul that are already present in ordinary life but whose ordinary nature suggests that they are capable of being developed further. Now even philosophers acknowledge that our capacity of memory points in the direction of what I will call the more spiritual nature of the human soul; that in other words we cannot regard memory in the same way as those soul faculties that are directly bound up with impressions of the outer sense world. But let us avoid philosophical reflections for now and keep in mind the role our ordinary, everyday experience of memory plays in our life. Through memory we can call up images of experiences we may have had many years ago. Depending on our inherent capacities, these images may be more vivid or more shadowy, but they stand before us. When we give ourselves up to ordinary sense observation and perception, what we picture has to be present before us, whereas what memory offers us is not present, may have happened a long time ago. Through our picturing capacities we conjure from with ourselves something that once existed but no longer does, that can no longer exist in the present. By this means we become aware of our ability to draw forth from within us powers of perception that embody or represent something not presently there. So the question is this: is it possible to further develop soul faculties we have developed since childhood so that we enhance what underlies our powers of memory? Can we do this so that we now not only picture something that no longer exists, that did once exist at some point in our lifetime, but picture instead something that does not exist at all? At this point we would effect a transition into a higher reality, one from which ordinary life on earth appears like the world of dream by contrast to our waking consciousness.

Anthroposophy attempts to develop what underlies the capacity of memory, using this inner discipline to arrive at the second awakening I spoke of. In doing so it turns to the human powers of thinking. These are, after all, what conjure forth pictures of what we have once experienced. Anthroposophic enquiry proceeds here by undertaking something with thoughts that is actually not done in the modern age. Modern thinking—and from a certain point of view rightly so—is more concerned with attention to the outer world. But allowing external impressions to act upon us, then processing these impressions by enumeration, measuring, weighing, and using thinking to combine them, is a passive form of thinking, one considered all the sounder for knowledge the more passive it is, the more it surrenders itself to the information received from our outer senses and organs of perception. Anthroposophy turns to this thinking and seeks to develop it further, and by so doing to avoid all fantastical conceptions such as many philosophers entertain. For this purpose, easily surveyed thoughts, of no special significance, are placed at the centre of ordinary awareness, and one then concentrates the soul entirely on these thoughts. We withdraw soul life entirely from outward impressions and outer life, trying to strengthen this soul life increasingly by focusing it upon one, or a series, of easily surveyed thoughts. In this process something occurs that may take a longer or shorter time to appear, depending on each person's inner capacities and constitution. One person may take three months for it while another may need many years. If you repeat these exercises in a rhythmical sequence, after a while you begin to notice a change in your inner life, which I would like to compare with something in outward life: if you keep exercising a muscle, it grows stronger. In the same way, you feel your inner picturing and thinking capacity strengthening from this work of focusing upon an easily surveyed thought; and eventually you will feel how your whole thinking grows active, how real life, inner life in a true sense, enters and informs this thinking. Gradually you will feel the great difference that exists, a real difference and not just a figurative one, between dead, abstract thinking and the kind toward which we strive and through which we seek to cultivate inner life in the element of thinking.

As I said, one has to start from a thought that can be surveyed clearly. The soul exercises I will describe today involve every step that is taken being observed in full, conscious reflection, in the way that mathematicians trace the stages of their calculations, or geometers consciously derive one form from another, each form leading to another form, and each calculation leading to the next. This consciousness of acting responsibly as an enquirer and producing reliable findings is one that the anthroposophic investigator experiences with as much stringency and discipline as a mathematician. It is essential to maintain such consciousness.

Any self-suggestion, all subjective aspects, must therefore be excluded. They cannot be avoided as long as we reflect upon random thoughts which have many resonances with life and often have a suggestive quality. But if we assemble thoughts that perhaps have no outward importance for us—such as 'light-wisdom'—and concentrate our whole soul life upon them while remaining indifferent to their reality value, then our thinking capacity will strengthen. And by this means—though as I said it takes longer for some and less time for others—we come to know what it means to live in thinking. You see, gradually our higher aspect is released from the mundane aspect that, as we know, inhabits our physical body. Just as, inhabiting the physical body, we know that there is life in the movements of our legs, the motions of our hands, so we become aware through such an exercise that there is something real, alive, vital in the motions of my strengthened thought.

To put it very roughly we could say that through these phenomena of strength in thinking, by means of which we spiritually touch realities as we otherwise only physically touch with our fingers, we come to experience a higher human aspect. Gradually we find that we can detach the higher aspect in us, which we experience in such thinking, from our physical being. And thus we arrive at an experience of our supersensible being as it lives between birth and death in earthly life. By raising ourselves to observation in our inner thought capacity, we become able to overcome the spatial realm by this means; we overcome the present moment altogether and come to experience in time. The second, released aspect of our being we experience is something that we do not feel to exist within a spatial dimension, which is the dimension of the physical human being. We find that we experience this second aspect of ourselves as a being fluctuating in time; and what we discern here forms itself into a kind of tableau which, in a relatively short time, enables us to survey our life on earth from the earliest infancy to the point at which we now are in life.

There is a great difference between these two things: the life-tableau and my memories. You might say that we can compose our life on earth so far from our memories of it. Using my faculty of memory I can put together what I experienced, either more recently or longer ago. And if I make the effort to do so, and if I take time for this, I will then possess an overall memory picture of my earthly life thus far. And it might be that I am mistaken, that in surveying the rapidly unfolding panorama of my life, I have something that I could also have with the help of subconscious soul forces, which introduce into my mind something like a conscious memory picture. But gradually you notice the great difference between what we compose in the memory and an inner life-tableau of this kind, which in fact stands before us as a first supersensible knowledge, as self-knowledge first of all. You see, if we compose all our experiences into a memory picture, we always only see, really, what has affected us from without, what has acted upon us in life. We see people, natural occurrences, outward things that have interested us.

The life-tableau is very different in this respect. Here we are far less concerned with what has come towards us externally, but attend instead to what has acted from within us. If I became acquainted with someone in my life, this life-tableau will remind me far less of how he approached me but rather of the longings within me to find something special or particular in him. If this life-tableau shows me a natural phenomenon of some kind, its aspects of interest do not come so much to the fore as the inner impulses in me of sympathy or antipathy toward it. What appears before me in this life tableau is myself, and how I conducted myself in response to what I experienced. You could say, to use a rough and ready comparison, that this memory tableau I have described relates to an ordinary memory like the embossed surface of a signet ring relates to the imprint in sealing wax. It is the negative in relation to the positive seal that we can compose through our ordinary memory faculty.

Having in this way passed through the first stage of soul practice, we thus come to a true self-knowledge of our life so far, in which various nuances will mingle. In this memory tableau we see what helped us progress, as well as other things that hindered or hampered us, or pushed us backward. We place ourselves with our human dignity and value into this memory tableau, and, through the knowledge awoken in us through it, we acquire an idea of what we are only now, in relation to outward reality and sensory powers, entitled to call the 'ether' of the world. This world ether lives only in a temporal realm, and now in a sense gives us a portion of what I have now described as the first form of the higher human being loosened and released from the physical.

But with this first step alone we have not yet achieved much. If we wish to get further, we must continue these soul exercises. The next exercises involve us applying our strongly activated inner will to banish these thoughts and pictures from our consciousness again, having first used the will to establish them in our awareness and concentrate on them so as to strengthen our thinking and being. As I said, full, conscious reflection must hold sway, as practised by a mathematician. It has to be said, you see, that our whole life of soul is in a certain respect absorbed completely by the thoughts we place at the centre of our awareness, and especially, when thinking has become sufficiently alive, by our own inner experience conjured before us in the mighty images of the life-tableau. We are strongly swayed by what appears before our inner eye in this way as a picture intensified into vivid reality. A still greater power is needed, then, to banish such thoughts and pictures once more from our awareness than we would otherwise need to rid our mind of ordinary thoughts. We should try to acknowledge this honestly.

When our senses fall silent, when also what we have perceived through the senses falls silent, when the interplay of thoughts falls silent, and thoughts and feelings are in a sense banished from our awareness, then we fall asleep. If thoughts do not stir and stimulate us, we do not have the strength to maintain our waking state. But if we have the strength of soul that is needed for what I described, then we also possess the strength to eradicate again the thoughts and pictures we have gained which, as I described, enter us by virtue of an inwardly strengthened life; we have the strength to keep our whole mind free of thoughts and yet still to remain awake. Only to be awake but to think nothing is the second condition that must be sought: waking consciousness empty of content! This waking but empty mind can be inwardly perceived, but does not long remain so. Yet having managed to establish it, the second stage of spiritual discernment arrives. Then we are no longer aware as was described above of what lives in us ourselves, but the spiritual content of our environment penetrates this waking, empty consciousness. The second person in us, who was first released from the physical, corporeal person, as we became aware of ourselves over the course of our whole earthly life, will now not only be self-aware but, through this higher self-awareness, apprehends a spirit world around them.

Again, something arises before our soul that appears far-fetched and alien to modern people, but is nevertheless intrinsic to what I have called the second stage of spiritual knowledge, or Inspiration. An exact Inspiration occurs—and in general nothing I have here described should be mistaken for what is often called 'clairvoyance' of a nebulous, mystical kind. If we are to use this term at all, we ought to speak only of exact clairvoyance, cultivated by the development of soul forces in the same way as mathematical thinking, which, after all, contains no outward reality but only one formed inwardly, prior to its application to the sense world as in procedures of measuring, enumeration, weighing and so on.

What we have first conceived in inner, living thinking, modelled on pure mathematics, must be augmented by what I have described here. And through these spiritual labours we come to findings and insights in the same way that we come to insights through measuring, counting and weighing. What occurs is a state of soul that we do not know in the ordinary mind because we do not need it. I want to clarify this soul condition that occurs when we have achieved an empty waking awareness.

Let us imagine for a moment that we are in a big, modern city, with all its hubbub and noise. We can't find peace or tranquillity here—it distracts us and fills our awareness. But then we leave the city and the noise and hubbub slowly fade as we put more distance between ourselves and all its commotion. Let us now imagine that we leave the city far behind and enter the quietness of a wood. Here we reach a stillness and degree of quiet that we could call 'zero' compared with the city's hubbub: silence around us, quiet within us. But now something else can happen, although such things are not observed in the ordinary course of life. For this we must resort to a second metaphor. As you know, if someone has a certain amount of capital, they can slowly spend it, and their assets grow ever less. If they do not earn any more but go on spending, then they arrive at zero assets. And if they still continue to spend, then they incur debt, and thus they have less than nothing, less than zero. Mathematicians use negative numbers to represent this situation, minus sums. Now picture this: we have distanced ourselves from the noisy hubbub of the big city, but we continue to descend into stillness: quieter than quiet and more silent than the zero point of silence. This is the soul condition that gradually arises as we pass through the empty and yet wakeful mind. Gradually we feel with great clarity what I would call the profound silence of the human soul. This deep silence is not only quietness but more—or if you prefer, less—than quiet. It descends below the zero point of stillness. And if we really experience this deep silence of the soul, then the spiritual presences surrounding us emerge from it; and the full state of Inspiration is present.

By truly experiencing this silence of the soul, we become able to hear spiritually what dwells in the world of spirit. The ordinary sensory world then becomes a means for us to interpret what lives in this spiritual world. I want to speak very specifically of actual spiritual perception. From the soul's deep silence resounds something that strikes me thus: it stirs me, it approaches me with a certain vivacity. It can give me, say, something like the impression the colour yellow gives me if I am sensitive and receptive to colours. Then I have something in the sense world through which I can express my experience in the world of spirit. My perception is one I can describe by saying that it affects me as the colour yellow does, or like the tone C or C sharp in music, or like warmth or cold. In brief, my sensory experiences offer me a means for expressing in ordinary words what appears to me in the world of spirit. In this way the whole sensory world becomes like a language to express what I experience in the spiritual world. Those who seek too rapid progress do not understand this and therefore come only to a superficial judgement. Patient investigators encounter an experience that strikes them in the same way as the effect of a colour on our sensibility, and this is why they describe their spiritual experiences in terms of colours, tones and so on. Just as we should not confuse the word 'table' with an actual table, so we should not confuse the world of spirit itself, which emerges for us from this deep silence, with the manner in which it is described.

Attaining this perspective, we arrive at the point of inwardly extinguishing this whole panoramic life-tableau that we first conjured forth. We do so not only in respect of isolated thought pictures but for the whole of our earthly life, in its inward form. This means that in a sense we extinguish ourselves as human being on earth. But by virtue of the fact that we have extinguished our earthly self, which is bound up with our physical human body, and have therefore come to an experience of the soul's deep silence, we also now experience what we were as human spirit-soul before we descended from the world of spirit. And in the same way as our physical body was the vehicle for relating to our physical surroundings, this experience of our existence in the world of spirit-soul enables us to perceive how, in pre-birth life, we were surrounded by spirit-soul beings and were ourselves a spirit-soul being of the same kind. We enter that world of spirit from which we descended to life on earth, and apprehend it fully.

It is noticeable that in ordinary life people are only concerned with the soul's eternal existence in one direction, that of the immortality of the soul after death. But this has another aspect, which an older idiom had a word for, though we have lost it nowadays. The soul's eternal existence does not only stretch forward, as its immortality, but reaches back to 'unbornhood'. Together, unbornhood and immortality compose the full scope of the eternal soul. Rather than indulging metaphysical speculation, we can come to an *experience* of the eternal nature of the human soul through the soul's deep silence: what has always been eternal and existed spiritually before we descended to earthly existence, and what remains eternal as we live our life in a physical human body between birth and death.

But this eternal character of the soul is something we can approach only gradually, even in anthroposophic spiritual research. As the third stage of development I must speak of something that may elicit some irritation and even mockery from those in the audience who come furnished with customary scientific ideas. I can very well understand such a reaction, as indeed I can understand all opposition to anthroposophy. But something we already possess in ordinary life can be developed further into a higher power of perception, in the same way that our childhood powers have developed further into our adult capacities—and this is the power of love. Love is something quite different when bound up with the human body as it surrenders to passions expressed in love than it is when, in the way I have described, the physical ego, and even the earthly I we know between birth and death, has been cast off; when we depart from physical existence into the condition in which we encounter pure spirit. When, in this process, we develop powers of love, of complete surrender, the experience we have had of perceiving and experiencing what we were in the pre-birth condition is transformed into knowledge. We learn what it means to experience the reality of full consciousness outside the body. And in surrendering ourselves to this spiritual experience, our I is given back to us again in a new way. The I that lives in self-seeking egoity here in earthly life, which is then overcome by acquiring the self-knowledge that can be gained when this I is twice extinguished, thus develops love in the full meaning of the word at a soul-spiritual level, and then something approaches us that initially appears to us as foreign to ourselves, someone quite different from us. Striving for this experience, we will assuredly not have it. We should strive, rather, for the kind of love I have described. And then, because we are now able to depart from ourselves entirely, we meet what we are ourselves, but as someone quite different; and only then do we see the nature of this self in a past life that we lived before this present life. Only then do we see how the I was present in a former stage of existence on the earth if we are able to feel, as it were, a second human being within us through enhanced, intensified love. Then we gaze back to a certain point of evolutionary time when the I began to be an I, when our recurring lives on earth began. But of this I cannot speak now.[19] All I can say is that we can gaze back upon a sequence of lives on earth, composing the full scope of our human life, between which lie periods of life in pre-birth or post-mortem existence between death and a new birth.

This is one thing we experience of the soul's eternal and immortal nature by working our way through to spiritual perception. The other, gained by love intensified into a power of knowledge, is an experience of the higher human being outside of the physical body. And what we further recognize and perceive is that this being is without body; we perceive how the body becomes a corpse at death, how this body falls away as we pass on into life after death. In the same way that we gained vision of our pre-birth life, of our 'unbornhood', so now we look into immortality, into life after death. The moral impulses we acquired in our earthly life, which we bear with us through the gate of death, and the way in which we prepare a new earthly existence in communion with the world of spirit, so as to descend again to birth on earth, now rises vividly before the soul which has begun in intellectual humility but has also succeeded in harbouring a certain trust in inward human powers.

This leads knowledge into the realm of life that lies so close to human longings and needs. We look at those whom we have come to love, whom ties of blood or soul connections have brought close to us; we think of the threshold of death and ask: What will become of the bonds that blood has woven, and the bonds that soul and spirit have woven, when we have passed through death's portal? Once we have this vision I described, this perception, we know that the outward, corporeal sheath falls away at death from our eternal being, and that we rise into the spiritual world by laws and powers that we brought down to earth at birth and with which we lived our physical life on earth. We learn that what we have in common with others as ties of blood, as bonds of friendship, as bonds of love, falls away too like the human physical body itself; and yet we know, with true knowledge, that we encounter again the souls with whom we had these ties in the pure community of the world of spirit, because physical hindrances no longer exist there. In this way, and not out of mere curiosity, we gain true knowledge of human dignity and the destiny of souls.

And something else becomes true knowledge for us. In dream, the reality of the outward physical world vanishes for us because the will is not incorporated in the physical body, not engaged. In dream, we think the picture world we see is reality. In the same way, before we come to the soul's deep silence, and waken to the life of the spirit, we regard much as reality. But on awakening to conscious spiritual life, after we make that second transition, when we find that the physical reality we experience in waking life appears as mere dreaming, then much that was a reality for us in physical-bodily life appears as a dream too from a higher perspective. Just as dream reality is superseded by physically perceptible reality, so what we experience in physical life as moral or religious people is superseded by our second awakening. And then we realize what someone like Knebel meant,[20] Goethe's friend, who said this when he was an old man: 'Once you've grown old you find that significant events in your life now appear as if they had been prepared long before. It seems that you yourself arranged everything that affected or influenced you as man or youth. And all the paths you chose as a youth seem to point towards each significant experience.' This idea, in still more developed form, is proven true if we imbue it with the insights we gain in the ways I have described. It becomes evident that this is indeed what happens in life. We experience something incisive, we are led to someone with whom we will walk a shared path throughout our lives. And we look at what led us to this person. The steps that led us to them have arisen from a longing to experience precisely what we can experience with them. In this experience we come to our goal, which rightly accords with a longing of the soul, a probation of the soul. What lives in us, through which we conjure our own destiny as if out of ourselves, must be connected with the insight into past earthly lives when we were a person of such or such a moral stance. And so we can see that what we now do in life instinctively, seemingly by chance, is connected by destiny, to what we were and how we lived in a previous life.

This may seem a devastating thought. But as little as our freedom, dignity or full responsibility is affected by whether we have blond hair or black, blue eyes or brown, spindly or thick-set hands, so little is our freedom and responsibility impaired by knowing that the soul configures us and that we must craft our destiny in life as free human beings upon destined foundations. But life become comprehensible when we are imbued with this idea of destiny, which is entirely reconcilable with freedom: that life is not random but that we feel ourselves engaged both in the world of natural necessity and in the world of a higher spirituality, in which is rooted our higher being with the moral powers with which destiny invests us. Such an insight leads us from external life toward the soul's immortality.

But there's a further possible objection: Yes, perhaps certain spiritual investigators can discern these things, but what does it signify for ordinary people? Well, it signifies exactly as much as an artist's work signifies for someone who is not a painter. It would be sad if everyone had to be a painter in order to appreciate a work of art. One needs only a certain healthy sensibility to experience the quality of an artwork, and only healthy human common sense to experience what the spiritual investigator describes. But if we place the sadly numerous preconceptions in our own path, as hindrances, then instead of revealing a whole world to us the pictures conjured by the anthroposophic spiritual investigator will appear to us as random blobs of paint. Even for those whose lives run in a straightforward, ordinary fashion, this world is fully comprehensible from accounts given by the anthroposophic investigator. And by drawing on books such as *Knowledge of the Higher Worlds*, people can always also embark on the path of spiritual research without altering their outward lives, and check what the spiritual investigator is saying, to see whether he is simply talking out of fantasy or whether his findings are firmly established, like mathematical judgements, like the results of measuring, counting and weighing and so on.

This is what spiritual science wishes to introduce into modern human culture, inevitably seeing it as meeting the inmost needs of numerous people. You see, today many people, as a result of their education and the prevailing scientific paradigm, have an unconscious yearning to know something, to have a real experience of, matters very close to the human heart. I have spoken of only one of these today—namely the soul's immortality and all that relates to this.

But in consequence something is introduced into the world which is very like the Copernican worldview when it was introduced into a culture wedded to an older outlook. People will reject it as 'idiocy', but slowly it will come to seem self-evident. The Copernican worldview took a long time to be accepted. Anthroposophy can wait. Yet it has a cultural obligation to state that ordinary science—whose methods are held to be sacrosanct—has developed a psychology based on external investigations, using external means of counting, computation and analysis, that is devoid of soul. Science even considers this to be an ideal state of affairs. Anthroposophy does not dispute the justification for such methods, founded on the scientific outlook, but it seeks to add to it a fully developed understanding of the inmost nature of the human soul, of what is soul-spiritual in the whole world, the eternal life that exists in the whole cosmos, so that human beings can discern themselves as eternal too, immortal, and inwardly connected with the eternal in the cosmos. Thus anthroposophy seeks to offer insight into our life at present and in the coming future, and by so doing to meet a need of our time, adding to modern, soul-devoid psychology a living psychology elicited from the human soul itself: a psychology founded on a world outlook pervaded and imbued with soul, with spirit. It is this that will be needed increasingly.

LECTURE 8

HUMAN DEVELOPMENT AND EDUCATION IN THE LIGHT OF ANTHROPOSOPHY

PRAGUE, 30 APRIL 1923

THE words 'Know yourself' resound to us from ancient Greece as a deep, spiritual admonition. This phrase can be related more to a general understanding of the human being, of human nature, than to personal self-knowledge, and as such it can be described as the culmination of all human knowledge and striving. From the way in which this phrase resonates in us we can also feel that it is not meant as a merely academic or theoretical exhortation but is intended rather as a spiritual admonition in a moral and religious sense. And it seems that at the end of an era in human evolution of much breadth and scope, a kind of answer and response now stands before the human soul. This response was expressed almost 50 years ago, and in fact has already been forgotten, really; in a sense has faded from human awareness. Nevertheless the whole of our modern condition of soul, the great conflict we carry within us, is influenced by this latter-day answer, which was expressed by Du Bois-Reymond. He stated that 'We cannot know', or, as he put it, 'Ignoramus, ignorabimus'.[21] Though many today think that this profession of unknowing has been superseded, the very way we relate as human beings to the world in our enquiries or our faith, is founded on this underlying idea. We can say in fact that this is the faith, either expressed or remaining unexpressed, in the findings of scientific research in their significance for our overall world outlook and view of life.

Now anyone who has participated in cultural life for the past few decades, and has recognized how it has evolved over the previous three to four centuries, will not gainsay the view of knowledge propounded by science. In its investigations of the outward world of the senses, its achievements are magnificent. These great achievements include the use of instruments, of experimental methods for investigating the sensory world and its laws, and its success in confirming and substantiating its findings through manifold empirical, technical and practical applications without which our modern life would now be inconceivable. This science starts from the premise of gaining knowledge of the world that is as independent as possible of the wishes, preconceptions and feelings we can bring to bear on our perception of things and phenomena. Science has achieved its successes specifically by excluding anything personal in its investigations. But someone who honestly upholds these scientific principles, who can see how beneficial science has been for our knowledge of the natural world around us, will inevitably also say in relation to the application of these methods, that they have their limit: that science, as it has so far developed, cannot extend into regions in which the human soul and spirit hold sway; and this is not because of any deficiency but precisely because of science's virtues.

If we survey what has been achieved in various scientific fields, we will recognize that this science of course seeks to turn its attention back upon the human being once more. It seeks to apply its methods to human nature, and yet it cannot investigate more than our outward bodily, physical being. We see this most clearly when the scientific method is applied in the form of experimental psychology, proceeding, by the use of what is a truly magnificent research approach, to examine mental and emotional phenomena within the human constitution. But at the same time it becomes apparent that none of these investigations lead us to what we can call the eternal nature of the human being: that aspect of human nature whose true reality people have a deep longing to recognize, harbouring a hope that this reality is something that passes beyond the limits of earthly life, beyond birth and death. I definitely do not wish to object to empirical methods such as those used in experimental psychology. The mode of research that underpins what I say to you this evening acknowledges the full validity of these methods. But it is because we recognize their limits too that we must state unequivocally that they cannot extend to the real nature of soul and spirit. In fact, some clear-sighted investigators have seen the necessity themselves of recognizing that science cannot extend to the intrinsic nature of matter itself on the one hand, and to the nature of human consciousness on the other.[22] But if we cannot study how our consciousness—that is, the soul properties active within us—encompass matter, then we are compelled to relinquish that great call for us to 'know ourselves'. In this case the epoch of human cultural evolution since the ancient Greek era would end with us acknowledging that 'Know yourself', albeit a fine and powerful exhortation, is ultimately an illusion. We would have to say that this exhortation must remain unfulfilled. The more deeply we engage with the spirit of scientific research, the more we must, from an anthroposophic perspective, give credence to those who affirm the 'ignorabimus', who state that ultimately we cannot know; who speak of the limits to science beyond which we cannot reach. And yet we must still ask whether the human mind can accept such limits willingly, turning aside without more ado from wishes intrinsic to the human heart.

An answer to this question can be found in the anthroposophic research I will try to describe this evening. Its enquiries examine the justification of these inner demands and promptings. Many people today who recognize the great achievements of science nevertheless feel that it cannot approach the realm of soul and spirit. Many, therefore, who do not wish to accept limits to human knowledge, turn instead to one or another form of mysticism, to modes of mystic vision that try to fathom through inner contemplation eternal dimensions of the human being. Through such mystic contemplation many fine and beautiful insights have been drawn forth from the depths of the human soul, from the depths of the life in us that otherwise remains subconscious or unconscious. Through such mystic contemplation, many have come to believe that what they draw up in this way from the depths of the soul, what they find within themselves, is rooted directly in divine, spiritual existence. By drawing it forth, they think, they will bring the divine spirit within the purlieu of human knowledge, making it manifest, and thus penetrate to apprehension of the eternal nature of the human being, and to our connection with the divine.

Someone who today asks the great questions of the human soul's existence, therefore stands, if you like, between two precipices which seem to set insuperable limits to knowledge: science on the one hand, mysticism on the other. Whatever promises mysticism holds out, however magnificent and beautiful are the writings of many mystics, which they draw forth from the human soul, most such attempts cannot stand up to the scrutiny of enquiries founded on disciplined, scientific training. You see, someone accustomed to the scrupulous methods of science, and used to evaluating everything, including human phenomena, will soon find that what the mystic draws forth from his inner depths is in fact nothing more than thoughts and feelings he first acquired many years before in the ordinary world, which, aided perhaps by a lively imagination, have since grown in him into images. These thoughts and feelings, having first sunk into the depths of a person's being, have been altered by the human organism, which, to outward investigation, has a secret and significant connection with the soul. Someone with a deep knowledge of the psyche will see that what has been gained by mystic paths, which is thought to be eternal, is nothing other than a store of memories that have been altered and transformed by the human organism itself.

And so, if we try to engage with a deeper mode of experience, with the great questions of human existence, we must ultimately acknowledge that science does not enable us to get further, for its findings are enclosed in a field in which knowledge is concerned only with outward aspects of the human being, and cannot reach intrinsic human nature. This admission is necessary. Serious and honest science does not try to delve further. And on the other hand mysticism, in the form it usually takes, cannot reach beyond subjective human experience. In exploring the world, science does not extend from the world to the human being; and mysticism, in delving into inner experience, does not reach out of this experience into the world. If we weigh up these two outlooks in our feeling, we can once again ask this: Is it not after all possible to go beyond what mysticism offers us on the one hand, and what science offers us on the other?

Now, in the lecture I gave at the 'Urania' a few days ago,[23] I pointed out that anthroposophy, as spiritual research, examines the workings of human memory. It turns out that we can deepen and extend our memory faculty. I did not embark before on deep philosophical or epistemological issues, nor do I wish to do so today, but will stay with easily accessible matters. I could go into deeper philosophical aspects of these things, but what I have to say today can best be understood if we stay in more everyday territory.

What lives in our memory, and renders us full human beings because, at any moment of our lives, we can conjure up things we have experienced in the past, has entered the human soul through sense impressions of the outer world. We receive sense impressions, and we process them in our thoughts. Hidden from sight they undergo a transformation within us, and then surface again. Either they rise involuntarily again, or we make an effort to recall them. If we wish to understand what really lives in memory in the human soul, we can only say this: it is like something that is reflected back, however much time has elapsed, by the mirror of the soul that lies deep and permanent in our human being. The outer world is reflected in our soul in the form of memory, the ability to remember. As I said, I do not have time and scope tonight to study the nature of this soul-mirror in detail, but this picture should suffice for now. Our memory does not take us into the very ground of our soul's being, however. If you look in a mirror, you see in the mirror what stands before it. In the same way, in mystic thoughts and images furnished by memory, we have only a mirror image of the outer world. If we want to see what lies behind the mirror, then either we must take the mirror away or must break it into pieces. In a certain sense we do have to break through this mirror within us, this power of memory, in order to look deeper into our being. And we do break through it, that is, we go beyond the mystic visions this mirror shows us, and enter more deeply into our being, if we activate our thinking inwardly, the same thinking that we otherwise expend on outer experiments and suchlike: when we meditate, focusing on a particular content and thereby continually strengthen our inner powers.

In the Urania lecture, I described this, and discussed it also in my books: how, through activating thinking in a particular way, we can descend below the memory mirror and look deeper into our being. You might think that this would show us our physical organization. It is certainly true that, in the ordinary mind, we only reach inwardly as far as the memory mirror, and, in doing so, physical processes in our organism change and distort the outward picture that we perceive in this mirror. But if we make our thinking ever more active, living with it in as inward a way as we live with our blood and breathing, so that our whole being participates in this inwardly living thinking, then we penetrate deeper into our human nature; and as we do so what is revealed is not our physical being, but a soul-spiritual nature that can only become apparent through this strengthened and empowered thinking. What is revealed to us is an aspect of us that is entirely soul-spiritual, which remains unconscious to the ordinary mind, but whose intrinsic nature shows us that it existed before we embarked on our earthly life at birth, or in fact at conception.

That this can be the case can become clear by recognizing how the intrinsic nature of memory gives us not present but past experience. We have the same certainty about the character of our experience in what I described above, which leads us deeper than mystic contemplation. Then we gain a spiritual picture of everything involved in the first phase of human life as the essentially creative principle, when a wondrous sculpting or modelling activity is working upon the brain and on the rest of the human organization. But in such contemplation we trace the human soul-spirit being beyond birth and death: we gaze into a world of spirit where we existed as human soul-spirit beings with our intrinsic core before we descended into this earthly world and mantled ourselves in what our forefathers have given us, a physical human body.

It is certainly true that we come to this perception not only through the nebulous kind of gift that is nowadays termed 'clairvoyance'. While we can use the word clairvoyance for what I have been describing here, it must be qualified by saying 'exact clairvoyance'. You see, someone who embarks on a path of spiritual research like a rigorous scientist, activates their thinking in a way that not only draws forth memory pictures but also things that lie beneath the threshold of memory, which were creatively active within us before the faculty of memory had developed, and before we began our earthly existence.

This is one aspect addressed by anthroposophic research as it engages with the two principles I have described. It seeks to deepen spiritual apprehension through exact thinking and, in one direction reaches beyond birth and death to a knowledge of the eternal core of the human being. But in the same way that we must recognize, if we seek rigorous knowledge and wish to go further than the mystic often goes, how the mystic's contemplations lead him to beautiful illusions, how we must in a sense take mysticism further to achieve knowledge of our pre-birth nature, so on the other hand, again by deepening our rigorous, scientific investigations, we must try to take a further step in spiritual perception. And this is done in the following way.

Yes indeed, we come up against limits if we honestly apply scientific methods to the world. We encounter limits precisely when we apply these methods to natural processes: limits we can formulate in the term 'material consciousness' and suchlike. But we have a choice here. We can stop at these limits and state that human beings cannot get beyond them, must simply accept this; or we can begin to wrestle with our whole being to overcome them. In doing so we can consider that we perhaps constrain and confine our innate faculties and capacities within these limits in order to perfect science. It may therefore be, if we continue in our struggles, and engage all our human capacities, wrestling with these thoughts as they encounter constraints and limits, that we can get beyond them. I know the objection that could be made here. People will say that it is indeed a good thing that science understands how to exclude human imponderables from its methodologies, adhering rather to measuring, weighing, computation and so on, everything valued as research tools. It is good to exclude subjective human aspects and it would be dangerous to muddy the waters again by including them.

But if we do this in the way anthroposophic enquiry seeks to do, first fully adopting the stance of science, fully achieving this objective separation of research methods from human aspects, but then reintroducing a personal quest into this objectivity, then something else emerges. Then we respect the demands of science but at the same time introduce the human element into its objectivity. And then the following must be said: if we have imbued ourselves with scientific enquiry and knowledge as it has developed in recent centuries and especially since the nineteenth century, as it were inwardly engaging with the spirit of science, yet at the same time also involving our whole person specifically in the things that science describes, then a human endowment, otherwise not seen at all as a power of cognition, does become a power of cognition, a means of enquiry. This devotion to something that is gained objectively ultimately becomes an objective elaboration of human love. If, with full respect for the scientific mode of thinking, we have surveyed natural phenomena in the world as far as possible from the scientific perspective, and then divest ourselves of this mode of thinking; if we can summon a sufficiently heroic approach to enquiry to immerse ourselves in scientific findings with the kind of devotion we only otherwise invoke in the realm of love, especially human love, then love itself becomes perception and knowledge, and then the love that has undergone this metamorphosis to become a power of enquiry will penetrate beyond what science is able to offer us.

It is not the work of a single day but of long spans of time in a human life to delve beyond the limits of science to the realities and beings that lie behind it. But when we do this, the following emerges. At the moment we break through these limits erected by science and look behind them, remarkably something becomes transparent in the human being that has always previously been opaque. In ordinary life we wake up in the morning, spend our days in waking consciousness with the powers of our earthly feeling and soul, and fall asleep again in the evening. But what occurs with the soul-spirit within our physical body is hidden from human awareness. Our confused dreams from the night time play into our waking life but have no real value for enquiry. And so we can say that all of human life is composed of what we experience when awake, and what we pass through in sleep. And we fail to observe, on the whole, that in looking back we always stitch the morning on to the previous evening, leaving out of consideration what escapes awareness—the periods during which we have been asleep. But now we must ask whether the soul-spiritual gifts we receive in sleep might not be just as important as what our waking life gives us.

Certainly it is true that in respect of outer life the waking state is paramount, and the more civilization came to esteem outward life only, the more it has attended to the state of wakefulness. And yet— as philosophers have acknowledged—what occurs in a good third of our life on earth, which we sleep through, is no less important than is our waking existence. But this only becomes vividly apparent when, by wrestling with natural phenomena through the thoughts I described above, we break through the barriers that limit our apprehension of things. And then the empty experiential space that we otherwise sleep through, which, apart from dreaming, is as a void for us, fills with content that is otherwise veiled in the obscurity of sleep. In the same way that we can look back on the knowledge that we gain in waking life, as physical sense beings, in relation to the earth and its phenomena, so now a soul-spiritual knowledge arises from the condition in which we pass the periods of sleep. The darkness intervening between falling asleep and awakening again, this third of our lives, becomes transparent; and what we then per-ceive is our true I, the shape of thinking, feeling and will. We perceive what continually works in us, without our awareness, our being of spirit-soul; and we recognize its content as what separates from the rest of us when we pass through the gate of death, when we lay aside the physical body. As sleep becomes transparent to us we come to discern the true nature of human immortality. If we look through and beyond mysticism, when we go further than ordinary mysticism, we come to know our pre-birth being; we do so if we respect science yet also start to wrestle with its limits. We come to perceive the immortal nature we contain within us. These perceptions show us how the human being is constituted and develops, revealing how a pre-birth human spirit enters and penetrates our physical organization, increasingly as it were submerges itself in this human organism and how the latter gains ever greater sway; how what enters us at birth disappears ever more through the course of physical human existence as we continue to develop so that we increasingly become a physical, corporeal being. But to the same degree that this development proceeds, that our innate spirit and soul submerge themselves in the physical body, something increasingly emerges that, as we observe sleep, appears as our future being.

As we move toward the end of a human life, we see at the same time that the declining spiritual being of our pre-birth existence gives way to the growing spirit-soul being of our coming existence after death. At every point in earthly life we see a balance between what we have brought with us out of the eternal world into earth existence and what we have fashioned so far and will carry with us through the gate of death into a spiritual existence. We gain perception of immortality. The path I have been describing which goes beyond both mysticism and science to gain real knowledge of human nature, is not one that can be dismissed as 'clairvoyant'. It is a path that proceeds step by step with the same exactitude a mathematician will practise, deriving each step from the one that preceded it. This path I have outlined—and in doing so I refer also to the books I mentioned—is the path of anthroposophy, which leads to perception and knowledge of both the soul's 'unbornhood' and immortality with the same rigour a strict mathematician will use at every step of an equation, and which demonstrates that in our enquiry into human nature we do not need to stop short with science's external, objective view nor with mysticism's inner, subjective one but that, rather, we can combine knowledge of the world with knowledge of human existence. If, in this way, science on the one hand and mysticism on the other are extended and developed, it will in turn become possible in humanity's future culture of the spirit to fulfil the admonition 'Know yourself', a phrase which so powerfully resounds for us.

Knowledge of the kind I have described is however different from the knowledge that is bound up with the nervous system, which is largely head knowledge. If you will allow me to make a personal remark here, though an entirely objective one, I would say this: when seeking as a spiritual investigator to study this realm, which I characterize as realms we pass through before birth and after death, one is aware that the kind of thinking otherwise serviceable in life is not sufficient. You have to develop a strengthened thinking that draws upon your whole being. This does not make you into a medium, but your whole being must be involved in such thinking. This kind of thinking penetrates into your feelings and sensibility, and in fact requires you to apply your whole content of will to it. At the same time, thinking about spiritual content is of a kind that, unlike other thinking, does not allow you to incorporate it into memory in the ordinary way. Here again I will make a personal remark: You see, if the spiritual investigator gives a lecture such as the one I am giving now, he cannot prepare it in the way ordinarily done for academic lectures. In this case he would only be calling upon memory; and what arises through deepened perception cannot in fact be drawn from memory but must be re-experienced anew at every moment. While it can be brought down into the regions where we formulate words about our insights, nevertheless we have to exert our whole being to do this. It has been my profound experience that I can only embody in words what I succeed in discovering in the world of spirit—and by embodying these things in words, they also embed themselves in memory—if I draw a few lines or write something down so that not only the head but all the other organ systems are involved. You have to feel the need to seek help from somewhere or other besides the head, for you cannot manage by grasping things in that way only, they flicker and fluctuate. The important thing is that I give expression to a thought in lines and sketches, and fix it in that way. I have whole wagon-loads of old notebooks filled with these things,[24] which I never look at again. Nor are they intended for that, but enable me rather to clothe in words what I have drawn from the spirit with great exertion, so that I can commend it to memory. Having written these notes or drawn these sketches, you have participated in spiritual production with more than the thoughts of the head alone, with more of your organism, and then it becomes possible to hold fast to what otherwise continually evades you. The rest of the human organism does not at first participate, is more unconscious and asleep than processes of the head. And whenever we incorporate something into our will, we employ the organs that are in a sense asleep even in our waking life. We are only really awake in our thoughts, in our mental pictures, for in the ordinary mind the way in which what we think penetrates into our organism as a will impulse or decision, so as to become a movement of the hands or fingers, say, is submerged in complete darkness. Only the spiritual investigator can observe what occurs between the process in the brain and the movement we perform. And thus spiritual perceptions, which are not ordinary head knowledge, have to be committed to the whole human organization. By acquiring knowledge of the human being from one's whole being, insights into human nature thus arising—which make pre-birth and after death existence tangible—can be applied in a quite different way to practical life than would be possible without this true knowledge of human nature.

Now those who draw upon anthroposophic research have taken the bold step, brought about by destiny, you might say, of introducing practical forms of education and pedagogy. You see, if you imbue yourself with knowledge of the human being based on the kinds of investigation I have described here, you acquire a finer, spiritualized instinct for how human beings develop through the different ages and phases of life from birth through to death. Then we need only have the courage to study human development in the same way, albeit at a higher level, as we otherwise study any field of science by the strict scientific methods applied to it.

And this gives rise, for instance, to the following: we will continually reflect upon how the destiny of the human being's soul and spirit is realized within bodily existence. Rather than speculative methods, we apply observational methods to such questions. If we develop true observation of human nature, then we can discover— and I am speaking in an easily comprehensible way now—how, in the child's early years, from birth to second dentition, the most significant human capacities emerge and release themselves from indeterminate depths of a person's being. We can observe the developing dynamic whereby a person, as a being who walks upright, finds balance as they place themselves into the world; how speech, how thinking, emerge from the depths of the soul and come to bodily expression. And what we see developing in this way culminates in the change of teeth. The singular thing about this is that it is a unique occurrence in human life. What occurs at second dentition is never again repeated. If you like, a sum of forces comes to conclusion in the human organism. Only those unacquainted with the nature of this human organization can believe that second dentition occurs separately from anything else. This is not so; it is, rather, the outwardly perceptible expression of something that occurs within the whole human organism. A person undergoes a process that will not occur again later in life, for otherwise we would continue to change our teeth at regularly recurring intervals. Someone who properly observes human development is aware of the significant transformation of the human soul and spirit that occurs at this time. But people do not properly attend to this change. If I were to fully describe things it is important for teachers and educationalists to know in this respect, based on the knowledge of the human being I wish to present, it would far exceed the scope of this lecture. I will outline them only briefly.

Take memory, for instance. To a superficial view, we might say that memory appears in a certain way up to second dentition, and

then it changes a little. Yet memory before and after second dentition is different in kind. Our scientific outlook today is not able to
study the intimate dynamics at work within the human being. To a
keener faculty of observation it becomes clear that the wonderful
memory we possess before the change of teeth is nothing other than
the action of habits that express themselves from within outwards.
Up to second dentition, memory arises from the forces and power of
habit. We can compare it to any habitual movement, and say that at
this stage memory involves the drawing of one thought from another
in succession.

In short, what we call memory undergoes a metamorphosis as the
child passes through second dentition at around six or seven. This
metamorphosis is one from a more physical, bodily mode of
experience to a more soul-spiritual one. Starting from such an
observation we can gain further insights that are hugely characteristic of the rest of human development. For instance, if we observe a
subtler observational instinct, if we incorporate the findings of
spiritual research, we can discover that the child is an imitative being
up to the change of teeth. Of course, these are not dogmatic truths
but in the first phase of life the child can be thought of as an entire
sense organ. We can compare the child's life in infancy with a single
sense organ, with the inward organism of the eye. In the same way
that the eye absorbs the outer world, and, by application of the will,
through the instrument of the organism, inwardly develops the
picture of what is exerted as impression upon it, so likewise children
continually endeavour to reflect what is present in their surroundings, to reproduce it through the imitation which emerges from their
inner being. The child is entirely sense organ, actively sensing and
absorbing. And precisely because of this, children not only imitate
and inwardly experience, unconsciously and in very dreamy fashion,
outward movements, gestures, words and tones of voice, and the
thoughts contained in these, but also—and this is the singular
thing—they observe and imitate the moral significance of each
gesture made by their father and mother. The moral significance of,
say, a person's facial expression, engraves itself in the child's physical

organization. Children are inwardly organized, right into their blood vessels, by living in sympathy with what occurs around them. Only by considering what this means will we be able to distinguish between inherited characteristics and what is acquired in the early years from a child's environment through imitation. And then also we can see the wonderful interplay between the environment and the child, and this will shed a very different light on scientific ideas about heredity, which can become a mystical concept to the rigorous investigator. This will also show how each person brings with them a particular nature and disposition as soul-spiritual being embarking on earth existence at birth; brings with them an etheric body—which is a term unfamiliar in modern thinking. The young child is characteristically a bodily-religious being. Young children are indeed bodily surrendered and devoted to the physical, outer world and its moral content in the same way as we can be surrendered and devoted to something that appears to us divine. They possess a bodily-religious mood. And since this mood is religious only in a bodily way, they naturally do not demonstrate piety or suchlike, the inward religiosity that may develop later. Yet if we can trace human development, we can see something that is entirely involved in the bodily, physical realm in the early years, enters a person's impulses of feeling and will. And when the time comes for the child to go to school, we must recognize that an inner metamorphosis occurs in the child's inner life. What was before bodily, physical experience, what emerged during bodily, physical development, is to some degree left behind at second dentition, and appears now in a different, soul-spiritual form, as inward feeling and soul. From what was first contained in forces of growth, in the modelling forces acting as spirit-soul within the body, a portion is released and transforms itself into independent soul and spirit after the change of teeth. And what we term growth, acting in the body, gradually changes into qualities of spirit and soul. If we take note of this, if we are equipped with this insight, then as teachers and educators our whole stance toward the child will be on the right footing. We will know that into this physical, sensory, bodily being, who possesses a mood of religious devotion to the surrounding world, is now growing a being of spirit-soul that lived in pre-earthly existence. If we put ourselves in the shoes of teachers with this outlook who have the care of children at this stage, we can see that they will be aware of their responsibility. They will know they are present on behalf of worlds of spirit to guide souls in their care and to fathom and decipher these children's bodily expressions. They will have a sense of dedication to the beings before them, a desire to help children really fully unfold everything they have brought with them from worlds of spirit-soul. Teachers will look upon children with reverence for their profession, seeing with each month and year that passes that everything they have brought with them from the world of spirit-soul transforms into physical and bodily reality. They will reflect on the ways in which they can affect the child, and will be aware of what was present as physical, bodily characteristics before the transformation that occurs with the change of teeth. Then, in the second period of child development, from second dentition to puberty, this transforms into soul qualities; and only at puberty does it metamorphose again into qualities of spirit.

Our view of the human being is then one in which what was experienced in earliest infancy now comes to expression in the person's spiritual engagement with the world: the bodily-religious quality becomes a spiritual-religious one. And now we can discern how bodily qualities become soul-spiritual. We no longer speculate about bodily-physical characteristics, or about spirit and soul but we can see, rather, how at different stages in a person's development the spirit-soul either manifests directly or how, at an earlier stage, this eternal spirit-soul works within the body. We gain a view of the human being founded on the reciprocal interplay between body and soul, based on observations that can properly underpin an education worthy of the name.

The workings of destiny made it possible to apply the insights gained from such observations in practical ways in school education, thus for children at an age when it is still possible to exert an effect upon their destiny. The 'Waldorf School' was established in Stuttgart by Emil Molt,[25] as an independent elementary school, and the lower middle-school classes were later added as well. I was entrusted with directorship of the school, and was able to introduce methods drawn from the view and knowledge of the human being I have described. Here it is a matter initially of leaving to one side what are known as 'learning objectives', for we derive these instead from the realities of human development itself.

I have only briefly outlined these things, but they rely on observing the developing, changing child each day, using one's pedagogical instinct, which arises precisely through working with the child, in relationship to the child, and which enables us to discern what we need to do each week, each month as educators, what we need to impart to the child, reading this, as it were, from the child's own nature. For instance, we can discern that when children first start school they have a natural disinclination for learning to write and read as such. And this is understandable if we consider that these distinctive signs we call letters, by means of which we read and write, are actually quite foreign to us initially since they have arisen through a long process of cultural development. Written script originated from pictures and signs that represented what they signified, and to begin with more closely resembled what people directly perceived, bore a more direct connection with what they signified. The child who comes to school for the first time, and who is supposed to learn these now abstract signs, feels no affinity with them; they seem alien to him. This understanding only awakens with puberty. The child has a quite different mode of understanding around the age of 6 or 7 compared with the teenager at age 13, 14 or 15. The young child, still only just forming emotionally and mentally, is dependent on the pictorial element to which he relates naturally, as to sense perception. If we know this, then we can introduce the right educational principles for this age. But then we have to resort to things which we applied in our educational practice in the school in Stuttgart. We have to get the child to engage in a kind of painting-drawing or drawing-painting. We have to get children to work not only with their head and eyes but with their whole being; and it is wonderful to see the remarkable pictorial quality achieved by the children as they paint and draw in this way. If we guide this properly, then we can develop letters, writing and reading, from something with which children have a natural affinity. In fact we introduce reading *after* writing, since reading involves only the head whereas writing calls upon the whole of us.

This is one example of practical steps by means of which we try to achieve a human-scale education. By observing the intrinsically religious disposition in human beings, we can also find the means to introduce ethical and religious impulses into education. And in this way the following becomes apparent. It is fascinating to observe children around the age of 9, in the first third of the second seven-year phase, and to recognize what they are going through at that time. All this unfolds unconsciously in them. We see that once children have passed the stage of second dentition, they make a transition from imitation to accepting everything upon the teacher's authority, to learning by this means. But do not think, I beg you, that the speaker, who wrote a book 30 years ago entitled *The Philosophy of Freedom*, is any kind of authoritarian. And yet, if you read that book and discover the meaning of freedom embodied there, you will also be able to see how it accords with a law of human development that, from second dentition to puberty, the child is a being who imitates everything the teacher does. He orientates himself not only by the words a teacher speaks but, out of an inner lawfulness, wishes to take his lead from the teacher's whole bearing. Once the child has found his way in to this natural sense of the teacher's authority, we see how he undergoes a kind of crisis around the age of 9. Everything occurs in the realm of feeling and the child is not consciously aware of it. And yet the child looks to the teacher and seeks something particular. And if we were to put this into words, the child would say roughly: Hitherto the beautiful was beautiful because my teacher considered it to be so; hitherto the truth was true because my teacher thought it so. But henceforth the child asks: Who justifies this authority before the whole world, and where does this knowledge of what is true and beautiful originate? The child passes through a crisis. He knows nothing consciously of what I have expressed but it lives in his feeling. And as teachers and educators we must observe this moment, and ensure that where necessary we continually say the right thing to the child in response. How we conduct ourselves at this critical moment will determine whether the child, throughout his life, will have a self-confident delight in life or will be as if alienated from it and inwardly constrained.

Thus a method of education which encompasses the whole human being is one that obliges us to educate in a way that is beneficial for the whole of a person's life. If we cultivate this overall observation of life, we will see that the way we educate a young child only comes to maturity later on. I'd like to offer an example of this. No doubt you know people who, when they are getting on in years, or perhaps are very old, radiate a sense of peace and tranquillity. They may not say very much at all but their presence is a blessing to those around them. Such people can spread grace and blessing upon the world around them often simply through the tone of their words, the way in which they speak, which embodies a wonderful sense of moral goodness. If we enlarge our study of human life beyond short phases, instead making efforts to observe the whole of life, we will find that people of this kind, whose presence brings blessing, had the good fortune when they were children to look up with reverence either to other people or to something that they received. This reverence around the age of 9 develops into something later in life that issues from us as blessing or benevolence. To sum this up in a picture, you could say that hands cannot bless in later life if they have not learned to fold themselves in prayer when young. This is only a pictorial way of saying that true insight into human nature offers the child something that enables a feeling for morality, for goodness to grow and live in him; that enables also antipathy for what is bad to grow and live, as the human body itself grows. You can have the sense that if you present the young child with sharply delineated, fixed and defined forms of knowledge, then this is like laying chains upon his organism. We must give the child concepts, impulses that can grow like the organism, that can grow soul-spiritually, that bear spiritually within them the inner capacity to become ever richer. And then, later, the person can look back gladly to these experiences so that his childhood springs anew again in a now elderly human body. These are just a few pictures, some instances, to show how true understanding of human nature, achieved by the means I described at the very beginning of my lecture, can be applied to education and child development. The Stuttgart school offers a demonstration of what I have described here; it shows these things in living practice, although we also wish to remain modest in our appraisal of the outcomes.

Now someone might object that such an understanding of human nature can only be of interest to those who have developed the capacity to perceive the world of spirit. But this is not so. It is true that someone who pursues the path of knowledge described, for instance, in the book, *Knowledge of the Higher Worlds*, will be able to check for themselves the results of spiritual enquiry. And yet this is not necessary in order to judge the fruits of this research, just as it is not necessary to be a painter to judge the beauty of a painting. While it is true that only a spiritual enquirer can describe the world of spirit, anyone who retains their healthy sense of things can certainly recognize the truth or untruth of the findings of spiritual investigation. For this reason we should not dismiss those who propound and pursue such spiritual research as a misguided sect.

Anthroposophy certainly does not seek to be this. Rather, it advances and continues forms of scientific enquiry that have been developing for centuries up to their culmination in the nineteenth century, in a trajectory that still continues today. But science can only become a real knowledge of human nature by applying the methods and guidelines I have described, and then it will also form a sound basis for a human-scale education appropriate to human beings. You see, investigation of the outer world alone will not help us live better, since neither science nor mysticism can lead us to full insight into human nature. It is like breathing: there has to be an interplay between inbreath and outbreath, between knowledge of the world and knowledge of the human being. And only such all-round knowledge can form the basis for an education that traces the spirit-soul's transformation into the physical body, and sustain the cultural transformation that is needed. If you look at life today you can see that this culture of ours cannot be transformed by outward changes in a way necessary for a civilization now under threat. Social progress will be possible only through what comes to us from the spirit, only through human deeds, human actions sustained by the spirit.

Let me sum up: spirit perception gives us ideas which can fill our whole being, and lead to spirit-filled deeds, spirit-filled actions, and spirit-filled social community imbued with the power of love. And in the near future this is what we so greatly need; what we need above all else.

LECTURE 9

SUPERSENSIBLE PERCEPTION.
ANTHROPOSOPHY AS A
CONTEMPORARY NEED

VIENNA, 26 SEPTEMBER 1923

ANYONE who speaks of supersensible worlds nowadays lays themselves open to the very understandable objection that they are out of tune with the needs of the times; and that science can only engage seriously with the biggest existential questions by remaining aware of its limitations, retaining clear insight into the fact that it must restrict its enquiries to the earthly sense world, and would succumb to fantasy to some degree if it were to exceed these restraints. In fact, the school of spiritual science that I described at the last Vienna Congress of the anthroposophical movement,[26] and which I wish to speak of again today, not only does not feel itself to be in conflict with the scientific outlook and scientific conscience of our era but, on the contrary, seeks to work absolutely in the spirit of the most rigorous modern scientific enquiry. We can however speak in a variety of ways of demands that we now encounter as a result of the magnificent theoretical and practical developments over the past three to four centuries, especially the nineteenth. Today, therefore, I want to speak of supersensible perception in so far as it seeks to meet these contemporary needs; and then, in the following lecture, I will speak about supersensible knowledge of the human being as a need of the human heart, of our human soul and sensibility in the present era.

Right up to the present moment, scientific research has produced magnificent results in its enquiries into conditions and phenomena in the outer world. Yet we can also speak in another vein of the achievements granted to humanity in the course of such developments. You see, very particular capacities have developed in association with serious scientific observations of the laws and facts of the outer sense world. Observation and experiment have in fact shed a light also on human capacities and faculties themselves. But many who are immersed in the most worthwhile way in scientific enquiry tend to disregard this light shed upon human beings themselves in the course of these investigations. If we reflect for a moment on what this light illumines, we will find that human thinking, studying through microscope and telescope the laws of minute, detailed phenomena as well as grand and far vistas, has also gained enormously in its capacities of discernment, in its incisive power to connect things in the world in such a way that they disclose their secrets and reveal their underlying laws. And as this thinking has developed, we see how a challenge has come to inform it—one posed, at least, by the most serious and dedicated investigators: a need for this thinking to become as selfless as possible in observations of external nature, and in empirical trials in laboratories, clinical research and so on. In this regard humanity has gained a great power, increasingly succeeding in ensuring that inner human desires do not infiltrate this thinking, that it is not tinged with views and perhaps even fantasies about human nature; that these are not projected on to what scientists seek to discover about life and existence with microscope and telescope, and through their measurements and calculations.

The cultivation of this outlook has gradually led to a thinking that, we can say, is very intent on developing its passive role. Thinking as it has developed through empirical observation and experimentation, has become so abstract that it now no longer allows itself to invoke knowledge or truths from within.

This quality of thinking as it has gradually emerged is one which, it seems initially, must dismiss our own whole intrinsic human nature. You see, what we are ourselves must be actively brought forth, externalized, and this can never really be entirely devoid of the engagement of our will. And so—and rightly so in the field of outward enquiry—we have come to a point where we specifically dismiss the activity of thinking that enables us to become aware of our significance within the whole fabric of the cosmos. In our enquiries, therefore, we have in a sense excluded ourselves, have forbidden ourselves from exercising our own inner activity. And we will see in a moment that what it is right to exclude and prohibit in relation to outward research and enquiry, must now be especially cultivated when we seek to enquire into the spiritual and supersensible nature of our being.

And then there is also a second element, an aspect of our being that comes to the fore but which modern scientific enquiry excludes. Its exclusion is alien to us as human beings though this exclusion facilitates our enquiries into the cosmos. I am thinking of human soul response and feeling. In modern research this human feeling is not allowed to figure. We should remain cold and prosaic. And yet the question remains whether this very feeling might not contain powers that would aid us in knowing the world. On the one hand we can say that our inner human intentionality is at work in our feelings, our human subjectivity; that it is a fount of imagination. But on the other hand we must also acknowledge that this feeling aspect of our nature, as it appears in daily or academic life, cannot play any particular role in human knowledge. And yet, if we remember, as science itself teaches, that the human senses have changed over the course of human evolution, that they have evolved from relatively imperfect conditions to their present state, and that in former times they certainly did not convey the world to us in as objective a way as they do now, then we gain an intimation that there might be something in our subjective feeling life that could be drawn forth and developed, like the human senses themselves, leading us from an experience of our own human interiority to a higher grasp of the cosmos. Precisely when we consider how feeling is suppressed within modern science, we can ask whether a higher meaning might not reside in our feeling life, one capable of elaboration and development from it.

But when we turn to a third element in our human nature, we can discern in a wonderfully vivid way how we may be propelled onwards from the scientific view, however genuinely commendable it is, to something else. I refer here to the will aspect of soul life. Anyone rooted in scientific thinking will know how impossible it is, within these parameters, to regard world phenomena in any terms other than original or intrinsic necessity. We rigorously connect spatial phenomena with each other, and likewise phenomena that succeed one another in time. We connect cause and effect according to unbending and necessary laws. In the rigorous pursuit of science we know what power is exerted simply by the observation of scientific realities. We know how this idea of universal causal imperatives holds us in its thrall, and how this idea of causality rises in our thinking to meet all the phenomena we investigate.

But then there is human will, this human will which tells us, at every moment of our waking lives, that what we undertake by inner intention is not causally determined in the same way as all other natural phenomena. This is why someone who observes themselves with an open mind and natural feelings will scarcely do other than ascribe free will to themselves. But if we then adopt scientific thinking, we are compelled to deny this free will. And this is one of the conflicts we find ourselves in today. During the course of these two lectures, we will consider various such conflicts. If we feel them in their full intensity, if we inhabit them, as it were, with our feelings, then it is likely—since we must pay authentic heed both to science on the one hand and to our own experience and self-observation on the other—that they will shake us and disturb us, to such a degree that we may despair of ever finding a sound basis in life for discerning the truth.

We have to regard such conflicts from the proper human per-spective. We have to be able to see that science compels us to refuse to accept our own daily experience and perceptions. And therefore that there must be something somewhere that offers us access to the world other than that irrefutably given by science. Driven headlong into such conflicts by the natural order of things, it becomes an urgent need today for us to acknowledge that we can no longer speak of supersensible, spiritual realms as was still possible only a relatively short time ago. We need only look back to the first half of the nineteenth century to find that minds at that time who paid all serious heed to science nevertheless also still pointed to the supersensible dimension of human life; to the realm that reveals to us the divine and our own immortality. They still pointed then to what we might today call the 'night aspects' of human existence. People deserving of great attention and respect pointed to that wondrous yet highly problematic world we enter every night, the world of dreams. They pointed to mysterious connections between the chaotic world of dream images and reality. They showed that our interior organization, especially during illness, is in some respects mirrored in the fantastical pictures of dream, and that healthy human life impinges upon chaotic dream experiences in the form of symbolic images. They described how much that we cannot properly survey in our waking senses is shifted into semi-waking states, and they drew their conclusions from such observations. These things are close to subconscious states of human soul life that express themselves in similar ways, and which many people today are still intent on exploring and cultivating.

Everything of this kind that approaches us was in some respects sufficient for early humanity, but can no longer serve us. It cannot do so because the way in which we now observe the natural world outside and around us has changed. If we consider eras when, let's say, people possessed a mystically tinged astrology, we find that they looked upon the sense world in a way very different from the exactitude we nowadays expect of science. And because they were content with sense perceptions of a less clear-cut kind than we nowadays have, they were able to find in mystic realms, in certain semi-conscious states, something that could teach and inform them. This is no longer so for us today. Just as little as we are able to draw from the direct information science offers us anything other than *questions* about the true nature of the human being, so we cannot satisfy our supersensible needs, as an earlier humanity did, solely by recourse to science.

The supersensible mode of perception that I wish to describe here takes full cognizance of these contemporary needs. It studies how human thinking, feeling and will have developed in consequence of science; and on the other hand it asks whether it is possible, with the thinking, feeling and will that modern people have mastered, to delve further and with the same clarity as science requires, into the supersensible realm. This cannot be done by logical deductions and suchlike, for here science rightly acknowledges its own limits. But something else can be done: we can develop our inner capacities of soul further from the point at which they now stand in ordinary scientific enquiry. And by so doing, we can apply the exactitude we are accustomed to in outer research in the lab or clinic to the development of our own spiritual capacities. I want to examine this first of all in relation to the power of thinking itself.

The thinking that has become ever more aware of its passive role in outward enquiry, and need not deny this, can inwardly intensify its activity. It will then no longer be exact in the way scientists otherwise are when they measure, weigh etc., but it will be exact in relation to its own procedures, in the same way that the research scientist, or a mathematician, is accustomed to tracing each step taken in full consciousness. And this is done by replacing old modes of muddled meditation, old modes of muddled self-contemplation with the supersensible mode of perception I am describing, so that this thinking instead develops in a very precise and exact way.

There is no scope here to do more than outline this precision of thinking, which I have described in full in my books, *Occult Science, an Outline* and *Knowledge of the Higher Worlds*. What we must achieve here—and this will take varying amounts of time depending on each person's inherent capacities—is to exchange the role of passivity in which thinking otherwise, rightly, surrenders itself to the outer world, for another mode in which we place our whole inner activity of soul into this thinking. We do so, for instance, by a short daily practice during which we withdraw from our engagement with the outer world to place before the soul some thought or other—its content is irrelevant—and direct all our inner powers of soul to this one thought in inner concentration. As a result something occurs that has an effect on the development of soul capacities comparable to efforts, say, to develop the muscles of the arm by exercise. Through use and exercise the muscles gain strength, and in the same way soul capacities become inwardly stronger and more active by this focus upon a particular thought. We have to do this in a very precise way, surveying each step we take in thinking with the same attention a mathematician will apply to his calculations when solving a problem in geometry or arithmetic. There are various ways to do this. It may sound banal, but you can find the content for your concentration in any old second-hand book you come across, as long as you are quite sure you have never read it before. It does not matter how true the thought is or not but whether you can survey the thought in its entirety. This is not possible if you simply draw a thought from your memory since this may have many vague connections and ramifications, much that lies in your subconscious or unconscious, so that you cannot be precise when you focus upon it. So it should be something that is entirely new to you, whose content lies before you in direct and immediate fashion, without any emotional experience connected with it or prior importance for you. What counts is the concentration of soul faculties involved, and their consequent strengthening. It is likewise good to avoid any prejudice against seeking the advice of someone who has made some progress in this field, and asking them to give you a suitable content. Then also the content will be new to you and you can survey it. Many people fear that this might render them dependent or reliant on the person who provides them with such content. But this is not so. In truth, you will be less dependent in this case than if you were to draw the thought content from your own memories and experiences, since this will be connected with all kinds of subconscious elements. Someone who has experience of scholarship or science will do well to use scientific findings as the content of their concentration. In fact these can turn out to be the most useful material of all.

If you do this for a longer period, maybe years—patience and perseverance are required, for some it may take only a few weeks or months to achieve the desired result, others may need years—then you can come to the point of inwardly elaborating your thinking in just as exact a way as physicists or chemists apply methods of weighing and measuring to eavesdrop on nature's secrets. Things learned in scientific procedure can be applied to the further development of our own thinking. And at some point or other, a significant experience arises: we no longer feel that we think in pictures which depict outer occurrences and realities, a thinking which basically is all the more faithful to these realities the less inner strength of its own that it possesses, the more it is mere image. No, we add to such thinking an inner experience of thinking itself, of inwardly invigorated thinking. This is an important experience. You can say that in consequence thinking begins to resemble the experience we have when we activate the power of our muscles, when we take hold of something or push against something. It is an experience of reality such as we otherwise have of our breathing or our muscle activity. This inner activity enters into our thinking and inhabits it. And since we have exactly investigated every step upon this path, we experience ourselves with full clarity and awareness in this strengthened, active thinking. It may be objected that science should be based on empiricism and logic, but this does not contradict what I am describing. You see, what we experience in this way possesses full inner clarity but is at the same time like putting out feelers: not like a snail extending a feeler in the physical world, but putting out feelers in a world of spirit—which, if we have got to this stage, is as yet only there for our feeling apprehension initially. And yet we are right to intimate it. You have the sense that your thinking has changed into a spiritual probing, and if this increasingly develops you will be right to expect that this thinking encounters real spiritual essence just as your finger, if you extend it, will encounter a physical reality.

If we live for a period within this inwardly strengthened thinking, it becomes possible for us to gain full self-knowledge, since this form of concentration enables us to apprehend the soul realm as an experienced reality.

We can now progress further with this practice by excluding, erasing these thought contents we have been focusing on and which have brought us to the point of having a real, soul-probing thinking; we empty our mind, as it were, of these soul contents which we ourselves introduced into our awareness. It is relatively easy to empty your mind in ordinary life, for you need only fall asleep. But having accustomed yourself to concentrate fully on a particular thought content, a keen power and energy is needed, especially with this invigorated thinking, this realized thinking, to dismiss such a thought content once again. And yet, in the same way as you first developed the strength to concentrate, so now you can also succeed, in turn, in getting rid of this thought content from your mind. Having achieved this, something arises before the soul which previously we could possess only in the form of an episodic memory picture: in a new way our whole inner life rises before the mind's eye, the life we have passed through on earth since birth or since the time to which we can remember back to in childhood, when we became conscious of ourselves in earthly existence. Usually our life is present to us only in memory pictures, pictures of what we have experienced. But what we now experience through this invigorated thinking is not of the same kind. It rises before us as in a mighty panorama so that what we experienced ten years ago, say, is not present as a pale memory only but it seems that we return in spirit to that time. Let's say you undertake this exercise when you're 50, and it leads to what I am describing, then time opens to draw you back to what, perhaps, you experienced when you were 35. You walk back through time. It is not just a pale memory of what you did 15 years ago but you feel yourselves inhabiting a past experience in a vivid, living way. You stride back through time, and space loses its meaning. Time presents you with a mighty memory tableau, an exact picture of life, a phenomenon which even scientists acknowledge sometimes occurs—

for instance when someone suffers a terrible shock, is drowning and close to death, say, and sees his whole life in images before him for a while, later recalling this with a certain horrified rapture. What occurs in such instances, induced by natural causes, is then really summoned before the soul through practices I have described, revealing a mighty panorama of the whole of one's earthly life, in chronological sequence. Only now do we really perceive ourselves in true self-observation.

It is easy to distinguish this picture of our inner experience from a mere memory picture. The memory image shows us how other people, natural occurrences or artworks have impinged on us from without. In a memory picture of this kind the way in which the outer world approaches us figures more largely. But in the supersensible memory tableau that rises before us, we see more of what issued from ourselves. For instance, if, at a certain moment of our lives, we embarked on a friendship with someone we love, we see in memory how this person approached us, how they spoke to us, what we owe them and so on. But in the memory tableau we perceive how we ourselves yearned for this person and how, ultimately, every step we took must inevitably have led to the other whom we had discerned as deeply suited to us.

What has formed through the development of our soul forces comes to meet us in this life-tableau with exact clarity. Many people do not care for such clarity and exactness since it shows them many things that they would prefer to see in a light other than that of truth. But this is something we must endure: to gaze upon our own inward nature with a fully open mind, even if this inner life must appear to our penetrating enquiry as worthy of reproach. I have called this stage of perception that of imaginative perception or Imagination.

But we can progress further from this stage. In what we perceive through this memory tableau, we have the powers that actually formed and shaped us as a human being. As we stand before this panorama, we recognize that forces develop within us that shape the substances of our physical body. In childhood especially, forces developed which, after birth, and up to around the age of seven, modelled and shaped what was at first an unformed mass of brain and nerve substance. We cease to ascribe what inwardly shapes us to forces that pertain only to material substances. Gazing upon this memory tableau, we cease to think this, seeing how the contents of this tableau—which are themselves powers—stream into all our forces of nutrition and respiration, and into our blood circulation. Without such powers, no blood would pulse in us, no breathing could occur. We come to discern, in fact, that our inner being is spirit-soul in nature.

What thus dawns on us can best be characterized with a comparison. Imagine that you are walking upon ground that has been softened by rain, and everywhere you go you see tracks or footprints made by passing people or wheels. If we imagine that an inhabitant of the moon came to earth and saw the state of the ground, but had not yet caught sight of any people, he might ascribe these tracks to various forces at work in the earth itself, forces that had somehow churned up the earth and left these traces. Such a moon being could perhaps analyse the earth in a search for the forces that had produced these markings. Of course we know in reality that they are made by passing people or vehicles.

Someone who understands the matters I have been describing will not therefore look with any less reverence and wonder upon the brain's convolutions. But just as we know that footprints are made by people and do not originate from the forces of the earth itself, so we can also realize that these furrows in the brain do not derive from forces inherent in the brain's material substance. Instead, the human being's spirit-soul, that we can apprehend as I described, works upon the brain to create these furrows. That is the key thing: to recognize our own spirit-soul being, to direct our eye of soul to the spirit-soul and its manifestation in outward life.

And now we can go further. Having first focused on a particular thought content, strengthening our own inner activity, then emptying the mind so that instead of the pictures we ourselves form, the whole content of our life rises before us, we can now also remove this memory tableau from our consciousness again—just as previously we erased a single thought and emptied the mind of it. And now we can learn to apply an intense strength to extinguish from the mind once more what we first perceived in enhanced self-observation as our spirit-soul being. In doing so we are extinguishing nothing less than our own inner soul life. Extinguishing something outward by our own volition was what we first learned to do in concentration; then we learned to direct our inner gaze to our own spirit-soul, the latter filling the whole memory tableau. If we now succeed in extinguishing this tableau itself, then what I call a truly 'empty' mind is achieved. Previously we lived in the memory tableau or in what we ourselves placed before the soul. Now something else arises. We have suppressed what lived within ourselves, and now we expose or offer our empty consciousness to the world. This is extraordinarily important for the soul's experience. And basically I can only metaphorically describe what happens to the soul in consequence, when we invoke a strong inner power to extinguish our own soul life. We need remember only how someone whose outer sense impressions gradually fall silent, in whom sight, hearing, perhaps also definite touch, cease, sinks into a state that closely resembles that of sleep. But when we extinguish our own soul content, though our mind is emptied we do not sleep. We enter a state I would call that of 'mere wakefulness', wakefulness with an empty mind. We can perhaps picture this empty mind or consciousness as follows. Imagine a big, modern city with all its noise and hubbub. You can leave it behind, so that everything grows ever quieter around you. Then perhaps you reach a wood and walk deeper into it. A complete contrast to the noise of the city: complete silence and stillness surrounds you.

But now I must resort to a banal metaphor to describe what I need to. The question is this: can this peace and stillness progress still further? Let's call this peace and stillness 'zero' in relation to the outer world. Now assume you have a certain amount of capital but you spend it until there is nothing left, can you go on spending? It may not be desirable, but many do it nevertheless: they go into debt. Then they have less than nothing, and can have less and less than nothing. Quietness and stillness can be thought of in the same sort of terms: quiet, equal to the zero point of wakefulness in the world, can be driven further into a kind of negative state, giving rise to an excess of stillness and peace. This is the experience of someone who extinguishes their own soul content: they enter into a state of negative inner quiet that lies below the zero point. Intensified, enhanced stillness of soul arises although we remain fully awake.

But this cannot be achieved unless it is accompanied by something else. It can only be achieved if a certain state connected with pictorial thoughts, also of our own self, is felt to pass over into another condition. Someone who initially feels and perceives the supersensible within their own self, is in a certain state of wellbeing, of complacency even and inner happiness, as has been remarked by various religions when they point to the supersensible realm and at the same time describe the happiness granted to those who inwardly experience it. Until we reach the point of extinguishing our own inner life, we can experience a certain wellbeing, an enhanced state of happiness. But the moment we enter this intensified stillness of the soul, inner wellbeing is replaced by inner pain, inner renunciation, of a kind we have not previously known, at the fact that we are now far removed from things we were previously very much connected with: far removed not only from a sense of inhabiting our own body but also far removed from our own experiences since birth. This is a renunciation that intensifies into a huge pain of the soul. Many shy away from persevering further at this stage. They do not find the courage to make the transition from a certain low-level clairvoyance, extinguishing the content of their own soul, to enter a state of mind where this inner stillness exists that I described. But if we push on further here with full consciousness, then Imagination starts to be replaced by what I called Inspiration in the books I have referred to here—though I beg you not to take offence at the terminology: the experience of a real world of spirit. Having first extinguished the sense world and having created an empty mind in unspeakable soul pain, the outer world of spirit comes to meet you. In Inspiration you become aware that a world of spirit surrounds you in the same way the sense world surrounds your outward senses.

And the first thing we perceive in this world of spirit is our own pre-earthly existence. In the same way that ordinary memory shows us past experiences in life, so now a cosmic memory is granted us: we look back into pre-earthly experiences, seeing our own nature as soul-spirit being in a world of pure spirit before we descended to birth for this current life. We see how our spiritual being took a hand in shaping our own body. Thus we look back into the spiritual, eternal aspect of human nature, to what becomes apparent to us as pre-earthly existence. And now we know that this existence is not dependent on the birth and death of the physical body, for it is what existed prior to birth, prior to conception, and what first made our material, genetic physical body into the human being we are. Only now do we gain a true concept also of physical heredity, by understanding that supersensible forces play into it, and that we acquire these from the purely spiritual world. We now feel connected to this world as we feel connected in earthly life with the physical world. And now we become aware that, despite the great advances humanity has made in its evolution, many things have also been lost that were once intrinsic to older, instinctive outlooks that are no longer any use to us today. In early times, people had perception of this pre-earthly life, as well as of human immortality, which we will come on to speak of shortly. You see, in olden times people saw and understood eternity in a twofold way. Nowadays we speak—and our language itself has only this term—of the soul's immortality. But once upon a time people spoke of 'unbornhood'—and some older languages still retain this idea—as the other aspect of the human soul's immortality. Times have changed. People nowadays are interested in what happens to the human soul after death since it still lies ahead of them. They are much less interested in any existence prior to birth or conception, since it is 'past', and they do after all now exist. But true insight into human immortality can only develop if we consider both aspects of eternity, both immortality and unbornhood.

But to connect with the latter, and to do so through exact clairvoyance, a third element is needed. Really we feel ourselves more wholly human if our sense of things is not entirely absorbed by earthly life. You see, the pre-earthly life we can learn to perceive enters us in pictorial form, and augments our sense of our humanity, making us fully human. This imbues our feeling with something like an inner light, and we know that we have now developed our sensibility, our feeling, into a sense organ for the spirit. But we must go beyond this and must also be able to make the will element into an organ of perception for the spirit. To this end, something must imbue human perception that is otherwise, rightly, not regarded as a power of perception by those who would be seen as serious researchers. We only become aware that it is, in fact, a power of perception, when we enter supersensible realms. I mean the power of love. We need only begin to develop this power, a power of love higher than the love that nature endows us with, the latter of course very significant for natural and human life. As I must describe them, the first steps in developing higher love in human life may seem paradoxical to you.

If, fully conscious of each step you take on this path, you try to feel the world differently from how you usually feel it, then you arrive at this higher love. Let us assume that you undertake to review each day in the evening, before you go to sleep, starting with the last thing that happened in the evening, and picturing it as precisely as possible; then in the same way you work backwards to the next-last occurrence, then the one before that and so on, back to the morning, surveying your whole day. This is a process that requires far more inner energy than simple picturing a single occurrence more or less vividly. This 'reversal' of thinking is the important thing here. Usually we regard what happens in advancing chronological order, one thing after another as they happened. But by the exercise I'm describing here, we turn all life on its head: we think and feel what has happened in the opposite order from how it happened. We can practise this with the events of each day, as I suggested, and will need only a few minutes to do so. But there is another way to do it also. Try to picture the progress of a play in reverse, for instance, starting with the fifth Act, then working back through the fourth, the third and so on to the beginning. Or imagine a melody in which the sequence of notes is reversed. By inwardly experiencing such things, you will find how your inner apprehension frees itself from the natural outward course of events, so that you become ever more independent of it. But despite increasingly individualizing ourselves by this means, developing ever greater autonomy, we also learn to give ourselves in full consciousness to the other, to outward life. Only now do we become aware that the more we practise this and develop fully conscious surrender to another being, the greater does our selflessness and selfless love grow. In this way we gain a sense of how this 'not living in ourselves' but instead 'living in another being', this passage from our own being into the other, grows ever stronger. And then the faculties of Imagination and Inspiration we have first developed can be joined by true, intuitive immersion in something other than us: we arrive at the power of Intuition, no longer only experiencing ourselves now, but, while retaining our full individualization, learning nevertheless to experience the other in all selflessness.

Here love becomes something that gradually enables us to look still further back into the pre-earthly life of the spirit. Just as we look back on the past events of this present life so, by intensifying love in this way, we learn to look back upon former lives on earth, discerning human life to be a sequence of successive lives on earth. In the next lecture I will touch on the fact that these successive lives began at a certain point, and will one day end. And human life in its entirety is composed of this succession of lives, between each of which lie lives of purely spiritual existence between death and a new birth. Death too, you see, is something we learn to see in its true significance through this enhanced, uplifted love, which becomes a power of perception and knowledge. Having advanced through Imagination and Inspiration to the point where these enhanced inner powers become capable of spiritual love, we come to the following experience in direct, exact clairvoyance: we experience ourselves spiritually without our body, outside our body. It really does become possible for the soul to experience emerging from the body in, if I can say this, a tangible way. Having experienced this spiritual realm outside the body through 'clairvoyant' knowledge, we know what it means to lay aside our body at death, to pass through the gate of death into new, spiritual life. Thus, at the third stage of development, that of exact clairvoyance, we come to understand the meaning of death and thus also the significance of human immortality.

The mode of supersensible perception I am concerned with here aims to introduce into human cognitive faculties something that proceeds step by step and very exactly. Scientists apply exactitude to outer experimentation, outer observation. They try to discover the secrets of phenomena through precise processes of comparative weighing, measuring and calculation. Spiritual scientists apply the same kind of exactitude to the development of their own soul faculties. What they make of themselves so that a world of spirit, and with it the eternal essence of the human being, of human immortality, appears before the soul, is done with exactitude, as Goethe says. At every step that a spiritual investigator takes so that the spiritual world will at last lie spread before his eye of soul, he feels as much conscientious responsibility for his discoveries as otherwise only mathematicians feel for the steps involved in their calculations. The latter have to be able to survey and note each calculation in full clarity, and similarly the spiritual investigator must survey with great exactitude what he makes of his own powers of perception. And then he will know that he has shaped an 'inner eye' from the soul with the same inward necessity as nature configures a physical eye from the body. He knows that he is as entitled to speak of worlds of spirit as of physical sense worlds perceived by the physical eye. Thus spiritual research of this kind will meet the demands implicit in modern science. This science is a magnificent achievement that spiritual science does not in the least oppose, but which it seeks only to develop further.

I very well know that anyone nowadays who wants to promote a cause, for whatever motive, enhances its importance by claiming that it is a 'contemporary need'. That was not my aim, nor will it be in the

next lecture. On the contrary, I will try to show that these contemporary needs already exist, and that the science of the spirit seeks
at every step to meet them. Spiritual investigators, of the kind I
mean, do not wish to be dilettantes in their view of nature but rather
seek to advance science in a rigorous and conscientious way. They
employ a truly exact clairvoyance to describe a world of spirit. But at
the same time they are clear that interpreting life by dissecting the
corpse from which it has fled, or turning a telescope toward the
depths of space, develops human faculties that accord only with the
microscope or telescope. These faculties also have an inner life that
such instruments constrain and deny. When we dissect the human
corpse we can perceive this truth: that nature did not directly create
the person who lived in it, but rather this body was fashioned by the
human soul that has now departed from it. We conclude the existence of the human soul from its physical outcome that lies before us.
It would be lunacy to assert that the forms and powers embodied in
the human being did not originate in something that preceded this
person's current existence. All that we hold back or retain as we
investigate dead nature with the powers whose inner activity is
rightly suppressed, can become the potential to further develop these
human soul forces. Just as the seed lies invisibly below the earth after
it has been planted, yet grows forth into a plant, so we plant a seed in
the soul, specifically if we are conscientious natural scientists. The
seed of imaginative, inspired and intuitive perception rests within us
if we are serious investigators. We need only develop it. And then we
can know that just as modern science meets contemporary needs, so
also does supersensible enquiry. It can be said that all who speak in
the spirit of natural science also speak in the spirit of supersensible
research, except that they do not know this. Today it is an unconscious yearning deep within many people—as we will see in the next
lecture—to unfold supersensible enquiry from this seed within.

I'd like to remind those who, on a supposed scientific footing,
oppose this spiritual enquiry, of a well-known saying that Goethe
puts into the mouth of his Faust: 'Folk never feel the devil's presence,
even if he has them by the throat.'[27] If we recognize that any scientist

who investigates the natural world conscientiously is already unconsciously uttering the 'spirit', then we can reverse this saying as follows: There are many who do not wish to acknowledge the spirit when its speaks to them, although they continually give expression to it in their utterances!

The seed of supersensible vision is today already far more widespread than people think, but it must be developed. The need for it to be developed is truly apparent in the grave events of our time. Next time I will go into more detail, as I said. But I'd like to end by referring to various stark signs of catastrophe that threaten all humanity, from which it can dawn on us that we face grave tasks and challenges, and that surmounting them will be a huge challenge to people of the near future. These grave outward aspects with which the world regards us today, the world of humankind especially, point to the need for inner gravity in response. And it is of this inner gravity that I wished to speak today, in directing our human sensibility to spiritual powers intrinsic to us, the powers that essentially comprise our nature. You see, while people today need to exert the most vigorous outward powers to meet the grave events that face us across the globe, they will also need great inner courage. We can, though, only find these powers and this courage by consciously encompassing our inmost being, not just theoretically but with practical knowledge, feeling and will. And this in turn can be achieved if we recognize the source from which our being in reality originates: the wellspring of the spirit. Increasingly—and not only theoretically but practically—we should learn to perceive and experience the human being as spirit, and spirit as the only source of our true fulfilment. Our highest powers and our greatest courage can come to us only from the spirit, in other words: from the realm of the supersensible.

LECTURE 10

ANTHROPOSOPHY AND THE ETHICAL AND RELIGIOUS LIFE

VIENNA, 29 SEPTEMBER 1923

IN the lecture last Wednesday I spoke of how supersensible knowledge can emerge through further development of our ordinary human faculties of soul, by methods that science too can acknowledge. I tried to show that systematic development of these soul faculties does indeed lead to a power of vision by which we can perceive a supersensible world in the same way that we perceive the sense world around us by means of physical senses. Through this higher power of perception we do more than acknowledge in the abstract that a spiritual world exists as well as a sense world. No, we delve into an actual experience, a real experience of spirit beings that form an environment within which we live when we raise ourselves to the level of spirit—an environment just like the plants and animals that surround us in the physical world.

This kind of supersensible knowledge is entirely different in character from what we normally regard as knowledge both in ordinary life and in the pursuit of science. In the latter case we appropriate ideas, such as those constituted by natural laws. Yet possessing such ideas does not enable us really to inform the soul with them so that they become an immediate power comparable, as spiritual capacity, to the strength of human muscles that is activated whenever we do something physically. Thoughts remain for us something shadowy, and we know from our own first-hand experience that by and large they do not exert much effect upon the human heart, compared to our deepest heartfelt concerns.

As I think I showed in my first lecture, the capacity of perception I have been describing, that actually enables us to penetrate the world of spirit, allows us to become aware of our own supersensible being as it was before we descended to earthly existence. And in consequence, what we acquire as knowledge of our own self in the world of spirit does not leave the heart, the deepest needs of our soul, untouched in the way that abstract insights do. Certainly, if we have pursued a life of enquiry and research, we will not underestimate the inner drama that can lie for us in a quest for knowledge and understanding. But the knowledge gained in scholarship and science is nevertheless confined to pictures of the outward world. Indeed, if we have undergone a scientific training, we will be proud, above all, of the fact that these pictures objectively reflect the outer world and no more; that they do not excite our inner life, do not pulse within it in the way that blood pulses through our veins. But the supersensible knowledge I have been describing is something that affects us in a way quite different from the knowledge we are accustomed to. And in order to clarify what I mean, I'd like to use a kind of metaphor, though it is more than that in fact, and does fully encapsulate the reality I am speaking of.

Let's consider the two states of consciousness within which we usually dwell. We could also say three states, but for our purposes now we will consider sleep and dream as one. During sleep we are cut off entirely from the outer world; in dream we inhabit only an inner world that can assume grotesque and chaotic forms. We may be in a room with many others, but our dream world will be ours alone, and we do not share it with them. If we study this dream world we can see how what we regard as our inner being is connected with it. Our bodily nature is already remarkably reflected in dream, in fantastical images. A certain pathological or over-active state in one of our organs can appear in a particular

dream image; or else such images will conjure symbolically, sometimes in very dramatic form, some outer noise or suchlike in our
vicinity. Thus dream creates pictures of what is happening within
us and outside us. And this is all connected in turn with our whole
life on earth. Dream draws into its dramatic pictures experiences
originating even in our life's most distant past. And the more we
study its workings, the more we can recognize that our inmost
human nature is, albeit in an instinctive and unconscious way,
connected with dream's unfolding activity. If we observe these
things carefully, we can discover that, at the moment of awakening, say, we can gain a deeper perspective on ordinary life than is
usually the case: what we experience in dream, in sleep, in encap-
sulated seclusion, in a way we do not normally share with other
people, is a soul-spiritual quality that descends into the body, as it
were, into the will and thus also into the will-pervaded thought
forces and sensory forces, and, in waking life, comes into relationship with the outer world via the body. Waking up means a transition into a quite different mode of consciousness than we have in
dream. We engage with outer occurrences by virtue of the fact
that our soul participates in the occurrences of our own organism,
which in turn are connected to outward occurrences. Naturally,
proof that my account of these processes is objective cannot be
furnished by abstract computational means, nor empirically. But
proof is apparent to those who can observe phenomena in this
domain, and in particular observe how something like a 'waking
dream' underlies ordinary, everyday, prosaic soul-life: a subconscious imagining, a life in pictures. It is true to say that just as
we can dive below the surface of water to the ocean floor or a
riverbed, so we can also delve down from our rational mind to
deeper regions of the soul. Here we penetrate to something which,
while having a less precise correlation with the outer world, more
intimately concerns us than rational thought. Here also we
encounter everything that can prompt this rational life to discover
its independent, inventive power, that instigates it to pass on into
artistic creativity and even—as I will be explaining—moves this

rational mind when the human heart turns from ordinary observation of and reflection on the world to a religious worship, to reverence for the spirituality in the world.

When we wake up ordinarily, through our soul's engagement with our bodily organs we enter into a connection with the outer world that enables our waking mind to judge the nature of our dreams, their rightness or wrongness, their truth or untruth. Dreamlife itself cannot do this. It would be sorely misguided to think one could find a 'higher reality' in the chaotic, albeit also dramatic images of dream, than waking experience can discern as its meaning.

We remain at the same level of waking experience when we engage with mundane knowledge through our rational preoccupations, through ordinary science. But through the contemplation, meditation and, as I will put it, the strengthening of the soul that I spoke about last time, we practise something at a higher level, consciously, that we unconsciously practise through our bodily organization when we wake up. Rising to this form of supersensible knowledge is a 'higher awakening'. And just as we can see a particular dream in the light of waking experience, drawing on memory and other soul faculties to relate this dream, say, to a bodily disturbance or an outward occurrence while we were asleep, and thus embed it in the context of reality, so, through the supersensible perception I have described, we can contextualize our sensory experiences, as we ascertain them through observation and experiment, by reference to a higher world, a world of spirit. By means of the exercises I have described we relate them to this higher world just as, on awakening in the ordinary way, we engage through our organism in the corporeal world. This marks the dawning of a new world of experience, really an awakening to a new world, an awakening at a higher level. This is, really, the nature of supersensible experience. And such an awakening requires the one who awakens henceforth to evaluate the whole sensory, physical world from the standpoint of this new mode of experience, just as we evaluate dream from the perspective of waking life. What I do here in my life on earth, what I gain through my physical understanding, I now learn to relate to processes I passed through as a soul-spirit being in a purely spiritual world before I descended to the earthly world, just as I relate what I dream to my waking experience. I learn to relate everything in physical nature to a world of spirit—though not in a 'generalized' way, not to some fantastical spirit world, but to the detailed, tangible, densely populated reality of a world of spirit. Through the powers of enquiry that I described—those of Imagination, Inspiration and Intuition—this world of spirit becomes discernible around us.

And just as, in ordinary life, we feel we live in a quite different realm when awake than in sleep, so our whole state of soul changes when we awaken to this higher reality. Thus an account, as I have given here, of supersensible perception, is not merely concerned with conveying pictures of the supersensible world but represents our passage from one state of consciousness to another, from one state of soul to another. But this also means that the soul contents with which we are concerned in ordinary life become very different too. Just as we become a different person, when we wake up, from who we were during sleep, so, through this supersensible perception we likewise become different in a sense. The thoughts and ideas we possessed in our ordinary mind now change. This is not just a change of concepts and ideas, an increase in understanding, but a radical shift in life and it affects our deepest human concepts. We become different in the very depths of our thinking, at the very root of our soul existence, by virtue of the fact that—albeit only for brief moments—we can enter into the realm that is perceived supersensibly.

Let me cite two thoughts which play the greatest conceivable role in ordinary life, where they possess their full and deep validity. But at the moment we ascend into the supersensible world, they acquire a quite different form. These are the two terms that underpin our view of the world: true and false, right and wrong. Truly supersensible perception has no interest whatsoever in shaking or unsettling the sound foundations of ordinary life. No, but this supersensible perception does add something to ordinary life, complements it, without taking anything from it. Those who become untrue to ordinary life through an impractical mysticism, are incapable of developing authentic supersensible knowledge. Authentic supersensible perception and knowledge is not born of fantasists or dreamers but rather of those who can engage their full humanity in practical realities of earthly existence. Thus I will not unsettle the foundations of ordinary life by tearing up the roots of what we think of as true and false, right and wrong. On the contrary, truthfulness and authenticity are strengthened and consolidated in our feeling sensibility through the metamorphosis these terms undergo in the light of higher perception.

On really entering this higher supersensible world, one no longer speaks in such abstract ways as to say: this is true, that is false, this is right, that is wrong. Instead the idea of what is true and right transforms into one we also know in ordinary life, albeit in a more instinctive way there. This concept of ordinary life transforms into a spiritual apprehension. 'True and right' changes into the idea of 'sound or healthy', while 'false' and 'wrong' translates into the idea of 'unhealthy'. In ordinary life, when we reflect on something, or feel something, or intend something, we say, 'this is right, that is wrong'. But when we live in the realm of supersensible perception, instead of these terms 'right and wrong' we gain the sense that the one is healthy, the other sick. You will say that healthy and sick are vague terms. But this is only so in ordinary life and the ordinary mind. This vagueness ends when higher knowledge is sought in the exact way I described in my first lecture. Thus exactitude also enters in to what we experience within this realm of higher knowledge. There, 'healthy' and 'sick' are terms we use for what we experience in communion with the beings of the supersensible world, whom we behold through such perception.

Just consider how intimate to us this can make whatever becomes the focus of supersensible perception: it affects us as closely as the body's health and sickness. Of one thing I experience in the supersensible realm I will say: I live my way into it, it raises, enhances my life, exalts it; in a certain way I become more 'real' in consequence, it is healthy. Of another thing I will say that it deadens, even destroys my own life, and I perceive therefore that it is sick or unsound. And in the same way that, using the terms 'right' and 'wrong', we find our place in the ordinary world, integrating ourselves into ethical life and the life of society, so we integrate ourselves into the supersensible world through 'healthy' and 'sick'. But this means we are rooted in this supersensible world with our whole being in a far more real way than we are embedded in the sense world. In the sense world we separate ourselves from things by these terms, right or wrong. I'd put it like this: 'right' invokes a less intense sense of wellbeing, and 'wrong'—especially to some—invokes a less intense sense of pain. But in the supersensible world it is not possible at all for experiences to be kept at arm's length in this way. There our whole being, our whole reality is involved in the way we experience this supersensible world. And because of this all dispute ceases there: Are things realities? Are they mere phenomena? Do they simply show us how our own sense organs respond to a stimulus? And so on—matters I do not wish to embark on here since there would be insufficient time. This kind of discussion of things within physical reality really has no meaning in the spiritual, supersensible world, for its reality or unreality is tested by observing that one thing has a healthy effect upon me and another an injurious effect, if we take that word in its full weight and seriousness. The moment we ascend to the supersensible world we notice that what was otherwise knowledge devoid of potency becomes an inward power of the human soul itself. We pervade the soul with this supersensible knowledge in the same way that our body is suffused with blood. In such knowledge, therefore, we also come to know the whole relationship to the human body of soul and spirit, learning thereby to perceive how the human being's spirit-soul descends from a supersensible pre-birth existence and connects with the inherited body. To comprehend this we must first so fully acquaint ourselves with the spirit-soul that we can experience its reality first hand, inwardly, in the same way as health and sickness.

Thus supersensible knowledge is not really mere understanding but, however reluctant we may be to use this phrase since it easily sounds sentimental, an 'ensoulment' of ourselves. It is soul itself, soul content that enters us when we penetrate to this supersensible knowledge. We do not after all become aware of our eternal existence, our immortality, through philosophical analysis and discourse. We become aware of it, rather, in direct experience just as we perceive outward things in direct sense experience.

But an objection may be raised to what I have said here: Yes, someone who has faculties of supersensible perception can speak in such a way, but what about those who do not yet possess these faculties? Well, the finest form of human community is when people nurture each other's soul development. This establishes human community on a wonderful foundation. And so we can say this: not all people will become botanists or astronomers, but nevertheless the major findings, at least, of astronomy or botany will be of importance for everyone, and will become common knowledge through people's sound and rational acceptance of them. Similarly, the healthy human soul can directly absorb and understand what is presented by a spiritual investigator capable of enquiring into the supersensible world. After all, we are born for truth not untruth! And what a spiritual investigator communicates will always be clothed in words and formulations that depart from what we are accustomed to receiving as images of the physical sense world. When the spiritual investigator presents perceptions and findings, this can act upon other people's whole being, upon their ordinary, sound common sense, awakening it in a way that can really lead it toward that higher awakening of which I spoke yesterday. And so I keep saying that, while I have tried in books such as *Occult Science, an Outline* and *Knowledge of the Higher Worlds* to show how, through systematic practice, we can achieve what I have called 'vision of the world of spirit', so that everyone can, to a certain degree, become a spiritual investigator, nevertheless this is not essential. You see, our sound human faculties can receive what the spiritual investigator communicates: it can resonate in the human soul, if this soul is open and receptive enough, and such knowledge will figure to those receptive to it as something long known. That is the distinctive thing about this spiritual enquiry, about supersensible knowledge as I have described it: that it does not convey anything that is not already subconsciously present in every person. And so each and every person can feel this: Yes, I knew that, it lives in me; and if I had not allowed myself to be dulled or numbed by preconceptions originating in orthodoxies and science, one or another experience I have had in the past would have enabled me to comprehend aspects of the larger context that spiritual science can present.

By virtue of the fact, for instance, that ideas of true and false transform into those of healthy and sick, inner soul experience grows ever keener. At a higher level we engage more keenly and intensively with reality than we do simply by waking up in the morning and engaging with physical reality. By this means, feelings and soul experiences are aroused that are just as exact in perception as they can be in relation to outward things. But what supersensible perception can give us concerns our whole being, by contrast to sensory knowledge which really only addresses the head. Allow me to illustrate this holistic nature of supersensible perception with a personal instance—although the personal in this realm also has an objective validity since what is objectively perceived in this way has an intense connection to one's person.

To illustrate how supersensible perception can be more than mere head knowledge but encompasses our being in an infinitely more vivid and lively way, I'd like to say this: those accustomed—as every authentic spiritual investigator must also be—to ordinary knowledge and perception, will know how the head participates in this ordinary cognition. Specifically if we have spent our life in ordinary activities of research and enquiry, when we then ascend to supersensible perception we are compelled to exert all our powers to hold fast to this supersensible knowledge that approaches us. We can observe that the exertion needed to pin down an idea about the natural world, a law of nature, the outcome of an experiment or a clinical observation, is as nothing compared to the inner effort needed to hold fast to the perception of a supersensible being. And I always found it necessary to use more than my head, as it were, to fix these supersensible perceptions: to support the effort the head can make through other organs, for instance the hand. If you record in drawing something that appears to you supersensibly, just in a few strokes, or write it down in characteristic, aphoristic phrases or even single words, then the effort applied in such activity is more than one that merely draws on the nervous system, as is typical for ordinary enquiry. Instead such exertion draws deep upon your organism to support these perceptions. And this means that your supersensible perceptions will not be merely fleeting, that they do not fade like dreams but that they can be retained. This is how I always have to work, and during my life have acquired wagon-loads of notebooks in the process,[28] which I never look at again. Activity is necessary for this retention, allowing you to keep in mind the things that are revealed. It is not that you consult your notes or drawings again afterwards to read off what you discovered. This writing or drawing is of course nothing like mediumistic automatic writing. It is as conscious as that involved in any scientific enquiry or similar, and it serves only to hold fast with your whole being the supersensible perceptions that come towards you. In turn, therefore, this also affects your whole being, encompasses your whole being, does not remain as impressions received by the head alone. The impressions are ones that affect your whole heart and soul. And what we otherwise experience in earthly life, joys with all their inner vivacity, pain of a greater or smaller kind, all the experiences we have through the outward sense world, through our interactions with other people, the ups and downs of life, this again appears at a higher, soul-spiritual level when we ascend to regions of the supersensible where we cannot speak any longer of true and false but rather of health and sickness.

And when you have gone through everything I described last time, especially also the great feeling of pain at a certain stage on the path toward the supersensible, then you penetrate to a level at which, as you approach supersensible experiences, you pass through an inner drama in which these perceptions can cause joy and pleasure otherwise only possible in physical life, or where they elicit the deepest pain: where you have renewed your soul life at a higher level, with all the inner coloration and intimate inwardness of soul life and sensibility that we possess through having grown to be one with our bodily organization in daily life. And it is here that higher knowledge, supersensible knowledge, meets what plays into ordinary life as moral existence, this human morality with everything connected to it, with religious feeling, with an awareness of freedom. The moment we rise to direct experience of the life of spirit, with its healing or injurious qualities, in a sense we come to the root of human morality, the root of our whole moral existence. We only meet this root of morality by coming to perceive how physical sense life, along with what flows out of us, is really a kind of 'dream' in relation to a higher life, just as dream is dream in relation to ordinary life. And the conscience we feel rising up in us from inchoate depths of our human nature, and which governs our actions in ordinary life, which governs our beneficial or harmful effect on those around us—this conscience which I would say shines up out of obscure profundities of our being, and prompts us to act in moral or immoral ways—now grows clear and bright and is contextualized within a reality just as dream is contextualized within reality when we awaken. We come to discern conscience as something that exists in shadowy form within us, as a bright reflection of the meaning and import of the world of spirit— the supersensible world to which we belong as human beings in the very core of our nature. And now, when we contemplate the moral world order and try to discover the reality underlying it, we understand that we must pass on from what sensory knowledge gives us to supersensible knowledge.

This is what I attempted to describe 30 years ago in terms of a solely ethical problem, as a moral conundrum, in my book, *The Philosophy of Freedom*. Without considering supersensible knowledge in that book, but purely by tracing and exploring human moral impulses, I was trying to determine how morality invariably springs not from the thinking that focuses on outward things, outward occurrences or bodily processes, but from an inward life of thinking that encompasses soul and will: a thinking soul life that is self-founded and originates in the realm of spirit. At the time, in *The Philosophy of Freedom*, I was compelled to search for a life of soul that is also independent of human corporeality, which appears, by comparison with the robust reality of the outer world of the senses, to possess only shadowy reality, but which is intrinsically rooted in the spiritual foundations of the world. The way in which ethical impulses proceed from a thinking that is cleansed of outer sense qualities, yet is very much alive within us, is what gives us our ethical character. And if, through supersensible perception, we now learn to perceive the conscience rooted in us as, basically, a reflection within us of the real world of spirit which plays actively through the sense realm, then we come to discern human morality as something that—without our knowledge, even if we only hear it as a faint inner voice in us—binds us forever to the world of spirit that can become manifest to us through supersensible perception. This is not to say that this supersensible perception is therefore of no significance for ethical life since we do of course have this voice of conscience in us, and can act on it practically in life in each situation we find ourselves in. You need only consider that old spiritual traditions, supersensible insights from ancient times that have survived, have today faded and live on only as faint echoes, and you will see how greatly we need new stimulus for our humanity. Here many people succumb to a grave error. It is clear, as a result of scientific thinking, which nowadays many still regard as the only valid form of knowledge—this science with its 'ignorabimus',[29] its doctrine of the proper limits to knowledge—that many have relinquished the pursuit of knowledge. They believe that moral impulses, religious intentions cannot be gained by means of this pursuit. Instead it is thought that ethical and religious impulses, the way we lead our lives, must be derived not from insights and understanding but from predispositions of human nature intrinsic in us. It has now come to the point where people dispute that knowledge can offer any stimulus or motivation that will enrich our moral and religious life through assimilation of our own spiritual nature—for that is indeed what we assimilate in supersensible perception. It has come to the point where people doubt the value of this! But on the other hand it will become apparent—as long as you are not one of those 'pragmatists' who in fact only pursue routine orthodoxies, but instead a truly practical person—that if we engage with the *whole* world consisting of body, soul and spirit, we will require more than pale traditions to sustain us in each and every situation in life. In actual life these traditions can no longer provide a full, ethical or religious foundation from which to draw inspiration.

Let me give you a specific instance of what I mean. There is a great deal that is unsatisfactory in education today, and this begs the question of how children should be educated. With Emil Molt's pioneering project in Stuttgart,[30] the founding of the 'Waldorf School', we asked this question of the world of spirit in order to meet the challenge of education. I will just briefly set out the intentions that necessarily underpinned this.

Above all we had to ask how we can educate children to be self-possessed people, people who encompass their whole being and can also manifest their whole nature in an ethical and religious stance toward life. Real understanding of the human being, of body, soul and spirit, was necessary for this. But this insight into human nature cannot be derived from generally prevailing orthodoxies today, let alone lead directly to practical measures in education that can allow us to tackle the most diverse tasks that face us. I'd like to briefly illustrate why the external science of which we are so proud today, which concerns itself with the material realm in empirical research and analysis, is unable, in fact, to penetrate the secrets of matter. I will keep this brief, but you can read about it in much more depth in my books, especially in *Riddles of the Soul*, with all the necessary proofs furnished there. If we attend to the findings of modern science we gain from it, for instance, the idea that the human heart is a kind of pump that drives blood through our organs. But the science of the spirit as I have been describing it leads us to a view of the human being composed of more than the physical body alone. It identifies a being of spirit-soul within us and shows how this spirit-soul penetrates our bodily nature. Thus blood is not driven through the body by the action of this heart-pump but directly by the spirit-soul itself. It engages in blood circulation as the energy that makes our blood pulse through our organism. In this view, the heart is something like a sense organ. With my eyes I consciously perceive the world around me, and bring it to consciousness in my thoughts, thus make it my own; and in the same way I unconsciously perceive, through this inner sense organ of the heart, the blood's pulsation which I elaborate unconsciously by my soul-spiritual forces. The heart is not a pump; it is the inner sense organ by means of which we perceive what our spirit-soul inwardly elaborates in our blood, in the same way that we perceive the outer world through our outward senses. The moment we pass from rational anatomizing of the human organism to a view of the whole human being, the true nature of the heart becomes apparent, its true significance. It is an inward sense organ. In the heart become apparent the effects of human blood circulation with its living impulses. The heart does not instigate this pulsation. And this is an example of, I would say, the tragedy of materialistic science: that it cannot actually penetrate the secrets of material life. We can only do so if we observe the spirit in its true work, in its creative engagement with matter.

If on the one hand therefore we perceive the creative spirit at work within matter, then on the other, through supersensible perception, we can also become aware not just of the mind or spirit with its abstract thoughts but of the true spirit in its living being. And only then can we have a real knowledge of the human being, such as we need if we are to develop in growing children something that can live in them for the rest of their lives with strength and in full accord with life and reality. Through this keen enlivening of our understanding of human nature, the way the teacher can see the child will be quite different from the view afforded by only outward observation. From the very first moment of life, the developing child is basically the most wonderful earthly phenomenon. It is wonderful to behold something emerging in the child from an initially enigmatic and undefined interiority that makes the face ever more characteristic and defined, that turns the initially unfocused countenance into a physiognomy full of utterance; to see how the movements of the child's limbs, to begin with still ungoverned, become ever more governed and directed. We bear a great responsibility, too, for supporting and cultivating these developments.

We can stand before the developing human being and, with all the inner devotion that supersensible perception can elicit, can say this: Within the child manifests something that lived in pre-earthly, spirit-soul existence in supersensible beauty. It has departed from its supersensible beauty, in a sense, and has submerged itself in the body that physical heredity was able to supply. And you as a teacher must draw forth what rests as God-given endowment in the human body, so that, from year to year, from month to month, from week to week, it can take hold of the physical body and pervade it; so that it can model the body to bear an affinity with, and come to resemble, the soul. You must also awaken in the human being before you what reveals itself there. And with this stance you no longer engage in education, and tackle the challenge of education, equipped only with rational principles, but you bring your whole being to bear on the task, your whole human soul and sensibility, your whole human sense of responsibility. You gradually learn also that it is not enough only to observe the *child* when you must decide what this child needs at any moment, but you must also survey the whole of a human life.

This is not an easy or comfortable thing to do. But the truth is that what may be apparent in an infant, say, emerges distinctively only in advanced age, having long remained hidden within a person; it reveals itself as either health-giving or injurious. As educators we are concerned not only with the children as we see them now. The whole of a person's life lies in our hands. It a superficial and mistaken educational principle to teach children only what they can already understand. This is to address the moment only, not to consider the whole of a person's life. You see, there is an age of childhood, from second dentition to puberty, when it is extremely beneficial for children to take things that they cannot yet fully understand on the authority of a beloved teacher. This can be the greatest blessing for life: it awakens children's life forces if they can see, in the self-evident authority of their teacher, the embodiment of truth, beauty and goodness. This does not hinder human freedom. This self-evident authority of the teacher grows and develops into a source of strength throughout the rest of a person's life.

When, at the age of 35, say, we recall with our mature sensibility something that we received into our heart around the age of seven or eight, that we took on trust on the authority of a beloved teacher, and that we only now understand as a mature person; when we draw forth this inner possession that first lived in us through love, then the dawning understanding of something that lies germinally within us will be the source of a rich inner enlivening. The child is robbed of such inner enlivening if the teacher seeks only to teach what can already be understood. This is a trivializing of the scope of education. We only pay due heed to the child's experience if we are able to engage with the whole person and, above all, teach in a way that can embed itself in the human soul.

You may have met people who radiate blessing to others around them. They have a calming, soothing effect even when others are irritable and confrontational. And if we are really able to look back— and, as I said, this can be difficult—to see how such people acquired these qualities, not only through their inherent disposition but also through education and upbringing, we will often find that, at a very delicate age, such people learned to look up with reverence and regard to carers or teachers who had a very warm and intimate, heartfelt relationship with them. This esteem and regard, this ability to revere is like a mountain brook that goes deep underground and only springs up later again. What the soul acquires in childhood works down into the depths of the soul and only emerges again in advanced age, when it becomes a power that seems to radiate blessing.

To educate the child at a tender age so that these powers of reverence can transform into powers of blessing in old age, is something we can encapsulate in a single metaphor: our hands will never extend in blessing when we are old if we do not learn to fold our hands reverently in prayer at a tender age.

This can show us in one specific instance how a particular challenge—that of education—can lead toward an ethical and religious mood. It shows also what our engagement with spirit perception can make of our sensibility, our will, and how it can imbue our whole outlook on life. What we might otherwise only develop in an outward way as educational 'technique' can instead become central to our ethical and religious outlook. But imbuing with this kind of mood the education practised at the Stuttgart Waldorf School, and at other schools affiliated with it,[31] certainly does not mean that purely practical aspects of pedagogy have been overlooked. Practical details are taken full account of. The task of education has here really become something which, with all its educational techniques, with all its practical attention to detail, at the same time meets the child with an ethical and religious mood. The actions of teachers become ethical and religious actions too, since what is done is drawn from the deepest moral impulses. Because educational practice flows from the educator's conscience, and because the teacher sees a God-given soul being in the developing person, pedagogy becomes at the same time religious practice. This need not be sentimental at all, but can be precisely what our now very prosaic era particularly needs. By virtue of the fact that spiritual science becomes a lamp that sheds light on our actions in life and our whole outlook on life, life itself, as in the examples I have given about education, can become a kind of universal divine worship. Supersensible perception does not bring us abstractions but real human powers. The insights gained through supersensible perception become actual life forces, and therefore they can also flow into our whole stance and outlook and can lead us beyond our ordinary limitations, from the sense world to the supersensible realm; and this in turn raises us to be moral beings. And then, in devoted love, we really can unite with the spirit of the world and thus develop truly religious piety.

This becomes apparent in education particularly. If we observe children up to the age of six or seven, we find they are entirely physically wedded to their surroundings. Their being is an imitative one, right into language and speech. If we consider this physical immersion in everything around them, if we observe what remains a naturally given environment for the child whose soul has not yet awoken, then it seems right to say that what we encounter in the child is a naturally appearing form of religious surrender to the world. The child learns so much so quickly through this naturally religious surrender to the world. And then we detach ourselves from the world, and, from the age of 6 or 7 our educational environment gives our soul another, intimating orientation. At puberty we come to independent judgement, growing into what gives us direction and aim out of ourselves. We do well indeed if, now we are also released from our sensory organism, we can follow thought, follow the spirit, and grow into a realm of spirit just as we lived naturally in the world as children; if as adults we can rediscover in the spirit the naturalness of a child's intimation of the world. If, after puberty, our mind and spirit can live in the world as the body of the child lived in the naturally given world, then our inmost human nature penetrates the spirit of the world in true religious devotion. We become religious people.

If we are to grasp the very essence of supersensible perception and knowledge then we need to transform ordinary forms of thought and perception into living powers. The same is true if we observe and understand the human being through what I described last time as the supersensible capacity of Imagination. If we become aware that the human being is more than only a physical body as physiology studies it, as it is anatomized for the purposes of developing the field of physiology, if we recognize by powers of perception I described that a supersensible being lives in this physical body, then we will also discover this supersensible being to be a sculptor who works upon the physical body. But then we must also be able to pass on from ordinary abstract ideas embodied in natural laws to an artistic apprehension of the human being; then the laws by which we otherwise ordinarily grasp the human physical form must become configuring powers. Science must become art. The supersensible nature of the human being cannot be encompassed by abstract science. We gain a science of our supersensible nature only through a form of beholding perception that entirely transposes science into artistic experience. Science must not remain confined to logic and experimentation. Certainly we could assert this, but what does the real world care about our assertions? If we really wish to grasp the world, we must orientate ourselves to the world rather than to our own theoretical requirements, and even our own logical thoughts. You see, the world leads us from merely logical thoughts into an artistic domain. And therefore we only arrive at a true view of life if we can transform our conceptions of natural law, through 'beholding judgement' as Goethe so beautifully put it,[32] into living, configuring laws of nature. Then we rise through art, 'through the dawn glow of beauty' as Schiller said,[33] to knowledge but also, at the same time, to the realm of true piety, the land of religion.

And then—and I will conclude with this—we discover the real nature of all the doubts that come over people when they say that knowledge does not furnish us with any religious, ethical imperatives; that such impulses depend on other distinct powers that are far removed from those of knowledge and enquiry. Certainly I agree that no outward knowledge, as such, can ever lead us to an ethical and religious outlook on life. What does in truth lead us into an ethical and religious outlook does not lie in the sensory domain. It can only be studied in the supersensible realm. We can only truly and properly comprehend human freedom, therefore, if we penetrate into this supersensible realm. Similarly, a true knowledge and insight into the nature of human conscience only becomes available through supersensible enquiry, for by this means we reach the realm of spirit that does not subject us to natural laws but allows us to act as free beings, at the same time imbuing and infusing us with the impulses that become manifest in conscience. And here becomes manifest too the divine nature of the world which a naturally religious and pious person instinctively feels. It is true that to be a pious, religious person we do not directly need the kind of knowledge and enquiry I have described. We can be this quite naturally and instinctively. Yet, as history teaches us, religious and ethical life cannot spring from a root other than that of knowledge, for all religious emancipation—and the religious disposition is of course always inherent in human beings—has proceeded from insights and knowledge that were first available through supersensible sources in ancient times. There is no moral or religious idea that did not spring from the root of knowledge. In our era, scientific thinking has also now sprung from the root of knowledge, yet it cannot reach the spirit. Because of this, many people cling to traditions to sustain their religious outlook. They think that these traditions embody something like a 'religious spirit' but in fact these are atavistic remnants, things simply passed down, and today they have grown so weak that we now need a new impetus through knowledge—not in the abstract, but an impetus that enlivens and invigorates knowledge, that will give people a new impulse in their practical lives: an ethical and religious impulse that springs with fresh immediacy again.

That is what we need. And although it is said—and this is certainly true in some respects—that knowledge as such is not needed for us to lead an ethical and religious life, on the other hand, as history once again shows, knowledge must not hamper and mislead people in their religious and ethical sensibility. It must be possible for us to climb to the highest levels of knowledge and yet, in doing so, arrive at the very same place that was the God-given, God-governed home we inhabited before we had gained such knowledge. Something we intimated and felt, and were right to do so, must be rediscovered also as we strive for the brightest light of the highest knowledge. Then knowledge will not crush an ethical outlook on life but can only kindle and properly imbue it, strengthening all morality, all religious conduct. Through such knowledge we become aware of life's deeper meaning; and we may indeed speak of such a thing. We become aware that, through the mysterious workings of cosmic destiny, through the whole wise dispensation of the universe, we first stand here as spirit-willed beings; and that as such we can also further develop ourselves. But in doing so through outward knowledge we find ourselves only upon an uncertain, inchoate ocean where doubt assails and dissipates us by contrast to the unity we inhabited when we still retained our naiver intimations. But if we awaken from ordinary knowledge to supersensible knowledge, then we return to something in us that is God-given, God-imbued.

What these gravely troubled times so greatly need is a new impetus in our ethical and religious way of life. This can only be truly cultivated if the knowledge, which in human evolution until now has advanced from obscure intimations to a modern, wakeful clarity of thought, is taken further toward a higher awakening, toward a deeper connection with the supersensible world. And at the same time, at this period of such grave trials for humanity in every corner of the earth, this will supply the impulse we need particularly for renewing social co-existence, indeed for the renewing of all modern thinking about society. We cultivate a religious and ethical outlook on life by advancing from ordinary knowledge through artistic and supersensible awakening. Understanding this, we nurture the very root of such an outlook, a truly unsentimental piety that enables us to serve the spirit by the way we live. We nurture it by seeking to lead our powers of perception and enquiry toward the supersensible realm so that its light allows us to awaken in a supersensible world— where, for the first time, we feel ourselves to be souls free of natural laws, where we can at last stand in our full human dignity with true piety, authentic inwardness and true religiosity as human spirit beings in the world of spirit.

LECTURE 11

HOW DO WE GAIN KNOWLEDGE OF THE SUPERSENSIBLE WORLD?

PARIS, 26 MAY 1924

ANYONE today who inwardly aspires to knowledge of the supersensible world is most often referred to methods and results that originated in ancient times. If we then delve a little deeper, we discover what were, at an earlier phase of humanity's evolution, called the 'Mysteries': centres which, firstly, cultivated religious life and rituals—these being infused by the spiritual principle—and secondly, which engaged in what we today would call scientific enquiry. The spiritual principle infused and imbued this other form of human apprehension too. And a third aspect expressed in these Mysteries was the artistic element. On the one hand, then, what imbued religion, ritual and science was made manifest at these centres to direct, tangible apprehension; and on the other, what imbued art was likewise embodied, made manifest. Basically, those today who seek the supersensible are still living from these things from ancient times as tradition has preserved them.

In my lecture today I do not wish to speak of these ancient traditions, nor of the ancient Mysteries. I want to speak, rather, of the potential for a new Mystery life, the possibility of a new path toward supersensible worlds, whose meaning and underlying conception can be equal to the standards nowadays set for scientific knowledge based on the huge advances in scientific thinking in the modern era.

If we look inwards we find our interiority to be actively con-stituted of thinking, feeling and will. Of these soul activities, only thinking is, if it is healthy, independent of our physicality. If we are able to devote ourselves fully and inwardly to the character of thinking, we will find that this thinking can only supply us with independent, logical laws because healthy thinking is naturally independent of our corporeality. Only if we start to think in pathological ways—if some kind of morbidity enters our thinking—does it become dependent on bodily processes. But what does this mean? It means nothing less than this: that as long as thinking is healthy, it keeps itself separate from the body; and it only submerges itself in the body, is only absorbed into the unconscious, if it becomes unhealthy.

The same is not true of our feeling, nor of our will. In its natural, normal condition, our feeling submerges itself in the body and is scarcely conscious to us, like anything dreamlike. It subsists entirely in our corporeality. The same is true of will. In ordinary life, we remain unaware of what actually occurs in will processes, because they are deeply immersed in our body.

If we now try to acquire higher knowledge, we must develop human capacities that are just as independent of corporeality as our ordinary thinking, but which are also able to perceive worlds higher than those available to ordinary thinking. In our present state of evolution, this thinking is only capable of perceiving and anato-mizing the physical sense world.

In the ancient Mysteries, this emancipation of spiritual faculties from the body was facilitated by outward means. Let us consider for a moment the effect on our soul of, say, a fleeting sound, noise or tone that frightens us. This sudden impression leaves no time for us to immerse in our bodily nature the feelings that occur in the soul. And if fright, fear, anxiety follow in quick succession, the soul element is retained outside of the body. The whole means used in the ancient Mysteries involved freeing the soul from the body through this kind

of shock. Terror, highly dramatic occurrences that lead the soul to a
pinnacle and then let it fall, were geared to giving a person experiences in which soul life is sustained outside of the body, and does not
immerse itself in it. When a person came back to themselves after
such occurrences, they recognized that they had been given insights
into a world otherwise closed to them—a world they called 'supersensible'. These outward means, which largely assumed a ritual form
in the ancient Mysteries, are no longer appropriate for modern
humanity. They also depended on isolating and secluding those who
were initiated into higher knowledge. The Mysteries were strictly out
of bounds for most, strictly organized and overseen by wise priests
who were able to establish external means that enabled those chosen,
over many years, to accustom their soul to achieving independence
from the body, and, with this independence of soul, to enter the
world of spirit.

People today would have no trust or confidence in anyone who
had to seek a path to the spiritual world by this means. And this is
because these methods required strict seclusion of the spiritual seeker
from the world. In ancient times, trust was only invested in spiritual
people if they secluded themselves from the rest of humanity,
whereas today we only trust seekers if they stand fully in life, if
nothing in the full reality and immediacy of life is foreign to them.
And for this reason, our modern era needs, and for now will go on
needing, methods to pursue the path into the spiritual world which
are more inward paths of the soul. In pursuing such methods we
must remain independent of external measures, external effects, to
advance us. I want to describe to you methods of accessing the world
of spirit that are very quietly effective within the soul and yet lead to
knowledge of the spiritual world as surely as the methods that were
used for initiation in the ancient Mysteries.

In my book, *Knowledge of the Higher Worlds* (whose French translation is entitled 'Initiation'[34]), I described modern methods of
initiation. This evening I would like to speak of these initiation
methods in general terms.

A particular inner engagement with our world of thoughts, our

powers of thought, is required to make a beginning on the path of
perception of spiritual worlds. In ordinary life we give ourselves up to
the outer world or to the thoughts that rise up in us from within.
And whatever relative activity we succeed in developing in this
ordinary mind, in general our thinking is nevertheless passive, surrendered either to the sensory world or the inner world of soul. In
fact, modern people actually place great importance on retaining this
passivity of thinking since they fear that if they shape their thoughts
arbitrarily, out of themselves, they will find themselves in an
imaginary realm. This whole approach to thinking has to change if
we are to enter the supersensible realm. We have to activate our
thinking. In line with old customs I have called this activation of
thinking 'meditation'. Quite contrary to the surrendering of ourselves to something objective in our thinking, it involves us placing at
the centre of our mind, through the inner power of our soul life, a
content of thought that can easily be surveyed and that is as simple as
possible. Focusing on this exclusively for a while, without any dis-
traction, we turn our whole soul's attention to this single inner
content.

In dwelling actively with our whole soul upon an inner content,
something happens with our soul faculties that otherwise occurs in
the physical body if, say, we keep using a particular set of muscles to
accomplish a specific kind of work. The muscles strengthen. In the
same way our powers of soul strengthen inwardly if the soul's activity
is repeatedly focused upon a content. The content of thinking must
be easy to survey since it should contain nothing that might come
from the unconscious. We must dwell upon this inner content in as
fully conscious reflection as we can manage. It is not good therefore
to take something complex, something perhaps that is drawn from
our memory, reminiscences that, as old soul experiences, have either
a rational or feeling connection with the content in question. It is best
therefore to find the meditation content in one of two ways. We can,
say, take a book we have never read before, whose content is entirely
unknown to us. We open it at random and read a sentence that is of
no particular interest to us. Yet we take this sentence and place it at

the forefront of our mind and ponder it. For a long time we focus our whole soul upon this content. But even better than this is if we have sufficient trust in someone who has real knowledge of these things: we can go to them and ask them for an inner content of the kind described. Such a person, if they are a spiritual investigator already, will be practised in knowing after a glance at us what spiritual content would be best for our meditation. If we then take an easily surveyed content that is wholly present in our conscious mind and concentrate upon it, dwell upon it in very meditative concentration, our thinking will gradually be entirely transformed; it will shed all abstraction, all coldness. Thinking becomes very pictorial. We gain the ability to think in images that are rich and vivid, even full of colour. Images that gradually become like vivid dream pictures yet have a quite different soul character, enter our conscious mind and we experience something that we have never before consciously experienced: the ability to think with as clear a presence of mind as the most clear-headed logician or mathematician can, though not thinking in terms of natural laws but in pictures whose origin we are initially unaware of.

Let us call this first level of knowledge of the supersensible 'imaginative perception'. We need to develop these capacities if we wish to enter the first sphere of the supersensible world. If we continue with such exercises for long enough—depending on the individual, it may take years, or perhaps only months—we can at last succeed in fully developing a pictorial consciousness, thinking in pictures in the same way as one otherwise thinks in abstract thoughts in the ordinary mind. We think, not dream, in these pictures. Having advanced far enough with this pictorial thinking, we will be directly conscious of the fact that this pictorial thinking does not submerge itself in the body but is free and independent of it. We now feel ourselves to exist in this independent picture thinking, we live in it fully: we live in it as we otherwise live in our physical body. And as we feel ourselves within our physical body, with all our bodily feelings, with both the pain and wellbeing that issues from it and is registered by the soul, so now we feel ourselves to be living in a finer, second nature. We have detached this second person in us from the physical body and can now say, out of inner experience, directly out of living experience that we no longer feel ourselves only within the physical body. Now we experience our human nature also in an etheric body, in a body of subtler substantiality. It becomes lived experience for us that a second human being is contained within the first. Just as we can perceive the physical world through the physical body's physical sense organs—colours through the eyes, tones through the ears—so now, feeling ourselves within the etheric body, which is as structured and organized as the physical body, and knowing this second nature of ours through it, we come to perceive a new world to which the physical body alone cannot penetrate.

The first new world we perceive is that of our own present earthly life. In a mighty tableau that unfolds majestically before us, everything that has occurred in life in chronological sequence stands before us now in its simultaneity, like a panorama: we survey everything in our life from the present moment backward to our birth, in retrospect. In the same way that things stand beside each other in space, so now, in this retrospective tableau, an experience that we had when we were 8 years old, say, is present simultaneously with other things that we experienced when we were, for instance, 20 or 50. It is as if time becomes space. And we learn to distinguish precisely between ordinary memory and what we now behold in tangible images in a majestic panorama of our whole life. Ordinary memory, which we draw forth from our being in isolated thoughts, ideas, pictures, is weak and pale by comparison. What we now survey as it unfolds before us is full, rich, vividly colourful, if I can put it like that. Yet everything also appears to us as outward things appear. From this panoramic view, which occupies a somewhat extended moment, we know how our life appears to the inner gaze. And it becomes apparent to us that a spirit-soul holds sway within us at every moment of our earthly existence since birth, or rather since conception. This spirit-soul compresses itself into forces of growth, forces of nutrition, into all activity holding sway in our physical body; but ultimately what we perceive here, having ascended to the first stage of supersensible perception, is a spiritual principle. At the same time, however, we discern not only our own etheric body but the etheric world that surrounds us, to which our etheric body belongs. We discern how differently we relate to this etheric world—which exists as definitely as the physical—from how we relate to the physical world. In the physical world, things are present. I am present. I speak of physical things as being strictly separate from me and can point to them. But I am connected to the etheric world through my etheric body in the same way that a part of my own organism is related to the whole organism. And just as a part of me, my finger say, can be distinguished from my whole body, so my etheric body, though it can be distinguished from the etheric universe, nevertheless forms a part of it. We are much more a unity with the world that stands behind the physical world than the physical body is a unity with the physical world. That is the first level of the supersensible world, and is also the first supersensible realm we reach on our journey toward supersensible knowledge.

At the level of supersensible knowledge that I have so far described, we do not gain more than an insight into this aspect of human nature that develops from birth to death as a unity that remains constant while also transforming throughout our life, by contrast to the separate substances that we assimilate and expel so that, as physical beings, we continually renew ourselves. The etheric body remains present as a unity from birth to death.

Now if we wish to advance further than this first level, a second stage of perception must be developed within the soul. Having, at the first stage, activated and invigorated our thinking so that we comprehend and encompass ourselves in our etheric body, to attain the second stage of knowledge we must now eradicate once more from consciousness everything that we gain in this way through strengthened thinking. Having very actively introduced a conscious content into our soul by concentrating on it with all our power, we must now let go of it again. You know what happens when we must rid ourselves of our usual soul content, the world supplied to us through our senses: we fall asleep. Gradually we lapse into a numbness of soul. This must not happen here, and does not happen. Yes indeed, it is difficult to rid ourselves again of a soul content that we have first exerted all our powers to consciously invoke. It is harder to do so in this case than with the contents of the ordinary mind. But if we succeed in expelling this content, something occurs that never otherwise happens. Our mind becomes completely empty. In the vivid experience of our own etheric body that we have first brought about, we become able to, as it were, abstract, look away from the whole sense world and from all ordinary thinking. We live then in a higher region. But if we now rid ourselves again of this higher region, erase this tableau of our own life, our consciousness becomes empty and we find ourselves in a state that is significant for all higher knowledge: that of mere wakefulness without inner content. We direct a strengthened, invigorated consciousness out into the emptiness of the world. We do not fall asleep as we do this, but remain wakeful. But if for a moment we face nothing but the void—this does not last long. Having maintained mere wakefulness in our consciousness, really empty consciousness, the world of spirit penetrates us: this is not our etheric body, nor anything that bears an affinity with it, but a spiritual world that is at first very far-off. The real world of spirit penetrates our merely wakeful and empty consciousness, though this empty mind and wakefulness has to be acquired through long-practised soul exercises that I have been able to describe only in general. You see, this suppression of all content does not succeed at the first try, but must be repeatedly practised. For some it will again take years while for others, if they have the right predisposition—which is a matter of destiny—it may take only months until they succeed in keeping the mind empty without falling asleep, so that the world of spirit can enter them.

Of course it might be said that this kind of experience of approaching the world of spirit could be mere suggestion, auto-suggestion. How, you may ask, can we distinguish such suggestion from what the spiritual investigator, the initiate, calls a real world of spirit? Only life itself enables us to make this distinction. Just as life itself will teach us the difference between the idea of red-hot iron and iron that actually burns you, one experiences realities in the world of spirit that stream into the empty mind. You simply know the difference between a spiritual reality and mere auto-suggestion in the same way that you can tell the difference between a red-hot piece of iron or just the mental image of it.

In the book I referred to, I called this second stage of supersensible knowledge by an old term, 'inspired knowledge'. Please don't take offence at the term. We need a terminology of some kind for these things. When we reach the stage of inspired knowledge we experience ourselves, in a sense, as inhabiting a third aspect of our being. First we have the physical person, then the etheric person. Now we experience ourselves as inhabiting a third entity. But as we do so we experience ourselves not only as independent of our body, as is true in strengthened, imaginative thinking, but we find ourselves entirely outside the body. We have attained the state that we can call living in the spirit outside of the physical body. Here we are also capable of departing from the etheric body too: that is, in the same way we eradicated all content, including all imaginative content, to achieve empty consciousness, so we also eradicate this life-tableau that we first achieved as I described. This means that we submerge what we possess in earthly life in the unconscious, and live outside of our physical and etheric existence. Having achieved this, our retrospective gaze no longer extends back only to birth or conception, but further back into the past: we gaze into a world of spirit in which we lived as spirit-soul before we descended to the physical world. We behold ourselves as living and acting in this spiritual world, just as we behold ourselves as physical human beings in the physical world. We come to discern how what nature develops as the physical germ of our being must connect and unite with what descends from worlds of spirit, for we can now ourselves behold this. And having gained this knowledge, in the course of which we depart entirely from our physical and etheric body, then we find as we return into our own physical and etheric body—that is, as the moment of our vision of the world of spirit ceases—that our soul-spiritual life on earth is a reflection, an image, of what we were as spirit-soul before we descended to the earth. And as we come back into our body, into the physical and etheric body, we master what I will call a configured, individualized power of perception or vision. Now, whereas we experience outside of our physical and etheric body a more general spiritual world which we passed through in pre-earthly existence, on returning to our physical and etheric body—not submerging ourselves in it but if you like tarrying or dwelling there—we learn to distinguish between the spirit beings of a higher world with whom we were united before we descended to earthly life, in the same way that we distinguish here between different human individuals. We learn to recognize beings who never descend to earth, never assume a physical body, divine beings of spirit. We are the co-inhabitants of the world of spirit with them before we descend to this earth. And, precisely through being able to move in our spirit-soul alternately between being outside and inside our body, we also learn to recognize that among these higher spirit-soul beings with whom we dwelt before we descended to earth, are human souls who are waiting to descend to the earth to experience it at a later time than we have experienced it.

Thus, through this stage of inspired knowledge, we come to recognize a part of the eternal nature of the human being to which very little heed is given in our temporal consciousness, even by religious people. Our modern era does not like to consider or contemplate pre-earthly existence. People do have an interest in thinking about what lies after death—even if only as a matter of faith or tradition—since this is something still to come. But since they are alive already, they do not feel any particular need to reflect on pre-birth existence. They are here after all! But they are interested in whether they will continue to exist. The second aspect of eternity, immortality, is of egoistic interest to them. In modern parlance we don't even have a word for the other half of eternity, for pre-earthly existence which extends as infinitely far back into the past as immortality extends forward. You see, in reality we only come to discern the eternal aspects of human life if we can once again employ terms which ancient languages possessed for eternity. They spoke of 'unbornhood' as much as of immortality. Modern initiation science recomposes the eternity of human nature from both unbornhood and immortality together. However, unbornhood is more intrinsic to real knowledge than to egoism. As far as immortality is concerned, people can maintain mere belief. But unbornhood, the certainty that my being existed spiritually before my physical body ever took shape, is something I only come to recognize if I am able to behold the unborn aspect of myself and not only the immortal aspect, which we will discuss in the last part of this lecture.

If in this way we have stepped outside our physical and etheric body, and feel ourselves to be amongst spirit beings as we previously felt ourselves to be amongst physical beings and things in the physical body, nevertheless we still know ourselves as a human being, as this specific individuality, this I. And in a sense we need only embark on the journey back in time to the world we passed through before this present life on earth. But when we thus feel ourselves within a world of spirit and outside our physical and etheric body, and if we then look downward to the world of stars, the stars no longer appear to us as stars but as worlds where higher or also lower beings dwell. Wherever our physical eyes would discern a star, we then perceive a cosmic sphere of other entities. If we now feel ourselves to be within a spirit world in the world of stars as we otherwise feel ourselves to be on earth in our physical body, we can speak of the astral body just as we spoke of the etheric body at the first stage of supersensible perception, because we now dwell within the spiritual nature of the world of stars.

If we desire to progress further than this, then, besides Imagination and a consciousness emptied of content, we must add a third capacity of perception, one that the modern mind very rarely regards as a faculty of knowledge. This capacity does play the greatest conceivable role in human life, but no right is assigned it to figure in knowledge. I am speaking of the human power of love: the love that leads people together with others so that we come close to those we love through the physical body, or the soul or spirit incarnated in the physical body. By further developing this power of love such that we can extend it into the experience of the etheric body firstly, but then also into the experience of the astral body, eventually we can go beyond discerning and experiencing our physical body. Gradually we can intensify love to the point where we not only see other beings but—ourselves being now spirit—we can enter into relationship with them in the same way that we enter into relationship with physically embodied people on the earth. Intuition enables us to communicate with spirit beings, just as physical capacities enable us to interact and communicate with physical people on the earth. If we enhance our capacity of love to such a degree that the spiritual becomes objective for us in the same way that the sense world is objective for us in the physical world, then, not only looking back into our pre-earthly spiritual existence we can also look back into former lives on earth. It becomes a reality for us that human life unfolds in forms of existence between birth and death, and then between death and a new birth, and then again between birth and death, and once more between death and rebirth: that we live successive earthly lives and in successive periods of purely spiritual existence. Thus we learn to look back upon former earthly lives and can perceive our present life as the recapitulation of these former lives.

Yet no one succeeds in beholding what they were, how they were, or that they even existed at all in a former life, unless they succeed in developing the capacity of love to the point where they can regard or confront themselves as they would another being. For this, our love-infused capacities of knowledge must be hugely different from ordinary capacities, so that we can behold our former periods of existence upon earth as we would regard the existence of another person in the present. If we ascend to this level, which I have called that of Intuition, of true Intuition, we can behold ourselves in recurring lives on earth as spiritually active beings who stand before our eye of spirit. Only then do we exist fully outside the life of our body. And if we experience this, then we know the nature of death. Death now stands before us as the outward, objective realization of what we ourselves have accomplished in knowledge and perception.

Just as we laid aside our physical and etheric body in the cultivation of higher knowledge so we can recognize now that at death we merely lay aside the physical and etheric body, and that we then pass through the gate of death into a world of spirit. Belief becomes knowledge, opinion becomes true perception. Thus, what we otherwise call immortality becomes for us certain, exact, tangible knowledge. We behold the immortality of our own human existence, the entry of this, our human being, into a life after death in the same way that we also behold a pre-birth life in the spirit, a pre-earthly life.

But we also look upon the interweaving of relationships between people in physical earth life: family relationships, relationships of love and friendship. We behold all this. Just as our physical corporeality is shed at death and the soul ascends into a world of spirit, so everything physical in our earthly friendships and loving relationships falls away to be replaced by an ensouled and all the more inward community when the people whose destiny leads them together here on earth have passed through the gate of death and find each other there again among higher beings. Modern initiation can only show the nature of the path whereby things that are otherwise matters of mere belief can actually be perceived, becoming assured knowledge of immortality as the other aspect of eternity.

Thus we rise through imaginative knowledge to sight of what lives between birth and death. And in gaining this perception we ascend at the same time to our etheric body. Inspired knowledge leads us to our astral body, so that we then enter the world we passed through before we were born, and which we will enter again after death. In the astral body we become acquainted with the pre-earthly and post-mortem life-sphere of human existence. Then, in ascending to intuitive knowledge, we come to know the fourth aspect of the human being, the true, eternal I that passes from one earthly life to another, and assumes purely spiritual forms of existence between each of these lives.

In conclusion, having outlined this path of modern initiation in general terms at least, allow me to say this: ancient knowledge, achieved in the way I described at the outset through outward rituals

and other methods, was more instinctive and dreamlike in nature.
And human convictions about the spiritual, supersensible realm have
remained with us in the form of traditions that once emerged from
this ancient, instinctive knowledge. Today, though, we can already
sense that many people feel an urge, a deep longing, to rediscover
paths toward spiritual worlds without being aware of this themselves. There are, as yet, only a few who know this consciously but if
we are able to see such things we can see how numerous are those
who in their subconscious mind yearn for Mystery knowledge
because they wish to find the path again into supersensible worlds.

The Goetheanum as we called it,[35] in north-west Switzerland, was
a very modest beginning in creating a Mystery centre to help people
find a modern, conscious path into the supersensible realm, contrasting with the more instinctive path of ancient times. Enemies
have robbed us of this Mystery centre, destroying it a little while ago
by arson. These things too have their eternal aspect. The physical fire
robbed us of the physical building, the Goetheanum, where we had
been cultivating the spiritual science I have briefly described to you.
But there is also such a thing as spiritual fire: it does not burn down
physical edifices but will continually re-engender them. Quietly,
with less noise and tumult than in the ancient Mysteries, pupils of
spiritual wisdom in the new Mysteries will come together and in turn
bring humanity the knowledge, so necessary to it, of the eternal
realities of human existence and of the world. This knowledge is
needed for our thinking, feeling and will, so as to gain inward clarity
and live harmoniously, and thus also find strength and security in
outward life. People need connection with the spiritual world. And
the longing will increasingly awaken in human souls—a longing
born from humankind's eternal search for the spiritual—to have such
a place as the spiritual school in Dornach, on the north-western
borders of Switzerland. This quest for the spiritual slumbered for the
short span of a few centuries, a period that brought us the outward
magnificence of science. But now, once again, the human being
stands at the gate opening on the supersensible, and is knocking at it,
since natural science alone cannot further advance the human soul.

Only modern Mysteries will quench the thirst that lives consciously in a few but unconsciously in a great portion of humanity. If we have true intentions toward the world of spirit, we will behold the human will for new Mysteries that is quite assuredly coming to birth, for spirituality will only return to humankind if new Mysteries arise in which people can discover the spirit in a more conscious, light-filled way than was true in the ancient Mysteries. Through such Mysteries they can be led back in a more developed, more perfect way to the divine world of spirit and thus to the very source of their full humanity.

NOTES AND REFERENCES

The title of the German volume was chosen by the editors of the first German edition, based on the first lecture in the book.

Only *the titles of the public lectures* originate with Rudolf Steiner himself.

Text sources: The printed text is based on full transcripts produced by the stenographers themselves from their short-hand scripts. The lectures in Basel and Dornach were recorded by professional stenographer Helene Finckh, who took down most of Rudolf Steiner's lectures from 1915/16 onwards. The two lectures given in Vienna were recorded in short-hand by Walter Vegelahn from Berlin, who was likewise responsible for many transcripts. The Paris lecture was taken down by Karl Day, from Dornach. The name of the stenographer for the two lectures in Prague is unknown.

Works by Rudolf Steiner in the Collected Works are referred to in the references with their GA number.

1. The First Goetheanum designed by Rudolf Steiner and built in wood under his direction between 1913 and 1922, and in use from 1920 onwards, was destroyed by fire in the night of New Year 1922/23. See also GA 286 and 287 on the art and architecture of the building.

2. Rudolf Steiner had given lectures in Basel from 1906 on general themes of spiritual science including education (GA 301) and social threefolding (GA 329 and 334).

3. Rudolf Steiner became acquainted with Goethe's works through his teacher in Vienna, Karl Julius Schröer, and from 1880 studied Goethe's scientific writings. In 1882 he took on the job of editing Goethe's scientific works, and writing a commentary on them for Joseph Kürscher's series, *Deutsche Nationalliteratur* (see GA 1). Between 1890 and 1897 he worked at the Goethe-Schiller Archive in Weimar. His preoccupation with Goethe and his ideas gave rise to *Goethe's Theory of Knowledge—An Outline of the Epistemology of His Worldview*, GA 2. See also *Autobiography*, GA 28 and the correspondence between Rudolf Steiner and Marie Steiner-von Sivers in GA 262.

4. Four Mystery Plays, GA 14.

5. A phrase often used by Steiner for the contemporary idea that there were fixed and insuperable limits to human knowledge. This was asserted with special emphasis by Emil Du Bois-Reymond (1818–1896) in his lecture given at the second session of the 45th assembly of German scientists and physicians on 14 August 1872. The lecture was titled 'On the Limits of Scientific Enquiry'.

6. For instance Henri Bergson (1859–1941) wrote as follows in *Matière et Mémoire*, essays on the relationship between body and mind (Jena 1908):

'...We now understand why memory could not proceed from the brain as such. The condition of the brain perpetuates memory, lending it power over the present through the materiality with which it endows it, but pure memory is a spiritual manifestation. With memory, we do properly enter the domain of the mind, of spirit.' (From the translation into German by W. Windelband.)

7. The great majority of these—several hundreds of larger and smaller note-books—have been preserved in the Rudolf Steiner Estate Archive. Many of the entries that relate to lectures have been published, either in the GAs themselves or in the supplements to the Collected Works. See *Register der Hefte 1–85/86*, Dornach 1985.

8. See Goethe, *Maxims and Reflections* 183.

9. The literal citation runs as follows: '...The second reflection is concerned exclusively with the art of the Greeks, and seeks to explore how those incomparable artists succeeded in elaborating from the human form the circle of divine creation, which is entirely self-contained and in which no salient character, no transition nor mediating part is lacking. I suspect that they followed the same laws as nature does, and which I am attempting to trace. Except that there is another quality present too, which I do not know how to express.' *Italian Journey*, Rome, 28 January 1787.

10. See note 1 and Carl Kemper, *Der Bau. Studien zur Architektur und Plastik des ersten Goetheanum*, Stuttgart 1966.

11. See *Eurythmy as Visible Song*, GA 278 and *Eurythmy as Visible Speech*, GA 279.

12. Goethe, *Zahme Xenien* IX.

13. From 1914 Rudolf Steiner and the English sculptor, Edith Maryon worked on a wooden sculpture which was still in the studio at the time of the Goetheanum fire and therefore survived intact. Today it stands in what is known as the Group Room at the Goetheanum. See also Åke Fant, *Die Holzplastik Rudolf Steiners*, Dornach 1969.

14. GA 306.

15. See lecture 1 in this volume and the introduction to the notes and references.

16. See note 14 above.

17. In *The World as Will and Idea*, Arthur Schopenhauer (1788–1860) writes: '...The act of will and the action of the body are not two different, objectively discerned states connected by the bond of causality; they do not stand in a cause-effect relationship but are, rather, one and the same thing, yet presenting in two entirely different ways: on the one hand very directly, and on the other in the mind's apprehension.'

18. Wincenty Lutoslawski (1863–1954), Polish philosopher, promoter of Polish messianism, Plato researcher and at that time associate professor at the University of Geneva. His stance towards anthroposophy was critical. The manuscript of his essay 'Rudolf Steiner's so-called "Occult Science"' was published in the journal, *Hochland. Monatsschrift für alle Gebiete des Wissens, der Literatur und Kunst*, edited by Karl Muth, 8th year, issue 1, October 1910, Kempten and Munich.

19. See Rudolf Steiner *Occult Science, an Outline*, GA 13, and also GA 11.

20. Karl Ludwig von Knebel 1744–1834. The literal citation runs: 'On closer observation one will find that a certain plan exists in the life of most people, as

it were laid down in advance for them due to their own nature or the circumstances that govern them. However varied and fluctuating may be the conditions of their life, in the end a whole becomes apparent: a certain kind of consistency and inner accord. However hidden may be the hand of a particular destiny, its clear traces become apparent, whether it be moved by outward influence or inner impulse. Indeed, contradictory motives often conform to its tendency and direction. However haphazard the course of a life is, its underlying foundations and tendencies still show through.' In *Knebels literarischer Nachlass und Briefwechsel*, ed. by Vanhagen von Ense, 2nd edition, volume 3.

21. See note 5.

22. Rudolf Steiner speaks in greater depth about this in the lecture he gave in Dornach on 27 September 1920, published in GA 322.

23. On 27 April 1923 in Prague.

24. See note 7.

25. Dr Emil Molt (1876–1936) was the owner of the Waldorf-Astoria cigarette factory and the founder of the independent Waldorf School in Stuttgart (1919), whose organization and leadership Rudolf Steiner accepted at his request.

26. From 1–12 June 1922. There Rudolf Steiner gave a cycle of lectures on 'The contrasting worlds of West and East', GA 83.

27. *Faust:* Auerbach's Cellar, line 2181.

28. See note 7.

29. See note 5.

30. See note 25.

31. By the autumn of 1923, other Waldorf schools had been established: in Dornach (1 February 1921), Cologne (1921), Hamburg-Wandsbek (22 May 1922), Essen (2 November 1922), King's Langley, Herts/England (beginning of 1923) and The Hague (1923).

32. Goethe uses the heading 'Beholding Judgement' ('Anschauende Urteilskraft') for an essay in *Bildung und Umbildung organischer Naturen*. See also *Goethean Science*, GA 1a.

33. In Schiller's poem 'The Artists'. In the editions where this poem appears, Schiller's phrase is 'Only through the morning gate of beauty...'. Rudolf Steiner referred to this fact as follows in the lecture of 4 December in Stuttgart, contained in GA 218: '...Schiller is right to say that "You only penetrate into the Land of Knowledge through the dawn red ['Morgenrot'] of beauty", which is usually printed as the "morning gate" ['Mortgentor'] of beauty.... If an artist makes a mistake in his writing, posterity naturally perpetuates the error. Of course, it should be "Only through the *dawn red* of beauty...". In other words, all knowledge originates in art. Basically there is no knowledge that does not have an inward affinity with art.'

34. Rudolf Steiner, *L'Initiation ou la Connaissance des Mondes supérieurs*, translated by Jules Sauerwein, Paris 1909 and 1922.

35. See notes 1 and 10.

RUDOLF STEINER'S COLLECTED WORKS

The German Edition of Rudolf Steiner's Collected Works (the *Gesamtausgabe* [GA] published by Rudolf Steiner Verlag, Dornach, Switzerland) presently runs to 354 titles, organized either by type of work (written or spoken), chronology, audience (public or other), or subject (education, art, etc.). For ease of comparison, the Collected Works in English [CW] follows the German organization exactly. A complete listing of the CWs follows with literal translations of the German titles. Other than in the case of the books published in his lifetime, titles were rarely given by Rudolf Steiner himself, and were often provided by the editors of the German editions. The titles in English are not necessarily the same as the German; and, indeed, over the past seventy-five years have frequently been different, with the same book sometimes appearing under different titles.

For ease of identification and to avoid confusion, we suggest that readers looking for a title should do so by CW number. Because the work of creating the Collected Works of Rudolf Steiner is an ongoing process, with new titles being published every year, we have not indicated in this listing which books are presently available. To find out what titles in the Collected Works are currently in print, please check our website at www.rudolfsteinerpress.com (or www.steinerbooks.org for US readers).

Written Work

Public Lectures

Lectures to the Members of the Anthroposophical Society

CW 200   The New Spirituality and the Christ-Experience of the 20th Century

CW 201   The Correspondences Between Microcosm and Macrocosm. The Human Being—A Hieroglyph of the Universe. The Human Being in Relationship with the Cosmos: 1

CW 202   The Bridge between the World-Spirituality and the Physical Aspect of the Human Being. The Search for the New Isis, the Divine Sophia. The Human Being in Relationship with the Cosmos: 2

CW 203   The Responsibility of Human Beings for the Development of the World through their Spiritual Connection with the Planet Earth and the World of the Stars. The Human Being in Relationship with the Cosmos: 3

CW 204   Perspectives of the Development of Humanity. The Materialistic Knowledge-Impulse and the Task of Anthroposophy. The Human Being in Relationship with the Cosmos: 4

CW 205   Human Development, World-Soul, and World-Spirit. Part One: The Human Being as a Being of Body and Soul in Relationship to the World. The Human Being in Relationship with the Cosmos: 5

CW 206   Human Development, World-Soul, and World-Spirit. Part Two: The Human Being as a Spiritual Being in the Process of Historical Development. The Human Being in Relationship with the Cosmos: 6

CW 207   Anthroposophy as Cosmosophy. Part One: Characteristic Features of the Human Being in the Earthly and the Cosmic Realms. The Human Being in Relationship with the Cosmos: 7

CW 208   Anthroposophy as Cosmosophy. Part Two: The Forming of the Human Being as the Result of Cosmic Influence. The Human Being in Relationship with the Cosmos: 8

CW 209   Nordic and Central European Spiritual Impulses. The Festival of the Appearance of Christ. The Human Being in Relationship with the Cosmos: 9

CW 210   Old and New Methods of Initiation. Drama and Poetry in the Change of Consciousness in the Modern Age

CW 211   The Sun Mystery and the Mystery of Death and Resurrection. Exoteric and Esoteric Christianity

CW 212   Human Soul Life and Spiritual Striving in Connection with World and Earth Development

CW 213   Human Questions and World Answers

CW 214   The Mystery of the Trinity: The Human Being in Relationship with the Spiritual World in the Course of Time

CW 215   Philosophy, Cosmology, and Religion in Anthroposophy

CW 216   The Fundamental Impulses of the World-Historical Development of Humanity

CW 217   Spiritually Active Forces in the Coexistence of the Older and Younger Generations. Pedagogical Course for Youth

CW 291   The Nature of Colours
CW 291a   Knowledge of Colours. Supplementary Volume to 'The Nature of Colours'
CW 292   Art History as Image of Inner Spiritual Impulses
CW 293   General Knowledge of the Human Being as the Foundation of Pedagogy
CW 294   The Art of Education, Methodology and Didactics
CW 295   The Art of Education: Seminar Discussions and Lectures on Lesson Planning
CW 296   The Question of Education as a Social Question
CW 297   The Idea and Practice of the Waldorf School
CW 297a   Education for Life: Self-Education and the Practice of Pedagogy
CW 298   Rudolf Steiner in the Waldorf School
CW 299   Spiritual-Scientific Observations on Speech
CW 300a   Conferences with the Teachers of the Free Waldorf School in Stuttgart, 1919 to 1924, in 3 Volumes, Vol. 1
CW 300b   Conferences with the Teachers of the Free Waldorf School in Stuttgart, 1919 to 1924, in 3 Volumes, Vol. 2
CW 300c   Conferences with the Teachers of the Free Waldorf School in Stuttgart, 1919 to 1924, in 3 Volumes, Vol. 3
CW 301   The Renewal of Pedagogical-Didactical Art through Spiritual Science
CW 302   Knowledge of the Human Being and the Forming of Class Lessons
CW 302a   Education and Teaching from a Knowledge of the Human Being
CW 303   The Healthy Development of the Human Being
CW 304   Methods of Education and Teaching Based on Anthroposophy
CW 304a   Anthroposophical Knowledge of the Human Being and Pedagogy
CW 305   The Soul-Spiritual Foundational Forces of the Art of Education. Spiritual Values in Education and Social Life
CW 306   Pedagogical Praxis from the Viewpoint of a Spiritual-Scientific Knowledge of the Human Being. The Education of the Child and Young Human Beings
CW 307   The Spiritual Life of the Present and Education
CW 308   The Method of Teaching and the Life-Requirements for Teaching
CW 309   Anthroposophical Pedagogy and Its Prerequisites
CW 310   The Pedagogical Value of a Knowledge of the Human Being and the Cultural Value of Pedagogy
CW 311   The Art of Education from an Understanding of the Being of Humanity
CW 312   Spiritual Science and Medicine
CW 313   Spiritual-Scientific Viewpoints on Therapy
CW 314   Physiology and Therapy Based on Spiritual Science
CW 315   Curative Eurythmy
CW 316   Meditative Observations and Instructions for a Deepening of the Art of Healing
CW 317   The Curative Education Course

SIGNIFICANT EVENTS IN THE LIFE OF RUDOLF STEINER

1829:   June 23: birth of Johann Steiner (1829–1910)—Rudolf Steiner's father—in Geras, Lower Austria.

1834:   May 8: birth of Franciska Blie (1834–1918)—Rudolf Steiner's mother—in Horn, Lower Austria. 'My father and mother were both children of the glorious Lower Austrian forest district north of the Danube.'

1860:   May 16: marriage of Johann Steiner and Franciska Blie.

1861:   February 25: birth of *Rudolf Joseph Lorenz Steiner* in Kraljevec, Croatia, near the border with Hungary, where Johann Steiner works as a telegrapher for the South Austria Railroad. Rudolf Steiner is baptized two days later, February 27, the date usually given as his birthday.

1862:   Summer: the family moves to Mödling, Lower Austria.

1863:   The family moves to Pottschach, Lower Austria, near the Styrian border, where Johann Steiner becomes stationmaster. 'The view stretched to the mountains ... majestic peaks in the distance and the sweet charm of nature in the immediate surroundings.'

1864:   November 15: birth of Rudolf Steiner's sister, Leopoldine (d. November 1, 1927). She will become a seamstress and live with her parents for the rest of her life.

1866:   July 28: birth of Rudolf Steiner's deaf-mute brother, Gustav (d. May 1, 1941).

1867:   Rudolf Steiner enters the village school. Following a disagreement between his father and the schoolmaster, whose wife falsely accused the boy of causing a commotion, Rudolf Steiner is taken out of school and taught at home.

1868:   A critical experience. Unknown to the family, an aunt dies in a distant town. Sitting in the station waiting room, Rudolf Steiner sees her 'form,' which speaks to him, asking for help. 'Beginning with this experience, a new soul life began in the boy, one in which not only the outer trees and mountains spoke to him, but also the worlds that lay behind them. From this moment on, the boy began to live with the spirits of nature...'

1869:   The family moves to the peaceful, rural village of Neudörfl, near Wiener-Neustadt in present-day Austria. Rudolf Steiner attends the village school. Because of the 'unorthodoxy' of his writing and spelling, he has to do 'extra lessons.'

1870:   Through a book lent to him by his tutor, he discovers geometry: 'To grasp something purely in the spirit brought me inner happiness. I know that I first learned happiness through geometry.' The same tutor allows him to draw, while other students still struggle with their reading and writing. 'An artistic element' thus enters his education.

1871: Though his parents are not religious, Rudolf Steiner becomes a 'church child,' a favourite of the priest, who was 'an exceptional character.' 'Up to the age of ten or eleven, among those I came to know, he was far and away the most significant.' Among other things, he introduces Steiner to Copernican, heliocentric cosmology. As an altar boy, Rudolf Steiner serves at Masses, funerals, and Corpus Christi processions. At year's end, after an incident in which he escapes a thrashing, his father forbids him to go to church.

1872: Rudolf Steiner transfers to grammar school in Wiener-Neustadt, a five-mile walk from home, which must be done in all weathers.

1873–75: Through his teachers and on his own, Rudolf Steiner has many wonderful experiences with science and mathematics. Outside school, he teaches himself analytic geometry, trigonometry, differential equations, and calculus.

1876: Rudolf Steiner begins tutoring other students. He learns bookbinding from his father. He also teaches himself stenography.

1877: Rudolf Steiner discovers Kant's *Critique of Pure Reason*, which he reads and rereads. He also discovers and reads von Rotteck's *World History*.

1878: He studies extensively in contemporary psychology and philosophy.

1879: Rudolf Steiner graduates from high school with honours. His father is transferred to Inzersdorf, near Vienna. He uses his first visit to Vienna 'to purchase a great number of philosophy books'—Kant, Fichte, Schelling, and Hegel, as well as numerous histories of philosophy. His aim: to find a path from the 'I' to nature.

October 1879–1883: Rudolf Steiner attends the Technical College in Vienna—to study mathematics, chemistry, physics, mineralogy, botany, zoology, biology, geology, and mechanics—with a scholarship. He also attends lectures in history and literature, while avidly reading philosophy on his own. His two favourite professors are Karl Julius Schröer (German language and literature) and Edmund Reitlinger (physics). He also audits lectures by Robert Zimmermann on aesthetics and Franz Brentano on philosophy. During this year he begins his friendship with Moritz Zitter (1861–1921), who will help support him financially when he is in Berlin.

1880: Rudolf Steiner attends lectures on Schiller and Goethe by Karl Julius Schröer, who becomes his mentor. Also 'through a remarkable combination of circumstances,' he meets Felix Koguzki, a 'herb gatherer' and healer, who could 'see deeply into the secrets of nature.' Rudolf Steiner will meet and study with this 'emissary of the Master' throughout his time in Vienna.

1881: January: '... I didn't sleep a wink. I was busy with philosophical problems until about 12:30 a.m. Then, finally, I threw myself down on my couch. All my striving during the previous year had been to research whether the following statement by Schelling was true or not: *Within everyone dwells a secret, marvelous capacity to draw back from the stream of time—out of the self clothed in all that comes to us from outside—into our innermost being and there, in the immutable form of the Eternal, to look into ourselves.* I believe, and I am still quite certain of it, that I discovered this capacity in myself; I had long had an inkling of it. Now the whole of idealist philosophy stood before me in modified form. What's a sleepless night compared to that!'

Rudolf Steiner begins communicating with leading thinkers of the day, who send him books in return, which he reads eagerly.

July: 'I am not one of those who dives into the day like an animal in human form. I pursue a quite specific goal, an idealistic aim—knowledge of the truth! This cannot be done offhandedly. It requires the greatest striving in the world, free of all egotism, and equally of all resignation.'

August: Steiner puts down on paper for the first time thoughts for a 'Philosophy of Freedom.' 'The striving for the absolute: this human yearning is freedom.' He also seeks to outline a 'peasant philosophy,' describing what the worldview of a 'peasant'—one who lives close to the earth and the old ways—really is.

1881–1882: Felix Koguzki, the herb gatherer, reveals himself to be the envoy of another, higher initiatory personality, who instructs Rudolf Steiner to penetrate Fichte's philosophy and to master modern scientific thinking as a preparation for right entry into the spirit. This 'Master' also teaches him the double (evolutionary and involutionary) nature of time.

1882:   Through the offices of Karl Julius Schröer, Rudolf Steiner is asked by Joseph Kürschner to edit Goethe's scientific works for the *Deutschen National-Literatur* edition. He writes 'A Possible Critique of Atomistic Concepts' and sends it to Friedrich Theodor Vischer.

1883:   Rudolf Steiner completes his college studies and begins work on the Goethe project.

1884:   First volume of Goethe's *Scientific Writings* (CW 1) appears (March). He lectures on Goethe and Lessing, and Goethe's approach to science. In July, he enters the household of Ladislaus and Pauline Specht as tutor to the four Specht boys. He will live there until 1890. At this time, he meets Josef Breuer (1842–1925), the co-author with Sigmund Freud of *Studies in Hysteria*, who is the Specht family doctor.

1885:   While continuing to edit Goethe's writings, Rudolf Steiner reads deeply in contemporary philosophy (Eduard von Hartmann, Johannes Volkelt, and Richard Wahle, among others).

1886:   May: Rudolf Steiner sends Kürschner the manuscript of *Outlines of Goethe's Theory of Knowledge* (CW 2), which appears in October, and which he sends out widely. He also meets the poet Marie Eugenie Delle Grazie and writes 'Nature and Our Ideals' for her. He attends her salon, where he meets many priests, theologians, and philosophers, who will become his friends. Meanwhile, the director of the Goethe Archive in Weimar requests his collaboration with the *Sophien* edition of Goethe's works, particularly the writings on colour.

1887:   At the beginning of the year, Rudolf Steiner is very sick. As the year progresses and his health improves, he becomes increasingly 'a man of letters,' lecturing, writing essays, and taking part in Austrian cultural life. In August–September, the second volume of Goethe's *Scientific Writings* appears.

1888:   January–July: Rudolf Steiner assumes editorship of the 'German Weekly' (*Deutsche Wochenschrift*). He begins lecturing more intensively, giving, for example, a lecture titled 'Goethe as Father of a New Aesthetics.' He meets and becomes soul friends with Friedrich Eckstein (1861–1939), a vegetarian, philosopher of symbolism, alchemist, and musician, who will introduce him to various spiritual currents (including Theosophy) and with whom he will meditate and interpret esoteric and alchemical texts.

1889:   Rudolf Steiner first reads Nietzsche (*Beyond Good and Evil*). He encounters Theosophy again and learns of Madame Blavatsky in the Theosophical circle around Marie Lang (1858–1934). Here he also meets well-known figures of Austrian life, as well as esoteric figures like the occultist Franz Hartmann and Karl Leinigen-Billigen (translator of C.G. Harrison's *The Transcendental Universe*). During this period, Steiner first reads A.P. Sinnett's *Esoteric Buddhism* and Mabel Collins's *Light on the Path*. He also begins travelling, visiting Budapest, Weimar, and Berlin (where he meets philosopher Eduard von Hartmann).

1890:   Rudolf Steiner finishes volume 3 of Goethe's scientific writings. He begins his doctoral dissertation, which will become *Truth and Science* (CW 3). He also meets the poet and feminist Rosa Mayreder (1858–1938), with whom he can exchange his most intimate thoughts. In September, Rudolf Steiner moves to Weimar to work in the Goethe-Schiller Archive.

1891:   Volume 3 of the Kürschner edition of Goethe appears. Meanwhile, Rudolf Steiner edits Goethe's studies in mineralogy and scientific writings for the *Sophien* edition. He meets Ludwig Laistner of the Cotta Publishing Company, who asks for a book on the basic question of metaphysics. From this will result, ultimately, *The Philosophy of Freedom* (CW 4), which will be published not by Cotta but by Emil Felber. In October, Rudolf Steiner takes the oral exam for a doctorate in philosophy, mathematics, and mechanics at Rostock University, receiving his doctorate on the twenty-sixth. In November, he gives his first lecture on Goethe's 'Fairy Tale' in Vienna.

1892:   Rudolf Steiner continues work at the Goethe-Schiller Archive and on his *Philosophy of Freedom*. *Truth and Science*, his doctoral dissertation, is published. Steiner undertakes to write introductions to books on Schopenhauer and Jean Paul for Cotta. At year's end, he finds lodging with Anna Eunike, née Schulz (1853–1911), a widow with four daughters and a son. He also develops a friendship with Otto Erich Hartleben (1864–1905) with whom he shares literary interests.

1893:   Rudolf Steiner begins his habit of producing many reviews and articles. In March, he gives a lecture titled 'Hypnotism, with Reference to Spiritism.' In September, volume 4 of the Kürschner edition is completed. In November, *The Philosophy of Freedom* appears. This year, too, he meets John Henry Mackay (1864–1933), the anarchist and Max Stirner scholar.

1894:   Rudolf Steiner meets Elisabeth Förster Nietzsche, the philosopher's sister, and begins to read Nietzsche in earnest, beginning with the as yet unpublished *Antichrist*. He also meets Ernst Haeckel (1834–1919). In the fall, he begins to write *Nietzsche, A Fighter against His Time* (CW 5).

1895:   May, *Nietzsche, A Fighter against His Time* appears.

1896:   January 22: Rudolf Steiner sees Friedrich Nietzsche for the first and only time. Moves between the Nietzsche and the Goethe-Schiller Archives, where he completes his work before year's end. He falls out with Elisabeth Förster Nietzsche, thus ending his association with the Nietzsche Archive.

1897:   Rudolf Steiner finishes the manuscript of *Goethe's Worldview* (CW 6). He moves to Berlin with Anna Eunike and begins editorship of the *Magazin für Literatur*. From now on, Steiner will write countless reviews, literary and philosophical articles, and so on. He begins lecturing at the 'Free Literary Society.' In September, he attends the Zionist Congress in Basel. He sides with Dreyfus in the Dreyfus affair.

1898:   Rudolf Steiner is very active as an editor in the political, artistic, and theatrical life of Berlin. He becomes friendly with John Henry Mackay and poet Ludwig Jacobowski (1868–1900). He joins Jacobowski's circle of writers, artists, and scientists—'The Coming Ones' (*Die Kommenden*)— and contributes lectures to the group until 1903. He also lectures at the 'League for College Pedagogy.' He writes an article for Goethe's sesquicentennial, 'Goethe's Secret Revelation,' on the 'Fairy Tale of the Green Snake and the Beautiful Lily.'

1898–99: 'This was a trying time for my soul as I looked at Christianity. . . . I was able to progress only by contemplating, by means of spiritual perception, the evolution of Christianity. . . . Conscious knowledge of real Christianity began to dawn in me around the turn of the century. This seed continued to develop. My soul trial occurred shortly before the beginning of the twentieth century. It was decisive for my soul's development that I stood spiritually before the Mystery of Golgotha in a deep and solemn celebration of knowledge.'

1899:   Rudolf Steiner begins teaching and giving lectures and lecture cycles at the Workers' College, founded by Wilhelm Liebknecht (1826–1900). He will continue to do so until 1904. Writes: *Literature and Spiritual Life in the Nineteenth Century; Individualism in Philosophy*; *Haeckel and His Opponents; Poetry in the Present;* and begins what will become (fifteen years later) *The Riddles of Philosophy* (CW 18). He also meets many artists and writers, including Käthe Kollwitz, Stefan Zweig, and Rainer Maria Rilke. On October 31, he marries Anna Eunike.

1900:   'I thought that the turn of the century must bring humanity a new light. It seemed to me that the separation of human thinking and willing from the spirit had peaked. A turn or reversal of direction in human evolution seemed to me a necessity.' Rudolf Steiner finishes *World and Life Views in the Nineteenth Century* (the second part of what will become *The Riddles of Philosophy*) and dedicates it to Ernst Haeckel. It is published in March. He continues lecturing at *Die Kommenden*, whose leadership he assumes after the death of Jacobowski. Also, he gives the Gutenberg Jubilee lecture before 7,000 typesetters and printers. In September, Rudolf Steiner is invited by Count and Countess Brockdorff to lecture in the Theosophical Library. His first lecture is on Nietzsche. His second lecture is titled 'Goethe's Secret Revelation.' October 6, he begins a lecture cycle on the mystics that will become *Mystics after Modernism* (CW 7). November–December: 'Marie von Sivers appears in the audience....' Also in November, Steiner gives his first lecture at the Giordano Bruno Bund (where he will continue to lecture until May, 1905). He speaks on Bruno and modern Rome, focusing on the importance of the philosophy of Thomas Aquinas as monism.

1901:   In continual financial straits, Rudolf Steiner's early friends Moritz Zitter and Rosa Mayreder help support him. In October, he begins the lecture cycle *Christianity as Mystical Fact* (CW 8) at the Theosophical Library. In November, he gives his first 'Theosophical lecture' on Goethe's 'Fairy Tale' in Hamburg at the invitation of Wilhelm Hubbe-Schleiden. He also attends a gathering to celebrate the founding of the Theosophical Society at Count and Countess Brockdorff's. He gives a lecture cycle, 'From Buddha to Christ,' for the circle of the *Kommenden*. November 17, Marie von Sivers asks Rudolf Steiner if Theosophy needs a Western-Christian spiritual movement (to complement Theosophy's Eastern emphasis). 'The question was posed. Now, following spiritual laws, I could begin to give an answer....' In December, Rudolf Steiner writes his first article for a Theosophical publication. At year's end, the Brockdorffs and possibly Wilhelm Hubbe-Schleiden ask Rudolf Steiner to join the Theosophical Society and undertake the leadership of the German section. Rudolf Steiner agrees, on the condition that Marie von Sivers (then in Italy) work with him.

1902:   Beginning in January, Rudolf Steiner attends the opening of the Workers' School in Spandau with Rosa Luxemburg (1870–1919). January 17, Rudolf Steiner joins the Theosophical Society. In April, he is asked to become general secretary of the German Section of the Theosophical Society, and works on preparations for its founding. In July, he visits London for a Theosophical congress. He meets Bertram Keightly, G.R.S. Mead, A.P. Sinnett, and Annie Besant, among others. In September, *Christianity as Mystical Fact* appears. In October, Rudolf Steiner gives his first public lecture on Theosophy ('Monism and Theosophy') to about three hundred people at the Giordano Bruno Bund. On October 19–21, the German Section of the Theosophical Society has its first meeting; Rudolf Steiner is the general secretary, and Annie Besant attends. Steiner lectures on practical karma studies. On October 23, Annie Besant inducts Rudolf Steiner into the Esoteric School of the Theosophical Society. On October 25, Steiner begins a weekly series of lectures: 'The Field of Theosophy.' During this year, Rudolf Steiner also first meets Ita Wegman (1876–1943), who will become his close collaborator in his final years.

1903:   Rudolf Steiner holds about 300 lectures and seminars. In May, the first issue of the periodical *Luzifer* appears. In June, Rudolf Steiner visits

London for the first meeting of the Federation of the European Sections of the Theosophical Society, where he meets Colonel Olcott. He begins to write *Theosophy* (CW 9).

1904: Rudolf Steiner continues lecturing at the Workers' College and elsewhere (about 90 lectures), while lecturing intensively all over Germany among Theosophists (about 140 lectures). In February, he meets Carl Unger (1878–1929), who will become a member of the board of the Anthroposophical Society (1913). In March, he meets Michael Bauer (1871–1929), a Christian mystic, who will also be on the board. In May, *Theosophy* appears, with the dedication: 'To the spirit of Giordano Bruno.' Rudolf Steiner and Marie von Sivers visit London for meetings with Annie Besant. June: Rudolf Steiner and Marie von Sivers attend the meeting of the Federation of European Sections of the Theosophical Society in Amsterdam. In July, Steiner begins the articles in *Luzifer-Gnosis* that will become *How to Know Higher Worlds* (CW 10) and *Cosmic Memory* (CW 11). In September, Annie Besant visits Germany. In December, Steiner lectures on Freemasonry. He mentions the High Grade Masonry derived from John Yarker and represented by Theodore Reuss and Karl Kellner as a blank slate 'into which a good image could be placed.'

1905: This year, Steiner ends his non-Theosophical lecturing activity. Supported by Marie von Sivers, his Theosophical lecturing—both in public and in the Theosophical Society—increases significantly: 'The German Theosophical Movement is of exceptional importance.' Steiner recommends reading, among others, Fichte, Jacob Boehme, and Angelus Silesius. He begins to introduce Christian themes into Theosophy. He also begins to work with doctors (Felix Peipers and Ludwig Noll). In July, he is in London for the Federation of European Sections, where he attends a lecture by Annie Besant: 'I have seldom seen Mrs. Besant speak in so inward and heartfelt a manner....' 'Through Mrs. Besant I have found the way to H.P. Blavatsky.' September to October, he gives a course of thirty-one lectures for a small group of esoteric students. In October, the annual meeting of the German Section of the Theosophical Society, which still remains very small, takes place. Rudolf Steiner reports membership has risen from 121 to 377 members. In November, seeking to establish esoteric 'continuity,' Rudolf Steiner and Marie von Sivers participate in a 'Memphis-Misraim' Masonic ceremony. They pay forty-five marks for membership. 'Yesterday, you saw how little remains of former esoteric institutions.' 'We are dealing only with a "framework"... for the present, nothing lies behind it. The occult powers have completely withdrawn.'

1906: Expansion of Theosophical work. Rudolf Steiner gives about 245 lectures, only 44 of which take place in Berlin. Cycles are given in Paris, Leipzig, Stuttgart, and Munich. Esoteric work also intensifies. Rudolf Steiner begins writing *An Outline of Esoteric Science* (CW 13). In January, Rudolf Steiner receives permission (a patent) from the Great Orient of the Scottish A & A Thirty-Three Degree Rite of the Order of the Ancient

Freemasons of the Memphis-Misraim Rite to direct a chapter under the name 'Mystica Aeterna.' This will become the 'Cognitive-Ritual Section' (also called 'Misraim Service') of the Esoteric School. (See: *Freemasonry and Ritual Work: The Misraim Service*, CW 265). During this time, Steiner also meets Albert Schweitzer. In May, he is in Paris, where he visits Edouard Schuré. Many Russians attend his lectures (including Konstantin Balmont, Dimitri Mereszkovski, Zinaida Hippius, and Maximilian Woloshin). He attends the General Meeting of the European Federation of the Theosophical Society, at which Col. Olcott is present for the last time. He spends the year's end in Venice and Rome, where he writes and works on his translation of H.P. Blavatsky's *Key to Theosophy*.

1907: Further expansion of the German Theosophical Movement according to the Rosicrucian directive to 'introduce spirit into the world'—in education, in social questions, in art, and in science. In February, Col. Olcott dies in Adyar. Before he dies, Olcott indicates that 'the Masters' wish Annie Besant to succeed him: much politicking ensues. Rudolf Steiner supports Besant's candidacy. April-May: preparations for the Congress of the Federation of European Sections of the Theosophical Society—the great, watershed Whitsun 'Munich Congress,' attended by Annie Besant and others. Steiner decides to separate Eastern and Western (Christian-Rosicrucian) esoteric schools. He takes his esoteric school out of the Theosophical Society (Besant and Rudolf Steiner are 'in harmony' on this). Steiner makes his first lecture tours to Austria and Hungary. That summer, he is in Italy. In September, he visits Edouard Schuré, who will write the introduction to the French edition of *Christianity as Mystical Fact* in Barr, Alsace. Rudolf Steiner writes the autobiographical statement known as the 'Barr Document.' In *Luzifer-Gnosis*, 'The Education of the Child' appears.

1908: The movement grows (membership: 1,150). Lecturing expands. Steiner makes his first extended lecture tour to Holland and Scandinavia, as well as visits to Naples and Sicily. Themes: St. John's Gospel, the Apocalypse, Egypt, science, philosophy, and logic. *Luzifer-Gnosis* ceases publication. In Berlin, Marie von Sivers (with Johanna Mücke (1864–1949) forms the *Philosophisch-Theosophisch* (after 1915 *Philosophisch-Anthroposophisch*) *Verlag* to publish Steiner's work. Steiner gives lecture cycles titled *The Gospel of St. John* (CW 103) and *The Apocalypse* (104).

1909: *An Outline of Esoteric Science* appears. Lecturing and travel continues. Rudolf Steiner's spiritual research expands to include the polarity of Lucifer and Ahriman; the work of great individualities in history; the Maitreya Buddha and the Bodhisattvas; spiritual economy (CW 109); the work of the spiritual hierarchies in heaven and on earth (CW 110). He also deepens and intensifies his research into the Gospels, giving lectures on the Gospel of St. Luke (CW 114) with the first mention of two Jesus children. Meets and becomes friends with Christian Morgenstern (1871–1914). In April, he lays the foundation stone for the Malsch model—the building that will lead to the first Goetheanum. In May, the International Congress of the Federation of European Sections of the

Theosophical Society takes place in Budapest. Rudolf Steiner receives the Subba Row medal for *How to Know Higher Worlds*. During this time, Charles W. Leadbeater discovers Jiddu Krishnamurti (1895–1986) and proclaims him the future 'world teacher,' the bearer of the Maitreya Buddha and the 'reappearing Christ.' In October, Steiner delivers seminal lectures on 'anthroposophy,' which he will try, unsuccessfully, to rework over the next years into the unfinished work, *Anthroposophy (A Fragment)* (CW 45).

1910:   New themes: *The Reappearance of Christ in the Etheric* (CW 118); *The Fifth Gospel; The Mission of Folk Souls* (CW 121); *Occult History* (CW 126); the evolving development of etheric cognitive capacities. Rudolf Steiner continues his Gospel research with *The Gospel of St. Matthew* (CW 123). In January, his father dies. In April, he takes a month-long trip to Italy, including Rome, Monte Cassino, and Sicily. He also visits Scandinavia again. July–August, he writes the first mystery drama, *The Portal of Initiation* (CW 14). In November, he gives 'psychosophy' lectures. In December, he submits 'On the Psychological Foundations and Epistemological Framework of Theosophy' to the International Philosophical Congress in Bologna.

1911:   The crisis in the Theosophical Society deepens. In January, 'The Order of the Rising Sun,' which will soon become 'The Order of the Star in the East,' is founded for the coming world teacher, Krishnamurti. At the same time, Marie von Sivers, Rudolf Steiner's co-worker, falls ill. Fewer lectures are given, but important new ground is broken. In Prague, in March, Steiner meets Franz Kafka (1883–1924) and Hugo Bergmann (1883-1975). In April, he delivers his paper to the Philosophical Congress. He writes the second mystery drama, *The Soul's Probation* (CW 14). Also, while Marie von Sivers is convalescing, Rudolf Steiner begins work on *Calendar 1912/1913*, which will contain the 'Calendar of the Soul' meditations. On March 19, Anna (Eunike) Steiner dies. In September, Rudolf Steiner visits Einsiedeln, birthplace of Paracelsus. In December, Friedrich Rittelmeyer, future founder of the Christian Community, meets Rudolf Steiner. The *Johannes-Bauverein*, the 'building committee,' which would lead to the first Goetheanum (first planned for Munich), is also founded, and a preliminary committee for the founding of an independent association is created that, in the following year, will become the Anthroposophical Society. Important lecture cycles include *Occult Physiology* (CW 128); *Wonders of the World* (CW 129); *From Jesus to Christ* (CW 131). Other themes: esoteric Christianity; Christian Rosenkreutz; the spiritual guidance of humanity; the sense world and the world of the spirit.

1912:   Despite the ongoing, now increasing crisis in the Theosophical Society, much is accomplished: *Calendar 1912/1913* is published; eurythmy is created; both the third mystery drama, *The Guardian of the Threshold* (CW 14) and *A Way of Self-Knowledge* (CW 16) are written. New (or renewed) themes included life between death and rebirth and karma and reincarnation. Other lecture cycles: *Spiritual Beings in the Heavenly Bodies and in the Kingdoms of Nature* (CW 136); *The Human Being in the Light of Occultism, Theosophy, and Philosophy* (CW 137); *The Gospel of St. Mark* (CW 139); and *The Bhagavad Gita and the Epistles of Paul* (CW 142). On May 8, Rudolf Steiner celebrates White Lotus Day, H.P. Blavatsky's death day, which he had faithfully observed for the past decade, for the last time. In August, Rudolf Steiner suggests the 'independent association' be called the 'Anthroposophical Society.' In September, the first eurythmy course takes place. In October, Rudolf Steiner declines recognition of a Theosophical Society lodge dedicated to the Star of the East and decides to expel all Theosophical Society members belonging to the order. Also, with Marie von Sivers, he first visits Dornach, near Basel, Switzerland, and they stand on the hill where the Goetheanum will be built. In November, a Theosophical Society lodge is opened by direct mandate from Adyar (Annie Besant). In December, a meeting of the German section occurs at which it is decided that belonging to the Order of the Star of the East is incompatible with membership in the Theosophical Society. December 28: informal founding of the Anthroposophical Society in Berlin.

1913:   Expulsion of the German section from the Theosophical Society. February 2–3: Foundation meeting of the Anthroposophical Society. Board members include: Marie von Sivers, Michael Bauer, and Carl Unger. September 20: Laying of the foundation stone for the *Johannes Bau* (Goetheanum) in Dornach. Building begins immediately. The third mystery drama, *The Soul's Awakening* (CW 14), is completed. Also: *The Threshold of the Spiritual World* (CW 147). Lecture cycles include: *The Bhagavad Gita and the Epistles of Paul* and *The Esoteric Meaning of the Bhagavad Gita* (CW 146), which the Russian philosopher Nikolai Berdyaev attends; *The Mysteries of the East and of Christianity* (CW 144); *The Effects of Esoteric Development* (CW 145); and *The Fifth Gospel* (CW 148). In May, Rudolf Steiner is in London and Paris, where anthroposophical work continues.

1914:   Building continues on the *Johannes Bau* (Goetheanum) in Dornach, with artists and co-workers from seventeen nations. The general assembly of the Anthroposophical Society takes place. In May, Rudolf Steiner visits Paris, as well as Chartres Cathedral. June 28: assassination in Sarajevo ('Now the catastrophe has happened!'). August 1: War is declared. Rudolf Steiner returns to Germany from Dornach—he will travel back and forth. He writes the last chapter of *The Riddles of Philosophy*. Lecture cycles include: *Human and Cosmic Thought* (CW 151); *Inner Being of Humanity between Death and a New Birth* (CW 153); *Occult Reading and Occult Hearing* (CW 156). December 24: marriage of Rudolf Steiner and Marie von Sivers.

1915:   Building continues. Life after death becomes a major theme, also art. Writes: *Thoughts during a Time of War* (CW 24). Lectures include: *The Secret of Death* (CW 159); *The Uniting of Humanity through the Christ Impulse* (CW 165).

1916:   Rudolf Steiner begins work with Edith Maryon (1872–1924) on the sculpture 'The Representative of Humanity' ('The Group'—Christ, Lucifer, and Ahriman). He also works with the alchemist Alexander von Bernus on the quarterly *Das Reich*. He writes *The Riddle of Humanity* (CW 20). Lectures include: *Necessity and Freedom in World History and Human Action* (CW 166); *Past and Present in the Human Spirit* (CW 167); *The Karma of Vocation* (CW 172); *The Karma of Untruthfulness* (CW 173).

1917:   Russian Revolution. The U.S. enters the war. Building continues. Rudolf Steiner delineates the idea of the 'threefold nature of the human being' (in a public lecture March 15) and the 'threefold nature of the social organism' (hammered out in May–June with the help of Otto von Lerchenfeld and Ludwig Polzer-Hoditz in the form of two documents titled *Memoranda*, which were distributed in high places). August–September: Rudolf Steiner writes *The Riddles of the Soul* (CW 20). Also: commentary on 'The Chymical Wedding of Christian Rosenkreutz' for Alexander Bernus (*Das Reich*). Lectures include: *The Karma of Materialism* (CW 176); *The Spiritual Background of the Outer World: The Fall of the Spirits of Darkness* (CW 177).

1918:   March 18: peace treaty of Brest-Litovsk—'Now everything will truly enter chaos! What is needed is cultural renewal.' June: Rudolf Steiner visits Karlstein (Grail) Castle outside Prague. Lecture cycle: *From Symptom to Reality in Modern History* (CW 185). In mid-November, Emil Molt, of the Waldorf-Astoria Cigarette Company, has the idea of founding a school for his workers' children.

1919:   Focus on the threefold social organism: tireless travel, countless lectures, meetings, and publications. At the same time, a new public stage of Anthroposophy emerges as cultural renewal begins. The coming years will see initiatives in pedagogy, medicine, pharmacology, and agriculture. January 27: threefold meeting: ' We must first of all, with the money we have, found free schools that can bring people what they need.' February: first public eurythmy performance in Zurich. Also: 'Appeal to the German People' (CW 24), circulated March 6 as a newspaper insert. In April, *Towards Social Renewal* (CW 23) appears— 'perhaps the most widely read of all books on politics appearing since the war.' Rudolf Steiner is asked to undertake the 'direction and leadership' of the school founded by the Waldorf-Astoria Company. Rudolf Steiner begins to talk about the 'renewal' of education. May 30: a building is selected and purchased for the future Waldorf School. August–September, Rudolf Steiner gives a lecture course for Waldorf teachers, *The Foundations of Human Experience (Study of Man)* (CW 293). September 7: Opening of the first Waldorf School. December (into January): first science course, the *Light Course* (CW 320).

1920:   The Waldorf School flourishes. New threefold initiatives. Founding of limited companies *Der Kommende Tag* and *Futurum A.G.* to infuse spiritual values into the economic realm. Rudolf Steiner also focuses on the sciences. Lectures: *Introducing Anthroposophical Medicine* (CW 312); *The Warmth Course* (CW 321); *The Boundaries of Natural Science* (CW 322); *The Redemption of Thinking* (CW 74). February: Johannes Werner

Klein—later a co-founder of the Christian Community—asks Rudolf Steiner about the possibility of a 'religious renewal,' a 'Johannine church.' In March, Rudolf Steiner gives the first course for doctors and medical students. In April, a divinity student asks Rudolf Steiner a second time about the possibility of religious renewal. September 27–October 16: anthroposophical 'university course.' December: lectures titled *The Search for the New Isis* (CW 202).

1921:   Rudolf Steiner continues his intensive work on cultural renewal, including the uphill battle for the threefold social order. 'University' arts, scientific, theological, and medical courses include: *The Astronomy Course* (CW 323); *Observation, Mathematics, and Scientific Experiment* (CW 324); the *Second Medical Course* (CW 313); *Colour*. In June and September-October, Rudolf Steiner also gives the first two 'priests' courses' (CW 342 and 343). The 'youth movement' gains momentum. Magazines are founded: *Die Drei* (January), and—under the editorship of Albert Steffen (1884–1963)—the weekly, *Das Goetheanum* (August). In February–March, Rudolf Steiner takes his first trip outside Germany since the war (Holland). On April 7, Steiner receives a letter regarding 'religious renewal,' and May 22–23, he agrees to address the question in a practical way. In June, the Klinical-Therapeutic Institute opens in Arlesheim under the direction of Dr. Ita Wegman. In August, the Chemical-Pharmaceutical Laboratory opens in Arlesheim (Oskar Schmiedel and Ita Wegman are directors). The Clinical Therapeutic Institute is inaugurated in Stuttgart (Dr. Ludwig Noll is director); also the Research Laboratory in Dornach (Ehrenfried Pfeiffer and Günther Wachsmuth are directors). In November–December, Rudolf Steiner visits Norway.

1922:   The first half of the year involves very active public lecturing (thousands attend); in the second half, Rudolf Steiner begins to withdraw and turn toward the Society—'The Society is asleep.' It is 'too weak' to do what is asked of it. The businesses—*Der Kommende Tag* and *Futurum A.G.*—fail. In January, with the help of an agent, Steiner undertakes a twelve-city German lecture tour, accompanied by eurythmy performances. In two weeks he speaks to more than 2,000 people. In April, he gives a 'university course' in The Hague. He also visits England. In June, he is in Vienna for the East–West Congress. In August–September, he is back in England for the Oxford Conference on Education. Returning to Dornach, he gives the lectures *Philosophy, Cosmology, and Religion* (CW 215), and gives the third priests' course (CW 344). On September 16, The Christian Community is founded. In October–November, Steiner is in Holland and England. He also speaks to the youth: *The Youth Course* (CW 217). In December, Steiner gives lectures titled *The Origins of Natural Science* (CW 326), and *Humanity and the World of Stars: The Spiritual Communion of Humanity* (CW 219). December 31: Fire at the Goetheanum, which is destroyed.

1923:   Despite the fire, Rudolf Steiner continues his work unabated. A very hard year. Internal dispersion, dissension, and apathy abound. There is conflict—between old and new visions—within the Society. A wake-up call is needed, and Rudolf Steiner responds with renewed lecturing vitality. His focus: the spiritual context of human life; initiation science; the course of the year; and community building. As a foundation for an artistic school, he creates a series of pastel sketches. Lecture cycles: *The Anthroposophical Movement; Initiation Science* (CW 227) (in Wales at the Penmaenmawr Summer School); *The Four Seasons and the Archangels* (CW 229); *Harmony of the Creative Word* (CW 230); *The Supersensible Human* (CW 231), given in Holland for the founding of the Dutch society. On November 10, in response to the failed Hitler-Ludendorff putsch in Munich, Steiner closes his Berlin residence and moves the *Philosophisch-Anthroposophisch Verlag* (Press) to Dornach. On December 9, Steiner begins the serialization of his *Autobiography: The Course of My Life* (CW 28) in *Das Goetheanum*. It will continue to appear weekly, without a break, until his death. Late December–early January: Rudolf Steiner re-founds the Anthroposophical Society (about 12,000 members internationally) and takes over its leadership. The new board members are: Marie Steiner, Ita Wegman, Albert Steffen, Elisabeth Vreede, and Günther Wachsmuth. (See *The Christmas Meeting for the Founding of the General Anthroposophical Society*, CW 260). Accompanying lectures: *Mystery Knowledge and Mystery Centres* (CW 232); *World History in the Light of Anthroposophy* (CW 233). December 25: the Foundation Stone is laid (in the hearts of members) in the form of the 'Foundation Stone Meditation.'

1924:   January 1: having founded the Anthroposophical Society and taken over its leadership, Rudolf Steiner has the task of 'reforming' it. The process begins with a weekly newssheet ('What's Happening in the Anthroposophical Society') in which Rudolf Steiner's 'Letters to Members' and 'Anthroposophical Leading Thoughts' appear (CW 26). The next step is the creation of a new esoteric class, the 'first class' of the 'University of Spiritual Science' (which was to have been followed, had Rudolf Steiner lived longer, by two more advanced classes). Then comes a new language for Anthroposophy—practical, phenomenological, and direct; and Rudolf Steiner creates the model for the second Goetheanum. He begins the series of extensive 'karma' lectures (CW 235–40); and finally, responding to needs, he creates two new initiatives: biodynamic agriculture and curative education. After the middle of the year, rumours begin to circulate regarding Steiner's health. Lectures: January–February, *Anthroposophy* (CW 234); February: *Tone Eurythmy* (CW 278); June: *The Agriculture Course* (CW 327); June–July: *Speech Eurythmy* (CW 279); *Curative Education* (CW 317); August: (England, 'Second International Summer School'), *Initiation Consciousness: True and False Paths in Spiritual Investigation* (CW 243); September: *Pastoral Medicine* (CW 318). On September 26, for the first time, Rudolf Steiner cancels a lecture. On September 28, he gives his last lecture. On September 29, he withdraws to his studio in the carpenter's shop; now he is definitively ill. Cared for by Ita Wegman, he continues working, however, and writing the weekly installments of his *Autobiography* and *Letters to the Members/Leading Thoughts* (CW 26).

1925:   Rudolf Steiner, while continuing to work, continues to weaken. He finishes *Extending Practical Medicine* (CW 27) with Ita Wegman.

On March 30, around ten in the morning, Rudolf Steiner dies.

INDEX

A NOTE FROM RUDOLF STEINER PRESS

We are an independent publisher and registered charity (non-profit organisation) dedicated to making available the work of Rudolf Steiner in English translation. We care a great deal about the content of our books and have hundreds of titles available – as printed books, ebooks and in audio formats.

As a publisher devoted to anthroposophy...

- We continually commission translations of previously unpublished works by Rudolf Steiner and invest in re-translating, editing and improving our editions.

- We are committed to making anthroposophy available to all by publishing introductory books as well as contemporary research.

- Our new print editions and ebooks are carefully checked and proofread for accuracy, and converted into all formats for all platforms.

- Our translations are officially authorised by Rudolf Steiner's estate in Dornach, Switzerland, to whom we pay royalties on sales, thus assisting their critical work.

So, look out for Rudolf Steiner Press as a mark of quality and support us today by buying our books, or contact us should you wish to sponsor specific titles or to support the charity with a gift or legacy.

office@rudolfsteinerpress.com
Join our e-mailing list at www.rudolfsteinerpress.com

RUDOLF STEINER PRESS